Human Behavior and Employment Interviewing

Other books by Dean B. Peskin

The Art of Job Hunting
The Building Blocks of EEO

Human Behavior and Employment Interviewing

Dean B. Peskin

American Management Association

**To Marcia,
my blessed navigator
during the lonely journey of discovery**

International standard book number: 0-8144-5243-4
Library of Congress catalog card number: 78-130915

First printing

Contents

	Introduction	1
1	A Survey of the Interview Process	7
2	The Perceptual Process and Attitude Formation	35
3	Decision Making, Problem Solving, and Programming	62
4	Breaking the Semantics Barrier	99
5	Evaluating Success and Failure	112
6	Motivation: Implications for Screening and Placement	140
7	Interviewing Techniques	164
8	Campus Recruitment	181
9	Testing and Conjunctive Interviewing	198
10	Interviewing Management Manpower	217
	Selected Readings	241
	Index	244

Introduction

Human behavior and employment interviewing is written for people in business and organizational work who make decisions about the quality of their company's job applicants, decisions based wholly or in part on the results of an employment interview. This obviously includes almost everyone who hires people because, of all the pre-employment screening techniques known today, interviewing remains the most universal. An employment interviewer may be a professional interviewer working for an employment or personnel department; or he may be a foreman or supervisor, a division manager, a corporate executive, a senior clerk, a physician, an engineer or welfare worker, an attorney, an educator, or a grocer. It is because interviewers come from such highly divergent social, economic, educational, and occupational backgrounds that every effort has been made to create a readable and easily understandable book that is practical and applicable for every reader, regardless of whether he has ever been exposed to behavioral science principles.

It should be noted that interviewing is used either as the only preemployment screening technique or in conjunction with other techniques such as job skills inventories, psychological testing, and reference checking. Interviewing, in this conjunctive sense, is perhaps the most common approach. Interviewing is universally used, but its practitioners sometimes justify it by counting advantages that are not always significant—for example, emphasis may be placed on attributes that are not of long-term value. Interviewing appears to be inexpensive, and does not require special equipment. In addition, it seems deceptively simple: Two people talk to each other—one is the interviewer and one is the applicant. The interviewer asks the questions he feels are important, and the applicant answers them. If the interviewer is not too dissatisfied with the applicant's answers—that is, if there are an insufficient number of reasons not to hire the applicant—then the interview is said to have gone well.

As if there were not already enough valid reasons inherent in the interview process to make it so popular, there is still another that probably has as much bearing on the popularity of interviewing as any other. Interviewing is gratifying for the interviewer. Even though the interview is a structured social situation in which generous portions of social lubricants, the amenities and courtesies (within a framework of ethical and moral guidelines), are typically in evidence, it also brings strangers together to sit down and to talk about the most personal aspects of life. In the usual interview situation, the interviewer is free to ask questions that he feels will elicit answers helpful to him in making a decision about the applicant. The applicant will generally answer any question even though some may be difficult or even embarrassing, because he wants employment and believes that the interviewer will not ask a question that is not germane. Thus, much like the physician who decides that in his best judgment a particular test, examination, or therapy is required, the interviewer proceeds, guided by his best judgment about how to elicit the facts he needs. The interviewer then relies on his knowledge of people to evaluate the quality of each answer and the interview as a whole. He may of course also rely on any of a number of screening tools, including test scores, personal references, comments from former employers, school grades, and the like. These screening tools may be used in various combinations; when properly combined, the tools reinforce one another.

Experience has taught the interviewer to ask certain questions; to make certain assumptions about the probability of future success or failure based upon the applicant's answers to interview questions and the applicant's history and biography; to assume a physical posture with appropriate facial expressions; and to use the language (or interview approach) that he finds works best in a set of given circumstances. Unfortunately, the interview does not always work; that is, it may fail to do what it was intended to do, and it may continue to fail again and again, and no one may ever be the wiser. The same or a similar interview approach is continued year after year; the hidden reasons for asking certain interview questions remain, and the same or similar meanings are continually read into applicants' answers to interview questions. Turnover rises steadily and morale is cause for concern. Proper placement of applicants becomes a worrisome problem; high-potential manpower continues to be scarce, and the need for its replacement increases. But some interviewers still fail to question their "knowledge of people." Not enough organizations review the performance of interviewers or make an effort to measure that performance. How many applicants did an interviewer recommend for hire? How many were subsequently accepted for employment? How many eventually became good employees? How many quit or were fired and over what period of time? What were the circumstances surrounding their terminations (both voluntary and involuntary)? Could some of the firings or resignations have been prevented? How might better interviewing in conjunction with improved testing methods and personnel research have helped reduce the probability of failure on the job? Granted, the interviewer has a knowledge of people that is made up of an accumulation of ifs and maybes—a kind of almanac of human behavior that keeps many an employment interviewer in surprisingly good stead in respect to turn-over and absenteeism, placement problems, and unending employee relations entanglements. Yet is the interviewer's knowledge of people really adequate for these problems? How good, in fact, is that knowledge, and upon what is it based? In other words, how good does the employment interviewer have to be? And how expensive is the interview process?

The single most valuable asset of any organization is the people who work for it. A company's growth and development, its ability to reach expected goals, to realize an acceptable return on investment, to provide quality goods and services, and to survive and prosper are direct reflections of its manpower. Finally, the ability of each employee in each organization to contribute to the quality of life and, in turn, to be enriched by that quality is largely a product of the successful interaction between man and the environment in which he functions.

When an interviewer reviews the background of an applicant, analyzes the applicant's responses during the interview, and weighs the results of other screening methods, the interviewer is, in fact, making judgments about the behavior of the applicant. It is the basic premise of this book that the applicant's behavior, like all human behavior, is not determined by chance. *Behavior is caused;* it does not just happen. The causes may seem unfathomable but they are there waiting to be discovered and understood; and so, for the behavioral scientist, the frontiers of his field are ever beckoning.

This book recognizes that there are two basic approaches to the interview process. One is the *utilitarian,* the other is the *functional.* The utilitarian approach is dominated by the *what* of the applicant:

For example, the number of address changes in the past several years, the pattern of employment, the skills inventory, the availability of transportation, the possibilities of a husband being transferred, minimum salary requirements, which shift is preferred, how often the applicant asks pertinent questions, appearance, voice quality (scratchy, choked, strained, or too loud) as evidence of nervousness, and the like. Although the utilitarian aspect of employment interviewing is important, it is given only mild treatment in this book. The functional approach is *why*-oriented and thus combines the what with the why. The why approach challenges both applicant and interviewer. It seeks to explain what has happened in the applicant's life, and it looks beyond the facts as they appear and probes for causative factors. It seeks to determine in what circumstances certain behavior has occurred and whether it will recur. It sees human beings in many dimensions, responding to internal and external stimuli (which the applicant may not be consciously aware of); it recognizes that the interviewer interprets what he sees and hears, and he thereby becomes a part of what he sees and hears because what he perceives as real or true is a function of the perceptual process. The interviewer's perceptions of the world are based on his life experiences, his emotional state, his understanding of the environment, his goals, needs, and values. The same process holds true for the interviewer's perceptions of the applicant. With the functional or why approach, the interviewer tries to understand how, for example, the applicant measures success and failure, what he thinks success and failure are made of, and why these concepts are not the same for all people. He must also understand how personal (internalized) concepts of success and failure can affect judgments regarding job placement and how such concepts are affected, in turn, by the goals, needs, expectations, aspirations, frustrations, and motivations of the applicant and the interviewer as well. The functional approach also recognizes the limitations of language as a medium of communication and endeavors to sift through abstractions in search of clear understanding.

It is possible for a well-programmed computer to evaluate the sum total of the what answers, but evaluation is much less easy where the whys are concerned. There are no simple answers, no formulas to be memorized or applied. This book attempts to demonstrate the value of behavioral science principles in employment interviewing and management in general. It also explains and justifies the behavioral science approach in practice and theory and encourages the upgrading of the interview process and the further training and self-development of interviewers. Thus it provides the means to reach beyond the self-imposed limitations of employment interviewing. The book defines employment interviewing as a distinct and wholly independent discipline separate from and unlike counseling or psychiatry. Academic theory and laboratory experiments are combined with marketplace reality to produce an interface of behavioral science and personnel administration.

This book discusses many problems inherent in organizational structure, performance appraisal, equal opportunity in employment, management methods and practices. There is no effort to give these topics a complete treatment. They are dealt with only as they are germane to the subjects of human behavior and employment interviewing. The chapter titles should not be interpreted to mean that the primary subject matter of one chapter will not be met again in other chapters. The subject of human behavior is not so easily compartmentalized. Chapter headings are an arbitrary way of highlighting the major message of a given chapter, expressing a specific point of departure, and bringing only general order to a subject that is by nature fluid. This fluidity, however, works to our advantage because it helps us view areas of human behavior organically and allows us to view the entire subject from different vantage points. For the most part, no specific effort is made to differentiate techniques used for blue collar and white collar workers or managers and clerks, although one complete chapter is devoted to high-potential managers. This is because (except for special, almost technical, problems involving management) behavioral science principles and theory, laboratory studies, and practical and personal experiences noted in the text have sufficiently broad applicability to both occupational categories. Where necessary, however, differentiations are made.

It would be impossible (and would serve no real purpose if it were possible) to indicate every conceivable human response to every conceivable interview question. It would also be impossible to imagine every conceivable human experience and ascribe to each experience specific behavioral interpretations with a scale indicating whether such configurations represent a good or a bad employee. What has been attempted is a combination or interchange of broad principles and experimental findings with practical operating experiences. In this manner, the particular subject under discussion does not become an academic curiosity but, instead, can be used to illustrate the dynamic and cataclysmic forces that come into focus when an individual and an organization meet. Thus the discussion helps direct and guide the interviewer in his approach to understanding himself and applicants, and it alerts him to the dynamics of his role.

One last comment about the importance of behavioral science principles and the need to apply knowledge of human behavior to personnel work and management in general. The values that members of a business organization believe in and the resulting operating policies and practices geared toward optimizing individual potential, creativity, and productivity, and the escalation of the ability of human technology to create and control change (not merely to react or cope with environmental changes produced by machine technology) are best achieved when we realize that man is not a product of technology but rather the creator of it.

1

A Survey
of the Interview Process

EMPLOYMENT INTERVIEWING is one of the most crucial responsibilities of any business enterprise because it is through employment interviewing that a business draws on that most precious commodity —manpower. Rarely does a business enterprise have comparable influence over any of the key determinants of its ultimate success or failure. When we analyze why one business is more successful than another, consistently more aggressive, profitable, ahead of the market or responsive to consumer demands, more efficient, and less costly to operate than comparable organizations, we discover that it is the people who constitute the business, from the file clerks to the chief executive officer, that make it a success. How large a part do breaks and timing play? What effect do economic resources have? The answer is that an organization must make its own breaks, by analyzing consumer moods, anticipating change, improving services, and making the most of its economic resources—all functions are performed by people. Therefore, the foundation of an organization is its people.

Perhaps as never before, the business community faces a make-or-break need to identify, attract, and retain productive manpower. Hangers-on will always be available, as will the marginally qualified, the corporate parasites who grudgingly give of their time but who feed upon the corporation with the instinct of predators, the "professional managers"—technical analysts and specialists—whose loyalty is to their trade rather than to their employer. There will be available for many years to come the unskilled, untried, hard-core unemployed, who are usually not members of the white majority but who, except for their lack of skills, often are surprisingly like much of the white workforce in that they are similarly undermotivated and underutilized. But highly motivated, capable, productive, and imaginative people are not always available for clerical and management jobs when business needs them. The shortage of such people, particularly for management jobs, will become ever more serious as one writer notes: "Evidence is accumulating that a 'no holds barred' scramble for executive talent—already in short supply—will develop in the next few years. Indeed, there are signs that the demands for this increasingly rare commodity could reach such boom proportions by 1975 that even the best-manned companies, which have executive talent in considerable depth today, would be unfavorably affected." [1]

According to the U.S. Bureau of Labor Statistics, there will soon be a serious shortage of 8 million new managers in American business, and within the next decade there will also be almost 750,000 fewer male employees in the 35–45 age range than there were in 1966. Equally alarming is the estimate that by 1975 one-third of today's managers will be lost to business by disability, retirement, or death.

Implications of the Growing Manpower Shortage

What the continued shortage of good people will require of business is threefold: First, business must master the art and science of manpower planning to more effectively evaluate and measure the quantity and quality of its available manpower in terms of corporate or operating goals as these define and direct the future course of the business enterprise. Second, business must evaluate meaningful programs designed to identify, motivate, develop, reward, and maintain (or protect) the manpower it values. Third, business must strengthen its ability to recognize productive and potentially valuable candidates for employment who are not yet a part of the workforce. These people are unknown quantities whether they apply for a job at the company's employment office, whether they are uncommitted candidates (such as campus recruits), or whether they are pirated from other organizations.

The growing complexities of the American business corporation

[1] A. Patton, "The Coming Scramble for Executive Talent," *Harvard Business Review*, May–June, 1967.

and of the management process itself increase the demand for people at every level of skill. When fewer high-potential managers are available (because there simply are not enough to go around because of the low birth rate of the 1930s or because some businesses do not or cannot compete on the basis of compensation alone), business must review its systems and procedures, begin work simplification programs, and even take on the torturous task of scaling down its manpower requirements, in effect settling for youthful enthusiasm instead of seasoned maturity. Business may even be forced to accept marginal contributors in the hope that management development programs and motivational efforts will work wonders. But lowering standards does not eliminate the need to identify, recognize, measure, and understand the current and future capabilities of an applicant. In fact, efforts to identify the potential of untried talent may create difficulties at the time of employment interviewing because there are fewer tangible evidences of success or failure and fewer identifiable career goals and objectives than might be prevalent among more seasoned and experienced applicants, and patterns of occupational behavior, including on-the-job performance, are not well defined.

At the same time, penetration interviewing is necessary for experienced applicants also, because past experience is a fertile field for gaining insights into an individual and for gathering significant facts about him. It is also important to determine whether he has fulfilled his potential and whether his future career aspirations are realistic in relation to his past performance. And so we must return to one of the realities of business life: the need to identify the right person for the right job. This is critical to business; unless an organization is able to identify productive, high-potential people, it cannot hire, promote, or effectively utilize them and will not get its share of the human resources that singularly distinguish one organization from another.

Limitations of Selection Techniques

After exhaustive recruitment efforts, after complex employment application forms have been completed, after tests have been taken (applicants sometimes require days to complete the tests and trained psychologists may require weeks to evaluate the performances), after credit bureaus have prepared a profile on the applicant, and after time-consuming character references have been obtained, the entire accumulation of costly data is set aside. Unless critically damaging evidence against the applicant appears, he will be granted an interview with a company representative, who may be the personnel director, an employment interviewer, or the company president.

Consider another set of circumstances. A job vacancy exists in an organization. The company reviews the records of its employees, analyzes work performance appraisals and the comments of present and former supervisors. It reviews and evaluates the educational and work experience of prospective candidates, and, then, with the careers of these candidates at stake, the decision makers rely on an interview to help point the way to the right decision. In both these instances, it is generally the rule that as the interview goes, so goes the applicant.

Without exception, interviewing is the one technique universally used to help make decisions about job applicants and promotees. Even when interviewing is practiced in conjunction with other screening methods, it emerges as the most critical, pivotal, and potentially powerful technique. Employers continue to spend large sums of money for all kinds of tests—from personality to job interest, from word association games to inkblots. Although the vast majority of companies in the United States spend more money on testing than on any other screening tool, the tangible direct results are marginal at best in terms of the predictability of success or failure on the job. It is not that tests are faulty but that the application of tests and test results to practical business circumstances is not yet perfected. Visions of testing as the ultimate screening and selection technique have dimmed because validation and reliability are seriously lacking.

Testing is rarely if ever used precisely as the test makers intended, rarely if ever applied with the academic sophistication and awareness of testing limitations that guided the development of the test. Too often subjected to criticism when used to make decisions rather than guide them, testing will be doomed not so much by the limitations of the testing method itself as by its misuse at the hands of practitioners who, faced with a drought of qualified applicants or an unequal share of the labor market's best, stretch testing to its unrealistic limits in a futile effort to find potential in applicants who seem least likely to have it. Within the limits of their validity, tests probably enable fairly accurate prediction of job success in terms of the capacity of the applicant to perform a job. But not all tests can indicate whether the applicant will apply his abilities to the job, just as a high score on an intelligence test may not be any more indicative of brilliant job performance than a moderate or just passing test score. The matter of testing and integrating test results with interview techniques is explored in Chapter 9.

Because people might take legal action against a former employer who gave a bad reference, references are not always reliable. Thus interviewing is still the dominant technique in screening; it helps make all other methods workable and understandable provided the interview process is conducted skillfully and correctly. An inept, misdirected, or otherwise misused interview thwarts the ability of an organization to staff itself effectively. Bad interviewing can destroy the public image of an organization and create morale problems for those hired through it. Because of the sensitive nature of the interviewing process, bad interviewing can haunt an organization and have untold adverse effects on candidates for employment or promotion.

Whether interviewing is used to identify qualified applicants or to make a decision about a promotion, it can and must be more than a tired and routine question-and-answer session. It should be a vital process that provides invaluable knowledge about the applicant and what makes him tick. It must give an idea of how applicants may respond under pressure; how they will think on their feet. It also must indicate what motivates applicants, what will satisfy them, what circumstances brought them to their present situation in life, and what inhibits them. In addition, it should help reveal what personality traits, idiosyncracies, emotions, habits, drives, and goals affect them.

Another highly critical consideration in employment interviewing is equal employment opportunity (EEO). This is laid down in statutes and in pertinent federal guidelines that must be respected in the interview process if companies are to be in compliance with the law. Also, the emergence of minorities as a factor in the labor market has created a need for totally different techniques that employers must be fully aware of. The importance of using proper interview techniques with members of minority groups is far-reaching; it involves the very stability of the society in which business seeks to operate. Traditional interview practices are inappropriate and do not provide the means by which such applicants can be understood or their potential and background recognized, defined, and objectively analyzed. Tests fall short of this objective as well; moreover, they are highly controversial and often misused; references are too often inappropriate or inapplicable.

What Employment Interviewing Is—and Is Not

And so our initial purpose is to focus our attention as much on what employment interviewing is as to what it is not. In so doing, we will survey employment interviewing and some of the applicable behavioral science concepts that are dealt with more fully in subsequent chapters. The squandering of precious manpower resources (with consequent increased operating costs), as evidenced by high turnover rates, is often the result of the tragic misplacement of applicants in positions where personalities, job needs, career objectives, abilities, aspirations, social goals, and educational and personal backgrounds are not considered. Complex and often abrasive performance appraisal systems, inability of salary programs to comfortably reflect and translate job performance into dollars, ineffective morale-building and development programs designed to mold, bend, or break the recalcitrant employee are often the consequences of such squandering and signal the need to face up to the fact that something is wrong.

A workable statement of the purpose and definition, the function and objectives of employment interviewing might be as follows:

> Employment interviewing is the open exchange of information between persons of acknowledged unequal status for a mutually agreed upon purpose, conducted in a manner that elicits, clarifies, organizes, or synthesizes the information to affect positively or negatively the attitudes, judgments, actions, or opinions of the participants, thereby making possible an objective and rational evaluation of the appropriateness of an employee for a specific job.

Let us analyze a few of the critical aspects of this definition of purpose as a means of measuring the scope of interviewing. Interviewing is "open" in the sense that there are no restrictions imposed by the interviewer or the applicant on investigation or inquiry. When such restrictions exist, they close off certain avenues of inquiry. Occasionally, interviewers restrict themselves because they feel that to investigate a certain area would be uncomfortable for the applicant. Such areas should not be avoided; instead the interviewer must be trained to handle sensitive inquiry discreetly.

The participants in an interview must not be of equal status. Each participant must exert pressure in an opposite direction, in terms of interests, decision-making authority, and the nature or impact of the decision each can make. This does not mean that either or both participants take an unalterable position for or against the other. An applicant has the power to withdraw from the interviewer's consideration or to decline a job offer. The interviewer has the power to decide that the applicant is not right for the job and to close the matter at that point. In other words, something must be at stake in the interview; something must be won—a job for the applicant, a filled vacancy for the interviewer, and increased manpower potential for the company—or lost—the desired job, the opportunity to fill the vacancy, and the potential manpower. When one or both participants cannot exert influence or pressure on the results of the interview, when one lacks the authority or responsibility to make a decision, or when either participant cannot directly affect or be affected by the outcome of the interview, then the relationship is not in the proper frame of reference.

It is important that the participants in the interview mutually agree on its purpose. This eliminates "gaming." We have all heard about the employee who is called into the boss's office and, through most of the discussion, believes the boss is going to give him a raise, when in fact the conversation is leading up to the employee's involuntary termination. The interviewer and the applicant must focus on similar objectives. The most common example of a lack of mutual purpose is the situation of an applicant for employment who is not told whether a vacancy exists. The interviewer who decides not to tip his hand may be proceeding along classic investigational lines, while the applicant, not cued to the interviewer's purpose, reacts either negatively to the seemingly pointless penetrating questions or passively to the entire experience. Nothing has been accomplished by the exercise, and both parties lose in this guessing game.

The evaluations, justifications, conclusions, and decisions at which the participants arrive need not be similar. For example, the interviewer may judge that the interview (in conjunction with other screening methods and investigative procedures) has gone well and that the applicant is qualified for employment. Believing that he can justify his conclusions, he decides either to recommend the applicant for hire or to hire him himself. On the basis of the facts that have emerged and on certain insights gained during the interview, the applicant may also conclude that the interview has gone well and on the strength of this decide that he is in a position to reject the subsequent offer of employment. For the applicant, the fact that the interview has gone well means that he has learned that he doesn't want the job. Both participants may have been objective, rational, diligent, and honest in their efforts, and yet each may have reached different decisions.

What the definition of purpose suggests is that employment interviewing has a narrow, specific, and predetermined function. If it is to do something other than what it was intended to do, then personnel administrators should either change the accepted techniques and call the new process by a different name or learn to apply them to the new function, supplementing them with new techniques. An employment interview is not intended to prove to the interviewer that his first impression about the applicant was either correct or incorrect; it is not designed for purely negative evaluation based on the reasons for *not* hiring the applicant; it is not intended to make the applicant feel better or worse than he did before the interview or to imbue him with inspiration or consternation; it is not intended consciously to restrict employment, to counsel, guide, advise, console, or serve as a confessional for past career mistakes. It is certainly not intended to satisfy the interviewer's curiosity or to serve as a mandatory, routine chore that must be performed regardless of the initial interest of the interviewer and the applicant. Furthermore, the interview is not intended to be the footbath before the plunge into the pool—that is, it is not a routine excursion before hiring the applicant; this type of interview is not an employment interview because it does not affect the decision in any way.

Interviewing as a Communication Process

Although an employment interview is a social relationship in that there is structured interaction between people, it is also fundamentally a communication process. When it is characterized as such, it begins to take on more meaning to the employment interviewer. Communication, in its most rudimentary form, is a sending–receiving process. A communication signal, be it an electronic impulse, a flag, a smoke signal, or a printed word, is sent, received, and presumably understood. But the communication process in employment interviewing is of a higher order. It begins with the basic linking of sending–receiving, to which is added acknowledgment, confirmation–confirmation. This total process requires the interviewer to send his message as an inquiry or statement; the applicant receives—that is, he hears—the message and acknowledges it by responding; the interviewer then confirms the response—that is, he perceives that the process he originated was completed in the manner intended. The applicant understood and responded to his sent inquiry correctly (even though a correct response to the inquiry could result in a wrong answer or an answer that does not advance the cause of the applicant). The final and more difficult confirmation comes from the applicant who sees that his response has been read correctly. He can usually determine this by the subsequent questions or actions of the interviewer or the outcome of the interview. This is a somewhat simplified description of a process that occurs each time a question is asked and a response is made.

But we have only touched on the problem of communication with all its semantic and perceptual implications. Later chapters deal with these areas in considerable detail. For the present, however, our purpose is simply to indicate that employment interviewing, if it is to be productive and to do what it is supposed to do, must include more than simply asking a question and hearing the answer. The employment interviewer must not only *hear;* he must *listen to* the language of the applicant.

There is a structural relationship between the language we use and reality. The matter of structure must be of interest to the interviewer, whose responsibility is to make sense of the abstractions, symbolism, extensionalization, assumptions, facts, and the consequences of the variability of words, and of what Korzybski calls the multiordinality of words—that is, the fact that certain words that can be applied to a statement and reapplied again to subsequent statements about the original statement without changing the meaning. These words include yes, no, true, false, love, hate, good, bad.[2] Language is limited in that words do not have a wide breadth of alterability, even though most English-language words have multiple meanings. Immediately, therefore, we see that the employment interviewer is handicapped from the start by a communication gap.

A very special circuitry characterizes the interaction in an employment interview, when the applicant and the interviewer transmit or convey certain facts about each other and what each represents. Perhaps "cues" would be a better word than "facts." Important judgments result from what the interviewer and the applicant perceive, but it is highly unrealistic to assume that perceptions simply register objective reality. The critical matter of perception is discussed in greater detail later, but suffice it to say here that our communication circuitry, semantic barriers, and the devilish challenges of perception are but a few of the many constructs that must be dealt with satisfactorily if we are to have an effective employment interview process.

It has been suggested that the employment interviewer's major responsibility and, in fact, obligation, during the interview is to listen. This, of course, means understand, comprehend, and gain insight into what is only suggested or implied or may even be hidden—the words behind the words. It also necessitates disciplined focusing of the interviewer's attention on the applicant. It does not mean defensive listening; that is, selective listening in order to reinforce biases about the

[2] A. Korzybski, *Science and Sanity: Introduction to Non-Aristotelian Systems and General Semantics* (Lancaster, Pa.: The Science Press, 1941).

applicant or use of listening time to decide the next move against the applicant—in effect, *offensive* listening.

Problems in Evaluation

How the employment interviewer deals with his load of information, how he synthesizes it, analyzes it, evaluates and uses it is another area of importance. It must be assumed that he has attained a certain level of education and experience. It must be further assumed that the interviewer is skilled enough and wise enough not to make a firm decision about the applicant during the interview and before all the facts have been considered. The interviewer must sift through his findings and ask himself what it all means. The extent to which the interviewer draws valid conclusions on which to base his decisions is the extent to which he is able to answer that question. It is not only the measure of his success as an interviewer, but it is also an indication of the probability of the organization's meeting its obligations and goals through its human resources.

The Interviewer's Alternatives

Perhaps a few isolated examples of the choices and alternatives that an employment interviewer must consider before reaching a decision will demonstrate the immensity of his responsibility. For example, after having reviewed the application, life history, and résumé, and after having interviewed the applicant, the interviewer knows that there have been successes and failures in the applicant's career history. What should previous success or failure indicate to the interviewer? (This will be discussed more fully in Chapter 5.) Success and failure influence goals, interpersonal relations, aspiration levels, and self-esteem. This influence lasts throughout our lives, and a successful act will be repeated because, as stated in Thorndike's law of effect, one quickly learns the responses that produce satisfaction, and one does not typically repeat a response or reaction that has previously resulted in a painful or unpleasant consequence. However, repeating in Company B those acts or responses that were successful in Company A may not always insure success; as a matter of fact, it may prove disastrous. What significance, then, does the interviewer attach to previous successes and failures?

The penalty for previous "failures" (in quotes because the term may be indefinable or invalid in any given case, and because the opposite of failure is not necessarily success but could be nonfailure) inflicted by employment interviewers is too often like the peculiar brand of justice that haunted the American West in the old days. This was typified by the whiskey-swizzling judge who ruled the territory from his favorite table at the saloon and announced to each prisoner that he would be given a trial before being hanged. Perhaps the penalty that applicants receive for previous failures results from their own inability to cover their tracks more skillfully, and to understand the nature and character of the failures. Success and failure are not only relative terms; they are also value judgments. How often in modern corporate structures is one able to isolate individual successes and failures? Isn't it more typical to find situations void of clearly discernible success or failure? This, of course, does not excuse employment interviewers who, sensing some failure in an applicant's background, strive relentlessly to uncover it and who view every experience negatively in its light. A series of failures, if in fact they can be isolated and clearly attributed to the fault of the applicant, must be considered, but with delicacy. One successful executive who had worked as a busboy during his days in college was fired after two incidents in which he dropped laden trays. After graduation he pursued a career entirely appropriate to his exceptional capabilities, but whenever he was confronted with a job application he would wonder whether he should indicate that during his college years he was fired from a job for being clumsy.

What is important, therefore, to the interviewer is not the nature of the success or failure but rather the effect the failure had on the individual. It has been demonstrated, for example, that aspiration levels and performance tend to drop during periods of negative feedback or failure. Performance seems to be directly affected by failures, which negatively affect personal goals and output. However, it was found that aspirations (goals), self-esteem, and productivity (performance) increased when failure-producing conditions were minimized or eliminated.

The Interviewer's Attitudes

The attitudes of the interviewer about success and failure obviously are critical. Typically, failure is viewed as bad and success as good. To some extent these evaluations carry over into our attitudes toward people, so that, unconsciously, successful people may be thought of as good and unsuccessful people as bad. Yet we rarely define what we really mean by "good" or "bad." "Bad" could mean morally corrupt, devoid of ethics, criminal in nature; it could even mean a state of health. The undeniable truth is that many morally deficient people have been successful in accomplishing their goals. The accomplishment of the goal (which is seen as good) does not deny the moral deficiency and vice versa—ethical, moral, and law-abiding people who fail in their efforts (which is seen as bad) remain law abiding and ethical. The tendency too often is to use the term "he's a loser" synonymously with "he lost"; the former indicates a general state of being and therefore embraces a person in all aspects of his life, whereas the latter applies strictly to a single situation.

Employment interviewers frequently describe an applicant as having "potential." Few who use this stock expression appreciate the full scope of its meaning; otherwise characterizations by interviewers using the expression would not rank second or third in priority after comments on appearance and personality. What the interviewer usually means by the phrase "he has potential" is that he *thinks* the applicant probably will not become a turnover statistic, at least through the next reporting period. But the primary emphasis is on turnover. The applicant is said to "fit." He will not leave the company too soon or before a reasonable time because he is the type of person who can "make it with us." Another meaning of "he has potential" is that if the applicant remains on the job he can be expected to advance. The key, of course, is the advance. Someone with potential might be able to perform one job well but not another. However, when an employment interviewer says an applicant has potential, it is generally taken to mean that he has the ability and the desire to strive for achievement. The fact is that, despite the employment interviewer's perception of potential, the applicant may be motivated to succeed or he may be motivated to avoid failure. These are totally different concepts. The little Pekingese who takes on the Chihuahua and not the German shepherd is playing the game of failure avoidance. Those who spend their time avoiding failure will probably strive for goals they feel reasonably certain they can achieve, regardless of their potential as indicated by employment interviews, colleagues' opinions, or test results. They do not seek success as avidly as they seek non-failure. To these people, the opposite of failure is the avoidance of failure. The success-oriented person, on the other hand, sets his sights on the stars and, although he may be uncertain of his chances for success, makes a valiant try, like the saucy Scottish terrier that defies a boxer. In short, the phrase "he has potential" does not clearly identify the applicant whose aspiration level is above his ability or judgment.

Supervisors and managers are familiar with the problem of a newly hired employee who is not fully utilizing his previous training and skills in his new situation. There is every reason to believe, on the basis of interviews, tests, and reference verifications, that the employee has the potential and knows what to do; yet for some reason he is failing or performing at a borderline level. This situation is not restricted to management or supervisory levels; it occurs on almost any kind of job. Sometimes it is referred to as "functional fixedness," the inability of previous training and experience to provide the skills required by a new employment situation. Past experience, after all, may affect the behavior of an individual when he attempts to solve problems, but the effect is not always positive or desirable. Preparation for problem solving can develop along several lines. In the final analysis, trial and error may be the primary manner in which we learn to recognize and attack problems, but past experience can be considered as a backlog or inventory of problem-solving memory—a kind of library from which the individual draws the knowledge that (with the necessary modifications) he applies to the problem at hand.

Functional Fixedness

One of the most obvious goals of the employment interviewer and subsequently of the manager is to determine how the applicant is likely to apply his past experience to a new job. After all, the applicant can be judged only on his experience and potential. Both must be recognized and, as well as possible, measured to provide the basis on which the employment decision is made. There has been considerable study on the subject of past experience and its role in problem solving. Past experience motivates problem-solving behavior on several different levels. Maier draws a sharp difference between reproductive and productive thinking.[3] By *reproductive thinking* he means the transfer of training or problem solving as a result of certain stimuli, inherent in the problem currently being confronted, that recall a similar problem successfully mastered in the past. *Productive thinking* goes beyond the application of previous behavior, in that previous experiences and the recollection of behavior are fabricated; that is, they are restructured and rebuilt. Productive thinking is more a reasoning process than a reaction to stimuli, a flexible, imaginative reasoning process that has matured as a result of past experiences but

[3] N. R. F. Maier, "Reasoning in Humans: III. The Mechanisms of Equivalent Stimuli and of Reasoning," *Journal of Experimental Psychology*, 1945, 35, pp. 349–360.

is totally impossible when the person is so completely chained to the past and dominated by what he knows "for sure"—a domination that reflects insecurity and failure—that he cannot produce innovative reasoning in a problem-solving situation. In a series of experiments Duncker, who was concerned with this problem, studied what he called functional fixedness.[4] He attempted to show that, when previous training must be used in a way it was not used before to solve the kind of problem for which the skill was originally learned, there is difficulty in calling up the previous training. Although Duncker's work has been criticized on the basis of his experimental theory, it suggested the need for further study of the problem of applying previous learning experiences. Subsequent studies have indicated that what is critical to the matter of problem solving is not so much that the employee's work performance is dependent on his previous work experience but that his problem-solving behavior will be influenced by the cumulative effect of various other kinds of experiences, which in turn affect problem solving.

Specific skills learned in preparation for a specific problem-solving situation are not nearly as important as how the skill or problem-solving behavior was learned, in what circumstances it was utilized, whether the utilization (that is, problem-solving behavior) proved to be successful, and, finally, what was learned.

But such knowledge is not enough for the employment interviewer and the businessman. A worker can refer to broad generalizations and then restructure his original learning experience into a narrow, limited, highly functional, and utilitarian problem-solving methodology. Functional fixedness in problem solving limits this kind of application of previous experience and perhaps inhibits it. Thus prior experience can affect perception and problem-solving situations negatively or positively; it may inhibit a new hire's performance. Therefore, past experience must be viewed in terms of the individuality of each applicant. Emphasis should be on how his experience has affected him and how he uses it. Consequently, the employment interviewer who attempts to analyze qualitatively prior job skills and training should make an effort to determine how the previous learning was accomplished.

Katona theorized that learning or problem-solving behavior is divided into two parts: senseless and meaningful.[5] The distinction, of

[4] K. Duncker, "On Problem Solving" (Trans. L. S. Lees), *Psychology Monograph*, 1945, No. 270.

[5] G. Katona, *Organizing and Memorizing* (New York: Columbia University Press, 1940).

course, refers to the difference between rote and reasoning or the result of understanding in the learning process. Performing a job by rote (memory) may produce a sharply rising learning curve or, in terms of job productivity, faster results than a learning process that endeavors to build understanding and reasoning into the worker. But although learning intended to build understanding is more difficult to acquire, there are long-range advantages for the worker who has learned a job task by understanding rather than by rote.

Learning by understanding has been shown to provide greater flexibility of thought or greater facility in transferring successful problem-solving behavior to a new situation. One of the problems involved with learning by understanding is that understanding is not always complete. Particularly where the concepts to be mastered are difficult, learners may fall back on rote (memory) to supplement understanding. Whether or not supplemented by memory, incomplete understanding can make the transfer of problem-solving behavior to a new situation quite difficult. In addition, there are some differences of opinion as to whether those who learn by memorization or those who learn by understanding can retain the skill longer. Certainly, utilization of the skill with sufficient feedback of success or failure is mandatory in either case.

Analyzing Applicant Motivation

An employment interviewer who announces that he finds the applicant "motivated" usually does not indicate what the applicant is motivated for, or what he is motivated by, or to what extent he is motivated. The interviewer fails to consider that motivation is only part of behavioral theory. True, behavior is motivated; it is caused by something. But it usually is biologically, culturally, and situationally determined as well. The interviewer who asserts that the applicant is motivated (and this statement might closely follow his pronouncement that the applicant has potential) probably is referring to the achievement-and-advancement kind of motivation. But this is not the total picture. The employment interviewer must look beyond the obvious "onward and upward" kind of motivation and not assume the applicants who do not have it are not motivated at all. The interviewer must, among other things, look into the biographical museum of the applicant's life and into what have been termed the predictors of managerial effectiveness. Using biographical information obtained from applications, transcripts, and résumés, he can develop specific criteria for evaluating the applicant's drive. Two specific areas to delve into are the applicant's relationships with his parents—particularly with his father—and the applicant's capacity for empathy, which is thought of as a prime enabling factor in managerial leadership. Groupings of personality characteristics such as ambition, achievement, and drive help the interviewer understand the stresses and personal conflicts, the goals and aspirations, the satisfiers and dissatisfiers that may affect the applicant's potential and may clarify his motivations and how he satisfies his needs.

Cognitive Style

Perhaps the most important concept for an employment interviewer to bear in mind when he attempts to describe the success-oriented, highly motivated applicant is contained in this comment: "There is now enough evidence to suggest that not the strength of need but the way in which a person learns to handle his need determines the manner in which motivation and cognitive selectivity will interact." [6] The concept of cognitive style may be helpful to the employment interviewer when he reviews a career that does not follow the usual pattern or when he is confronted with educational and occupational experiences that are not typical of similar applicants. The applicant may exert control over his career just as he may exert control over his interpersonal relations on the job. He comes to the interview having experienced both achievement and failure, both reward and punishment in highly structured educational and work environments. He may have satisfied his needs in ways that best suit him or in the only ways available to him. Note how this concept relates to the problem business faces with regard to the entire process of employment selection: the problem of treating each applicant as an individual, different from any other.

The Nature of Interviewing

In any discussion of employment interviewing, there are few matters of greater concern than the question of what employment interviewing is really all about. It is the unyielding nature and character, if you will, of employment interviewing that so misleads practitioners and causes employers to retain emotionally ill equipped and educationally unprepared employment interviewers year after year and to

[6] J. S. Bruner, "Social Psychology and Perception," *in* E. Maccoby, T. Newcomb, and E. Hartley (eds.), *Readings in Social Psychology* (3rd edition) (New York: Holt, Rinehart and Winston, Inc., 1958), pp. 85–94.

tolerate their pompous dissertations on neatness, freedom from body odor, and "potential." Employment interviewing is not a gentle business. Nor is it, when performed correctly, a function for which practitioners should feel apologetic. Employment interviewing, as our definition of purpose indicates, is a narrow, demanding, explicit procedure. Although the interviewer must be subtle, ethical, considerate, and even genteel in his approach, his pursuit of the basic goal—usable information on which to base a decision in the best interests of the organization and of the applicant—must be unremitting. The employment interviewer must refuse to be intimidated by the exigencies and complexities of the applicant's personal and career histories.

Probably the most common mistake made by employment and personnel departments in companies and by employment agencies and others directly involved in employment interviewing is to give the interviewer a title designed to impress applicants (and, in business enterprises, those who award salary increases, who establish salary ranges for such people, and who listen to their recommendations). Frequently the title attempts to describe what the holder does. The title employment counselor is more widely used than it should be when applied to an employment interviewer. Counseling and interviewing are two totally different functions. If the title employment interviewer seems less prestigious than employment counselor, it may be because insufficient use has been made of the interviewing function, or it may be that the full impact of the interviewer's job is not appreciated. If this is the case, an elaborate and inaccurate title only adds to the problem.

The marked differences between employee counseling and employment interviewing are not always clearly understood. This is the fundamental explanation for the fact that employment interviewing does not always reach optimum effectiveness. When the purpose and goal of the function are not clear, the conduct, style, and performance of the function may be ill defined as well, thereby making it even more difficult to evaluate interview performance. Part of the confusion may be found in similarities between counseling and interviewing. Both employee counseling and employment interviewing are communication processes. Both require discussion—exchange of ideas, listening, and understanding—and both are concerned with the ultimate satisfaction and productivity of the applicant and the benefits he can provide to the organization in terms of decreased labor turnover, decreased operating costs, improved efficiency, and the overall quality of the workforce. Both are people-centered and concerned with personal histories, strivings, and needs. But at this point, employee counseling and employment interviewing go their separate ways. Employment interviewing must move, almost relentlessly, toward a predetermined point. The interview is used with other screening methods to make possible a decision about the applicant's suitability for the job.

Employee Counseling

Employee counseling is markedly different since there is no predetermined point to which counselor and applicant can steer. This is because counseling is more concerned with solving or diminishing emotional problems. This is not to say that job applicants may not be troubled by emotional problems. But an interviewer's objective is not to relieve these problems—he must decide on the appropriateness of the job placement despite the emotional problem or in keeping with the limitations the problem imposes. The counselor is concerned about morale; he often supplies answers to the counselee and hopes to build his confidence. The counselor may also provide the means and the occasion for the counselee to release pent-up emotional tensions. Counselors often act as problem solvers and make efforts to effect some reorientation or realignment of the counselee's ideas and attitudes. The employment interviewer, on the other hand, typically deals with attitudes and ideas as he finds them; any advice or counseling he might offer is incidental to the discussion of job prerequisites and the qualifications of the applicant. Thus the objective of an employment interviewer is the collection of facts that will enable him to make a decision on whether an applicant should be hired or an employee promoted within the organization.

The employment interview takes place because a job vacancy exists. The employment interviewer must recognize that the *constant* he deals with is the job to be filled; the *variable* is the applicant. Presumably, the job has been clearly defined in terms of its function and its relationship to comparable or disparate jobs in the work unit, department, division, and company. The job description will define in sweeping, descriptive terms the relationship of the job to corporate goals and objectives and its influence on end results, and will list the duties and experience required of the employee who must perform the job. The job description will also indicate, in varying degrees of detail, the action, style, movement, and intelligence required of a worker; the job will be clearly and precisely named, and obligations, responsibilities, and accountabilities will be clearly delineated.

In addition, there will be a job specification that simply indicates the qualifications a worker must have to perform the job. Ideally, the job specification will indicate avenues for job enrichment and methods and procedures for appraising skills and growth. It is here that the motivational aspects are developed—the elements of recognition, authority, and responsibility that constitute the difference between job enrichment and job enlargement, which is little more than a treadmill from which the employee rarely escapes, except by termination. The personnel administrator must prepare a job evaluation that measures and describes the value of the appraisal standards and the highly specific skills related to such standards, production, or quality norms. He must also decide on salary ranges for a specific position. Salary should satisfy both the stated objectives of the company, which are to keep costs low, and to maintain the stability of the workforce while remaining competitive in the labor market, and the objective of the employee, which is to maximize his income.

The Manpower Planning Approach

In pursuing a manpower planning approach, the personnel administrator and the company management should define and explain as clearly as possible to the employment interviewer reasonable career path projections and training and development requirements. For each specific job, the interviewer should be provided with key information, including performance appraisal standards, why the job is vacant, its turnover history, what occupational and personal goals and achievements contribute to success on the job, and why the job could not be filled from within the organization. In addition, the interviewer should know how the continued expansion of the corporation, the complexities of the management process, and the net result of losses due to retirement alter the manpower resources of the company and in what ways these related factors affect and are affected by the job vacancies he must fill. It is not necessary to brief the interviewer each time there is a recruitment and placement effort. Instead, the manager should develop a manpower action plan incorporating the above points. By applying the plan to each job vacancy, the interviewer will have the insights he needs to probe the applicant in depth and with relentless efficiency. Thus the basic elements of manpower planning enlarge the personnel administrator's responsibility, strengthen the hand of the employment interviewer, and make it possible to relate the whole process more closely to the applicant.

Importance of Behavioral Analysis

The employment interviewer must understand that each candidate for employment is fundamentally different from every other applicant and fundamentally different from every other human being as well, and that unless these fundamental differences are recognized and understood, it is futile to search for predictors of success or failure, or to make random judgments about an applicant's potential, or to cling to tired stereotypes in order to explain away troublesome applicants. This means there must be no "red flag" zones or knockout responses in employment interviewing. In other words, no statement made by the applicant should automatically disqualify him on the grounds that it is incompatible with the "official" attitude of top-level management, the personnel administrator, or the employment interviewer. Such "official" attitudes—commonly concerned with motivation, with interests, status, the value of a retirement program or benefit package, security, or criteria for success or failure—usually reflect not corporate policy but personal beliefs. They are not necessarily valid; in fact, they may be no more than low-order stereotypes, and in the final analysis may have nothing whatever to do with ultimate success or failure on the job or with the capacity to contribute to an organization. Typically, such predetermined official opinions are applied without the slightest regard to the objective factors in favor of the applicant.

For example, suppose an employment interviewer upholds the belief—his own or that of high-level management—that money is the prime mover of men and that all employees will scale unprecedented heights to get it. And suppose he enforces this belief as a dogma, to disagree with which would be prejudicial to the employee. Now there is enough evidence to justify the view that money is an important incentive. But it is incorrect to consider that money is a substitute for job satisfaction. Adhering to his dogma, the interviewer might form an unfavorable opinion of an applicant who responds only passively to the company's salary scale, competition formula, or commission or bonus plan. In fact, however, the applicant might be interested primarily in the prestige he thinks he will gain by working for the company. This, together with the satisfaction from the work itself, could constitute an incentive comparable to money in the applicant's subsequent work performance. But the interviewer has already raised his red flag of alarm and categorized the applicant as an unknown quantity. The fact is that the response of a worker to an incentive plan may well depend more on his own background than on the plan itself. As one writer has suggested, "Management's power to motivate is effective only to the extent that from the employee's point of view management controls the means by which the employee can satisfy his needs."[7] He further indicates that while a paycheck and praise are among these incentives, so is prestige.

Let us take an example and explore it fully to see what considerations can enter into the process of choosing an applicant. Consider an applicant with excellent credentials and a completely likable, pleasant personality. His experience is satisfactory, but his earning history indicates that at this point in his career he will be susceptible to the "money game"—high bonuses, commissions, and competition for promotion. The applicant may give the impression of being cool under fire: He is rarely ruffled and is philosophic about the contingencies of life. He may be thought of as a deep thinker, silent and shrewd, the kind of person one would not want to bid against in poker. He may be hired for one reason but may accept the job for a totally different reason. The interviewer or employer may see a cool, even unemotional, likable, efficient, good-natured, level-headed person with just a hint of arrogance. The interviewer may decide that the applicant is the type that is deadly in the corporate clinches, a man who will survive to beat the money game in the pressured atmosphere of intercompany competition. The fact of the matter may be that the applicant is looking for a paternalistic type of company that will give him security. He may, in fact, shun competition, and properly interpreted his coolness, good humor, and uncomplaining philosophic attitude indicate that he will never take his work too seriously; that he is security-motivated, seeking a protective employer and a safe, quiet work environment; that he will rarely draw attention to himself and considers money and competition hazards rather than stimuli.

It is difficult to spot this type of person, even for the experienced interviewer. Yet behavioral scientists suggest that hidden motives may be brought to light through complex investigative methods as well as through examining physical characteristics, which indeed are often indicative of personality. The investigative procedures include skills inventory and other psychological testing procedures (although in the case of personality tests, more tangible indications of the applicant's motives are revealed). Much can be gained from a critical analysis of the applicant's biographical information as well, but such an approach must be handled delicately and prudently because indis-

[7] D. McGregor, "The Staff Function in Human Relations," *The Journal of Social Issues*, Summer 1948, pp. 5–22.

criminate interpretations may lead to unreliable and irrelevant conclusions. This is but one example of the challenges and responsibilities of employment interviewing.

An applicant like the one just described—who seems cool and competitive but who is in fact seeking security—is usually easy to recruit,
since experience has taught him that there is little he can do to shape
his own destiny. Because the employment interviewer has misread
personality traits that were actually part of a facade, the applicant
may be placed in a highly competitive, high-pressure situation. Here
he may find some measure of success since his performance may
fluctuate, and may never be quite disappointing enough to threaten
his position. He is a good fellow and well liked, and therefore he
may linger on for years. In this instance the employer's dogma about
the importance of money is negatively upheld—the mediocre employee was, in fact, unresponsive to the incentive of money.

The Motivation of Applicants

Let's return for a moment to one of the basic concepts of employment interviewing: The job to be filled is the constant; the applicant
is the variable. Behavioral researchers have repeatedly demonstrated
that people are motivated by their own needs rather than by the
efforts or policies of the organization, which often run contrary to
what the employee feels and wants. When an organization treats
human behavior as a constant rather than as a variable, the only
result is conflict. No one can be completely objective in judging another person. Prejudices and preferences exert a strong influence on
one man's opinion of another. Argyris asserts that a fully matured
person would find it totally impossible to function effectively in a
typical organization structure. He further contends that organizational
methods and practices are antithetical to the natural growth processes
of human beings.[8] What of the employment interviewer who seeks
to fill a job vacancy requiring a "mature" person to work in a highly
structured organizational environment? By way of an answer, we
might ask: Will the interviewer ever realize the absolute futility of
his search?

Treasuries of information can be gleaned from the objective analysis of life histories, which can help illuminate the why of test scores
(or job references, credit ratings, and many other predictors) and

[8] C. Argyris, "Understanding Human Behavior in Organizations: One View
Point," in M. Haire (ed.), *Modern Organization Theory* (New York: John Wiley
& Sons, Inc., 1959).

help explain more about the applicant's drives, motives, stress thresholds, and job needs. If we accept the widely held principle that something, call it X, causes behavior, then we are led to assume that an individual is motivated when these causal factors act on him in such a way as to make him aware of certain needs; he begins to want something. The desires may be positive—more and greater satisfactions—or negative—preservation of existing satisfactions. What he wants becomes a goal, and so his behavior is said to be goal-directed. But some needs are more demanding, more important, and more confining than others, and so there is an order of priority among needs, which applies also to goals. This persists almost unchanged for long periods of time—perhaps even for a lifetime.

Research has shown that the experiences of the child interacting with his family are major determinants of his personality. Moreover, it is now generally accepted that some of the best indicators or predictors of success and failure on the job are to be found in biographical information. Thus we are drawn irresistibly to the conclusion that decisions affecting employment and job placement (in any capacity, whether clerical, managerial, or executive) must result from diligently applied and pertinent investigative procedures designed to explain the total personality of the applicant in terms of his experiences, needs, strivings, motives, and goals.

Parent-Child Relations

Let us explore the dimensions of this interviewing challenge. What can we know about the job applicant, for example, whose parents were divorced when he was a child, who was in poor health, whose father was incapable of providing for the family, and whose mother assumed the father role? And what of the applicant who as a child was proud of his successful (success as interpreted by the applicant) father? Freud's reaction-formation and identification concepts can help direct the employment interviewer. Simply stated, reaction formation explains how and why the strengths, successes, achievements, and strivings of one generation come about in reaction to the perceived weaknesses and failures of the preceding generation. In other words reaction formation explains the process that stimulates and motivates a son, disappointed with his father's failure, to avoid the life pattern of his father and to strive to reverse that pattern in himself. Similarly, where the father is successful the son may experience a negative reaction and resign himself to failure. The son may feel that he is incapable of matching the father's successes, or that in today's world the father's pattern for success cannot be repeated. Today we see examples of reaction formation, not only in the black ghetto and in the poverty-stricken white slums, but also in suburbia, where the son or daughter forms a negative attitude toward certain life styles and values. The use of drugs by the children of executives has been viewed partly as a reaction to another generation and partly a result of a too permissive environment. It is clear that a feeling of alienation is prevalent among the younger generation and that drugs are used as a weapon against the older generation to help crack the facade of smug self-satisfaction that the youngsters perceive. In this connection, John Finlator, assistant director of the Federal Bureau of Narcotics and Dangerous Drugs, comments, "In affluent families, the kids know their parents are going to react by saying 'You're ruining me.' " [9]

A son may identify with a particular life style that he associates with his father's success. The criterion of success need not be material; the father's confidence, spirit, and even self-assurance may qualify him as successful in the eyes of the son. Thus in the drive for achievement—simply for achievement's sake—the individual may seek those channels in which he can succeed so that he can follow the pattern of success that has been building in him since childhood.

If a person is dedicated to a task, a job, an assignment, a career, or a profession, it does not necessarily mean that he likes what he is doing or that he is receiving any satisfaction from the job itself. He may only be satisfying his need for achievement. For example, a successful accountant who indicates during the employment interview that he dislikes accounting is telling the interviewer a great deal about himself. The salesman who likes the success he has achieved through sales more than the actual selling is not at all uncommon in the job market. This salesman is not necessarily less effective than one who likes to sell. Nor is the accountant who dislikes accounting necessarily less accurate, ambitious, or aggressive than one who loves figures. Each is motivated in his own way to do his own thing.

Behavioral Concepts and Job Placement

The validity of such behavioral concepts in job placement is determined by how relationships are measured and which relationships are selected as well as by statistical methods. Prediction (whether it concerns sales effort, business success, turnover, or human behavior)

[9] S. Margetts, "Why Do Executives' Children Take Drugs?" *Dun's Review,* June 1969, p. 43.

is ultimately a matter of selecting, weighing, and mixing observations about the past with what we understand about the present and with what we think will be true in the future. This means that there must be a logical relationship between what we want to predict and what is indicated, and between the degree of accuracy we need and the reliability of our measurements.

For example, almost every personnel department with a testing program uses some form of intelligence test. An intelligence test may indicate whether a man is intelligent. However, it does not differentiate between the kind of intelligence that may be beneficial to a business and the kind that may not. For instance, a highly intelligent manager, who sees many sides of a problem and many different ramifications and consequences of each alternative decision may become so immobilized by his own thought processes that he cannot make a decision. How effective, therefore, is he as a manager? On the other hand, a single-minded manager, who is guided in his decisions by the narrow purpose of his job, the goals of his company, his understanding of people, who shrewdly weighs the chances for success and failure—with his goal clearly in mind—makes his decision and drives for its successful conclusion with a singleness of purpose. Both managers are intelligent, but which would a company prefer to have working for it? There is also the problem that the single-minded man might not score as well on the test as the "deep thinker." Therefore, although intelligence tests may be helpful in some areas, they must be used as supplementary tools for interviewing until they can accurately measure and define what a company means by intelligence.

Since many statistical methods do not provide the accuracy desired, the absence of statistical certainty in behavioral analysis does not decrease the value of this approach. In fact, identifying the interrelatedness of personal experiences, educational background, and occupational goals helps build understanding and provides insights that may lead to a decision as to what statistical measures and screening tools will work best in the prediction of success or failure on the job. The researcher, therefore, has an impetus to develop more sensitive tools of measurement, building a partnership between the behavioral scientist and the personnel practitioner.

We explore the relationship between the employment interview and other screening methods in Chapter 9. For the present, suffice it to say that, just as the artist selects hues and tones rather than paint, so the personnel interviewer and administrator should select precise techniques, not tests or methods. From what we learn about the relationship between what we understand about the applicant, what we assume, and what screening and predictive techniques reveal, an organic process emerges having a synergistic effect on all the contributing screening methods.

What the Applicant Wants

Let us now draw together some of the concepts we have discussed and apply them to an analysis of the applicant who is being interviewed. Fundamentally, the applicant wants to be treated with dignity. In recognition of this, one of the first admonitions given student nurses concerning patient relations is that they must never refer to a patient as "the liver in 365," or "the Type A in 414." Similarly, applicant relations demand that the whole person be interviewed and dealt with and not just the dexterity of the typist's fingers, the mental capacities of the manager, or the technical knowledge and aptitudes of the skilled worker. Only in this way can the interviewer pick up the myriad clues that help explain the applicant, and only in this way can a bond of mutual concern be built.

In typical circumstances an applicant is free to decide whether to accept a job offer. The company has the same freedom where the applicant is concerned. Hence a business organization is a voluntary association, not a random accumulation of people. But, although the applicant does in fact exercise considerable discretion as to where and at what he works, he does not have complete freedom of choice. That choice is determined to a very marked degree by the applicant's self-esteem (ego) and his perception and understanding of his own needs and limitations. The interviewer who does not consider this selective discretion misses an important clue that, in combination with other clues gotten from the interview and from tests, could help him understand the applicant. Seemingly benign questions such as, "How did you happen to come to our company?" or "What is there about Pitfall Manufacturing Company that interested you?" are too often literally thrown at the applicant as little more than something to break the ice and to get the applicant to talk and relax. Usually, such questions meet with equally benign responses such as, "I have heard about the company and thought I would apply for a job here," or, "I think I would be happy here," or, "I know enough about the company to be interested in working here." Although they do serve the limited purpose of the questions, these answers are unsatisfactory in our frame of reference. The interviewer who expects nothing more misses a golden opportunity.

Need Fulfillment

An applicant selects an organization as a prospective place of employment because he thinks it will suit his purposes and will help him achieve his goals. If he considers monetary reward his prime objective, then of course he will seek a job with a firm that is known for its high salaries and bonuses. Perhaps he wants prestige and status, or glamour, or a good location, or security. In any case, he will seek a company that can fulfill his needs.

Often the employee's range of choice is limited by his skills, or he may have special aptitudes for which he can command a high salary, but which not every firm can use. And, of course, there is the applicant who has no real understanding of his capabilities or potential, who has low-order career and job objectives, and who sees no difference between one company and another. In this discussion we are not considering applicants referred by employment agencies. It is generally assumed that the agency is conducting its screening in a professional and ethical way, so that the most suitable company for the applicant has already been selected.

Typically, the well-educated applicant capable of making a tangible contribution to an organization will be more discriminating in his selection of a prospective employer than the passive one. The latter has long ceased to exert control over his destiny, in the belief that such control is futile. Also less discriminating in selecting an organization is the minimally educated, undermotivated person who is satisfied simply to find a job he can do and get paid for it. The security-oriented person is inclined to steer clear of jobs that offer feast or famine in the paycheck or that pay commissions or competitive piece rates. The person who demands some power over his environment, who needs involvement and challenge, and who craves the excitement of the unknown is right for a company and a job that emphasize experimentation, innovation, and "blue-sky" horizons. A person in this class often suffers from a deep-seated lack of confidence, which he seeks to eradicate by achieving success. When he attempts something he has never done before, he covers himself psychologically because in the event of failure he has the excuse that he is new.

The Applicant's Self-image and Career Selection

Occasionally, a misread self-image determines career choices. For example, a glib, fast-talking person who claims he has "never met a stranger" may in reality be fraught with anxieties. He affects a gregarious, self-confident manner to conceal his nagging insecurity and fear of people. He protects himself by overwhelming people before they can take advantage of him. He may choose the sales field because it offers an opportunity to deal with people. Thus his own misconceptions of himself guide his career along stereotyped lines. This type may seek to identify himself with an industry because he attributes to it some characteristic that he associates with himself, such as dynamism, exuberance, or imaginativeness. Of course both self-image and industry stereotype may be wrong.

Although it may seem that the applicant is able to make free choices, at least as to type of work, company, and industry, we have seen that these choices are, in fact, restricted by emotional needs. One of the challenges facing the interviewer is to determine why the applicant selected one particular career or company. Not to do so might result in misplacing an applicant in respect to the job, the supervisor, the company, or the industry itself. Thus we may find applicants who, within the limits of their choice, unnecessarily underestimate themselves or who challenge these natural limitations to the point of frustration. The consequence may be anomie, general disorientation—a situation that routine questions and answers or popular screening tests resolve.

Far too many employment interviewers are so concerned with affectations and styles they consider appropriate to their work, so concerned with superlubricated human relations, so relieved that the interview concludes on a note of warmth and friendship, so proud that throughout the interview the emotional level rarely gets off dead center that they never bother to evaluate the real effectiveness of the interview itself. Regrettably, most interviewers seem obsessed with the idea of relaxing the applicant. They work so hard at it that neither the applicant nor the interviewer is the least bit relaxed. Sometimes the atmosphere is so completely agreeable that it is almost sticky.

Far too few interviewers ever challenge a qualified applicant with questions of substance and purposeful direction that would enable the interviewer to build rapport with the applicant or create an atmosphere of mutual confidence. Rarely does the typical interviewer rise to the occasion presented by a capable applicant and deal with him as an intelligent person and as an equal. When the interview is over, the interviewer usually asks himself, "Did I step on any toes?" meaning did he touch sensitive areas? If only he had.

2

The Perceptual Process and Attitude Formation

THE EMPLOYMENT INTERVIEWER, by the nature and purpose of his job, must make certain judgments about applicants. To do this fairly, he must search for clues that will help him understand the applicant. The interviewer is influenced by what he perceives. We are, therefore, faced with the problem of *perception*. By simply looking at an applicant, an employment interviewer will be unable to form an objective opinion. Certain variables will interfere. It is unrealistic to assume that anyone can perceive anything objectively—even an inanimate object. But, when the object is animate and a human being—and the situation is by nature judgmental, highly structured, and enmeshed in and confused by semantics and uncertain screening methods—the task of making objective evaluations seems insurmountable.

Factors that Distort Perception

Indeed the task is complex, but it is more easily surmountable if those involved in the interview process have a greater awareness of their own impact on end results. The employment interviewer must understand that he himself influences his own perception. He will respond to certain cues he may not be aware of just as all of us are often influenced without our knowing it, by the size and shape of an inanimate object, by its color, and by the way light shines on it. In other words, there are certain unconscious, subliminal stimuli that affect perception. Psychologists speak of irrelevant cues in this respect; that is, human beings are influenced in their judgment by occurrences or situations that may have nothing whatsoever to do with the matter at hand. These stimuli are confusing and sometimes ill defined.

For example, physical characteristics have nothing whatsoever to do with morality any more than the shiny exterior of a car is indicative of a smoothly running engine. A facial expression might indicate a deep-thinking, serious, academic nature, when in fact none of these qualities is present. The manager or the interviewer who makes decisions about employment is going to be influenced by what he feels plus by what his experience tells him and by certain impulses that set into motion a chain reaction of thoughts. Thus the decision maker is affected by his emotions and it is reasonable to assume that, if the observer perceives that someone agrees with his preformed idea of what is good or favorable, then that person affects the observer's perception favorably.

But these influences or stimuli are not always obvious. The observer is a part of the perceptual process and brings to bear his expectations, emotions, values, and motives. Regrettably, the observer is a highly fallible link in the perception process. Even physical characteristics can cause an observer to form incorrect impressions about the abilities and character of people. Employment interviewers are especially vulnerable to first impressions. A letter from an applicant inquiring about the possibilities of employment or requesting an appointment, a photograph, a résumé, an application for employment, test results— any of these seen prior to an in-depth employment interview can be responsible for a first impression.

If employment interviewers are to fulfill their job responsibilities, if they are to be fair and just to the applicant, if they are to provide an ethical and professional atmosphere for the interview, and if they are to benefit the organization for which they work, they must avoid drawing conclusions from their first impressions. An interesting study regarding first impressions was performed by Dailey.[1] Through laboratory experiments, he was able to show that first impressions not only are lasting but that they also tend to be inaccurate. He further

[1] C. A. Dailey, "The Effects of Premature Conclusions Upon the Acquisition of Understanding of a Person," *Journal of Psychology*, 1952, 33, pp. 133–152.

found that those who do not draw conclusions from first impressions are better able to arrive at reasonable and just decisions about people.

The reason, of course, that first impressions can be so damaging in an interview is that they can carry over to the observer's evaluation and judgment about the applicant's ability to perform a job. The interviewer who does not guard against first impressions may make an unconscious effort to prove their correctness. He may reinforce his so-called knowledge of people by steering the interview in directions that either prove or disprove his first impression. A first impression may be so powerful and have such impact on the interviewer that, even if the applicant knew of the impression, he could do nothing to overcome it. In fact, however, the applicant rarely has the faintest idea of the impression he has made.

Stereotypes

The employment interviewer is also subject to the lure of stereotypes and bias—concepts that people form and that they feel they can rely on with certainty regarding the unalterable nature and character of certain types of people. Stereotyping cannot be relied on and is dangerous. The problem is a difficult one because it is so common and so widespread. No matter where you go, you will find people who share your stereotypes. This leads to a reinforcement that makes it easy to believe that stereotypes are truths. Expressions such as, "Where there's smoke, there's fire," and "An acorn of suspicion leads to a tree of truth," can be used to reinforce stereotypes even when they have long ago been disproved. Nazi propaganda during World War II shows how an untruth, no matter how fantastic, will be believed if repeated often enough.

Generalizations

It is, of course, possible to single out an individual, form an attitude about him, and then apply that attitude to all members of his group. But, obviously, one person's characteristics do not apply to all the members of his group. Stereotypes can affect judgments regarding members of certain religious, national, and racial groups. These generally refer to supposed innate qualities, such as frugality, money-making ability, rhythm, physical endurance, authoritarian or dictatorial tendencies, laziness, immorality, artistic and musical talent. But stereotypes can go beyond religious, racial, and national criteria. They even extend to income. Controlled experiments have shown that income levels shape attitudes about the social adjustment of individuals. Experiments indicated that the poor were considered to lack social adjustment and were probably unhappy. At the same time, those in higher economic categories were thought of as being happy, pleasant, well adjusted, and healthy. It is believed that various income groups harbor stereotypes of other income groups and that a particular attitude reflects the observer's income bracket as well as his own value system, self-concept, and perception of the outside world.

We can immediately recognize the impact such perceptions and interpretations can have on the employment interviewer. It must be remembered that the employment interviewer is a human being. Simply because he is in the profession of evaluating and judging others does not make him immune to the dangers inherent in the perceptual process. It is seen readily that stereotypes can markedly affect the direction and outcome of an interview. Even when the interviewer is sophisticated enough to be aware of the external factors that influence him, he is not aware of the subliminal stimuli to which he is also subject.

Halo Effect

Let us consider an additional hazard, the halo effect. Simply stated, the halo effect is a favorable or unfavorable future-oriented generalization made by an observer that becomes, in effect, a prism through which the observer views all characteristics—assets and liabilities— of another person. For example, an employment interviewer may decide that an applicant is dressed inappropriately. Therefore, the interviewer's perception of the way the person is dressed is linked with what the interviewer believes the mode of dress means or says about the applicant. This negatively affects the interviewer's further observations. The halo effect has often been cited in connection with performance appraisals in which one or a few achievements of an employee result in a high-performance rating, even though these achievements may not fall into any of the categories in which he is supposed to be evaluated.

The halo effect may be most marked when the observer must deal with unknown, intangible, or loosely defined traits as, for example, honesty, integrity, ability to follow through, and morality. In a study particularly pertinent to this discussion, Grove and Kerr found that employees at a company in receivership judged their working conditions, pay scale, supervisors, and colleagues harshly. This was a reflection of their insecurity and concern about the financial condition of the company.[2] Thus the halo effect produced negative attitudes when in fact as the study indicated, working conditions, pay schedules, and other circumstances of employment were probably better than in most other branches of the company.

An employment interviewer attempting to determine an applicant's attitude about a former employer must carefully weigh the applicant's comments, not because he is necessarily attempting to distort the truth, but because unconsciously and most probably without malice the applicant will view his former employer through the prism of the work environment. Interestingly enough, stereotypes, bias, and the halo effect do not always manifest themselves as individual or isolated distortions that march through the interviewer's mind single file. Instead, these perceptual blockages can appear as a kind of chain reaction, which the interviewer considers to be logical and perhaps even natural. For example, knowing that a person is of a certain national origin brings to mind a certain stereotype, which in turn draws together combinations of descriptions presumably valid for the individual. As the link of descriptive terms grows, each additional description, stereotype, or consequence of the halo effect becomes more specific, more certain, and more detailed, thus having an influence and impact on the observer that seems rational, logical, and even near the truth but which may be grossly misleading.

Let us now consider one other perceptual block that can affect the employment interviewer's observations. Remember that the observer is a part of the process and is influenced by his environment in how he perceives and what he perceives. The results of laboratory experiments have supported the conclusion that the observer's emotional state can directly affect his perception. He may project his own feelings into his evaluation of others. This could be described as a "mirror" effect, because instead of seeing the other party, the interviewer is actually seeing himself. For example, a person who feels threatened may observe others as being threatening. Or a man who has just left a motion picture theater feeling thoroughly frightened by a horror movie imagines each darkened alley and shadowed doorway to harbor fearful and threatening apparitions. The employment interviewer must be acutely aware of this form of projection. He must understand that his own weaknesses, frustrations, anxieties, and the like may be projected into applicants.

[2] B. A. Grove and W. A. Kerr, "Specific Evidence on Origin of Halo Effect in Measurement of Morals," *Journal of Social Psychology*, 1951, 34, pp. 165–170.

The tendency toward projection generally increases proportionately as a person's understanding of himself diminishes. People who recognize undesirable traits in themselves usually project these traits into others. They see in others even greater amounts of these undesirable traits than they are willing to admit exist in themselves. The employment interviewer who realizes that his emotions are affected and his understanding of himself shaped by feelings of inadequacy in some aspect of his personality may perceive a similar quality in others.

Perception

Perception is a matter of interrelationships that affect behavior. Observing someone else's behavior we might conclude that it was illogical, irrational, out of order, or inconsistent, but it must be kept in mind that the person thinks that his actions are perfectly in keeping with the situation as he understands it. We say that behavior is caused by something, and therefore it has an effect. This cause-and-effect relationship exists in what theorists term a field or a systematic bridging relationship between cause and effect. The perceptual field constitutes everything the individual perceives. A person's behavior, therefore, is subject to, and continually determined by, this perceptual field.

Whether our perceptions are accurate and real is of little importance. The environment, or situation, or instance to which a person reacts becomes real to him in terms of the behavior that it causes. In the final analysis, the perceptual field is affected by the individual's need to organize stimuli to satisfy his motivational needs.

In terms of Gestalt psychological theory, human beings respond to the perceptual field in terms of organized wholes. In other words, they react to a total situation, the interrelatedness of stimuli, and the organic relationship of cause and effect rather than to isolated stimuli. It can be expected, therefore, that changes in behavior will occur as the perceptual field changes. Obviously, a person must be ready for changes which are brought about by attitudes, mental set, misconceptions, physiological capabilities as well as by situations that are not easily understood, such as those the employment interviewer faces routinely. Because people share—to varying degrees—understandings about certain perceptual stimuli, they can not only communicate with one another but can also begin to predict behavior. It might even be suggested that, conversely, it is possible to observe perception by reading back from the behavior we observe.

The employment interviewer must make himself a student of human behavior. It is important for him to understand that the applicant will perceive the interviewer in his own special way just as he will perceive the applicant in *his* own special way. It is absolutely necessary for the interviewer to understand the influences on his own perception as well as the experiences an applicant may have had that influence his perception, behavior, and aspirations. If the interviewer understands the nature and cause of stimuli that may influence his perception and his objectivity, then he is able to shield against such stimuli as they arise during the course of an interview. This is why we are concerned with the mechanism of perception as it affects the employment interviewer's attitudes and decisions about an applicant.

Perceptual Selectivity

Employment interviewers must be sensitive to the fact that they will respond to an applicant on the basis of what has been called the contravaluant hypothesis. This means that the employment interviewer will be selective on the basis of his own dominant values regarding a particular subject. Understanding and extrapolation that lead toward a conclusion are influenced by the values of the observer or listener so that words that have, in effect, high dominance or high value will create greater interest, will stimulate the listener, and will channel his thinking; whereas low-dominance or low-value words are blocked; that is, in a way, avoided.

Other studies have indicated that the listener tends to block or defend himself against words or comments that are personally offensive. On the whole, therefore, the perceptual abilities of the employment interviewer are affected not so much by the degree to which he wants to obtain a favorable response from an applicant, as by the responses that force him to make positive or negative judgments at considerable frequency throughout the interview. The employment interviewer, in effect, seeks certain responses from the applicant that he considers positive or agreeable. He may, of course, seek negative or disagreeable responses as well. This is a consequence of the manner in which he structures the interview or the technique or approach he takes to obtain the information he wants. On the basis of the applicant's first few responses, the employment interviewer is then perceptually ready for responses to other specific inquiries and even to predict how the applicant would fare if hired.

We hear a knock at the door and assume that someone is standing at the door requesting that it be opened; we hear what sounds like a jet engine and assume that an airplane is flying through the sky above us. We learn, therefore, to predict certain consequences from certain causative factors. Thus the interviewer tends to match or compare his own perceptions about the applicant with what he considers to be logical or reasonable responses to his inquiries. This gives the employment interviewer a wide range in making assumptions about the applicant.

After we perceive things that simply should not be, it still takes us a while to see things as they actually are. It is possible for an observer to expect to see, on the basis of his experience, what he has always seen or what he has always expected to see; he thinks that what he observes or perceives is real or true. However, once an observer understands that his expectations may not be satisfied, he is prepared for the unexpected or the unpredicted.

Thus we might expect that an employment interviewer who has found incongruities in one applicant will be aware that they might exist in other applicants as well. Unfortunately, the pull that stereotypes, bias, the halo effect, experience, and projection have sometimes stifles this awareness. For example, an employment interviewer, when dealing with an applicant, may expect very little in the way of enlightened conversation, deep understanding of responsibilities, or oral proof that he is qualified for the position for which he is applying. If and when the interviewer's expectations are confirmed or reinforced, the accuracy of his perception is also confirmed. In the absence of any contrary indication he will expect what he considers the norm, in other words, a range of behavior that experience has taught him to regard as typical or acceptable. Thus perception leads the employment interviewer to establish reference points, which he feels are a reliable guide to understanding the applicant. These reference points will presumably accommodate his own perceptual responses and will be predictive enough to give him the insight he requires.

The Interviewer as the Norm

Employment interviewers often tend to use themselves as the ideal, standard, or "norm" for the type of person they would like to recommend for employment. Therefore, it is important for the employment interviewer to know himself, to understand his weaknesses and strengths, to have insight about his strivings, motivations, and frustrations because only in this way will he be able to evaluate an applicant accurately. Furthermore, the employment interviewer will be less likely to arrive at the kind of extreme conclusions about an applicant that are little more than critical generalizations. The employment interviewer must understand that he is likely to focus on those characteristics of an applicant that are most similar to his own. If a person is sociable, he is likely to be sensitive to, and highly aware of, the sociability of others.

It must be remembered that there are relatively few categories in which we can place people, partly because of limitations in our language and partly because of lack of information and training regarding variations in personality types. People, therefore, typically use categories that they are familiar with or that they would apply to themselves. Hence employment interviewers, like everyone else, may tend to be less sensitive, less aware, and less understanding of those traits and characteristics that do not necessarily match their own or that do not fit into familiar categories.

Our perception of others is affected by our own adjustment. An employment interviewer who is relatively pleased with his lot in life, who generally likes himself, and who accepts himself for what he is will probably avoid extremes of enthusiasm or antipathy, and will tend to be more understanding (although not necessarily more forgiving) and more broadly receptive to applicants than an interviewer who is unhappy with himself and his lot in life.

Even though people find solace in the thought that others are plagued with the same deficiencies and problems as they are, when they see their own unfavorable characteristics reflected in someone else they react negatively. It would be unrealistic to suggest that employment interviewers do not like or dislike applicants. This is to be expected. Now, when an interviewer likes an applicant, the qualities that he perceives are primarily those that he has in common with him. The interviewer will tend to perceive the other qualities inaccurately or vaguely. When the interviewer dislikes the applicant the situation is reversed. The qualities perceived are those that the interviewer does not have in common with the applicant. The interviewer has set up a defense to avoid identifying himself with someone he dislikes.

Pitfalls in Perception

The ability to control the perceptual process is not a skill with which we are born, any more than we are born with sales skill. The employment interviewer can sometimes avoid perceptual pitfalls as long as he is aware that they exist and provided he can look beyond himself to more established norms by which to measure applicants. It is considerably easier for an observer to understand personality types when he is familiar with them than to make judgments about people with whom he has had little contact. This is particularly true with respect to the interviewing of persons from certain ethnic or minority groups that the interviewer may be unfamiliar with.

An employment interviewer will form certain opinions about the status of an applicant on the basis of such factors as position applied for, education, social background, previous job experience, salary, and even age. An applicant who seeks to fill the position of janitor will probably be viewed as having less status than an applicant for a managerial position. In general, an observer tends to attribute more favorable characteristics and traits to high-status persons than to low-status persons even though they may respond identically to a given question. Therefore, everything the applicant does—what he says, how he responds, his humor, and even his physical posture—is viewed in terms of the interviewer's ideas about the applicant's status.

It is obvious that the observer must be conscious of behavior. It was suggested earlier that there are cues about which the observer is not always consciously aware. But there are also visible traits or characteristics that an applicant feels free to reveal and that seem apropos of a given situation. For example, an employment interviewer may wish to know how respectful a young clerical applicant is. The fact that the applicant may appear to act in a manner that the interviewer considers respectful does not really indicate the applicant's true attitudes about authority. Yet the applicant will probably be judged on the basis of the clue that the employment interviewer perceives. An applicant who is highly personable and outgoing may be a total failure at sales, but the employment interviewer could view him as a potential salesman.

The realization that others are different from or in conflict with us predisposes us to recognize and perceive differences. In challenging interview situations that create conflict and anxieties and that produce friction, the interviewer is confronted with someone he may see as a threat—a competitor of sorts. In such situations the applicant and interviewer may have difficulty communicating. The applicant may have trouble describing his successes or failures, the nature of the supervision under which he worked, and many of the circumstances of his previous employment.

The way in which employment interviewers evaluate clues—that is, information about the applicant—is largely determined by the interviewer's experience, training, and motives. A fact that an applicant relates about himself is not in itself important unless the interviewer thinks it is. But, because the interviewer is never absolutely certain about the validity and reliability of his perceptions, he must learn to expect certain responses so that he can analyze his own experiences and understand how they will affect his perception in relation to the responses. What we perceive is a result of our own background, needs and goals, life experiences, and education. These results are constantly reinforced by our day-to-day experiences. Cantril has said:

> We create consistencies concerning people and social situations. These provide us with certain consistent characteristics that will ease our interpretation and make our actions more effective so long as there is some correspondence between the attribution we make and the consequence we experience from it in our own action. The social consistencies we learn obviously involve the relationships between ourselves and others.[3]

Effects of Company Pressures on the Interviewer

Employment interviewers are usually under pressure to fill job vacancies. Widespread manpower shortages, noncompetitive salary scales, poor company image, accelerated expansion and growth, need for new technical skills, and high turnover rates are just a few of the factors that create this pressure. Consider its effects on an employment interviewer who must objectively analyze the qualifications of applicants for employment. Consider, too, the effect on the employment interviewer of abrasive comments by managers (who must fill vacancies in their departments) alluding to the personnel department's supposed inability to find people. These managers are often amazed that the job has stood vacant so long.

Now consider how this pressure affects the interviewer's perceptual process. Distortion in perception takes place in direct relation to the urgency of a need. Urgency is translated into emotional stress, and the greater the emotional stress the greater the tendency to interpret or to act on what we *want* to see, *need* to see, and *hope* to see. Thus it can be said, that *the ability and discipline to control perceptual pitfalls in the interviewing process is affected by the motivation of the interviewer.* If the employment interviewer is to be held strictly responsible for the quality of the applicants he refers for employment, if careful historical records are maintained concerning his ability to

[3] H. Cantril, "Perception and Inter-personal Relations," *American Journal of Psychiatry,* 114 (2), 1957, pp. 119–126.

judge potentially successful people, if the organizational environment is such that the interviewer can seek a high level of professionalism in his technique and of accuracy in his evaluations, then his perceptual process can more nearly be controlled. Obviously, to judge an applicant's potential and to weigh and evaluate his experiences the interviewer must be conscious of his own job responsibilities and of his own attitudes, expectations, experiences, and reinforcements, which necessarily affect his perception.

The work of Dearborn and Simon illustrates again the internalization of stimuli.[4] They demonstrated that an observer perceives what he is prepared or ready to perceive and in so doing selects from complex or multiple stimuli. However, as the object of the observation becomes less fathomable (such as generalized human behavior, work histories, experience, and job goals) the observer will be more influenced by what he expects and by his own personality and self-concepts and less by the object of his observations.

Employment interviewers must, necessarily, be cognizant of numerous responsibilities—to the applicant, to themselves as professionals, to the employment or personnel department, to the department where the vacancy exists, and to the company with respect to both present capabilities and future potential.

The perception, which affects the final judgment of the interviewer about the applicant, may be qualitatively determined by the sense of obligation and responsibility toward one of these several pressure points. For example, motivational as well as cognitive forces come to bear when it is necessary for the interviewer to make selective judgments about the stimuli he "chooses" to perceive. The employment interviewer who feels that his first obligation is to the applicant may follow a kind of counseling-interviewing approach that is highly applicant-oriented. The interviewer who is concerned about his department's inability to produce warm bodies for managers to interview could make highly arbitrary decisions. In his desire to improve the department's performance he might see only the applicant's favorable qualities and ignore anything that suggests the applicant is a poor or questionable choice. Thus the interviewer's perception is a selection process whereby he chooses from among various stimuli projected by the applicant and ignores others. Selection is based on the interviewer's needs, motives, and total experience, which are brought to bear at the time. Also perception may be affected by certain learned

⁴ D. C. Dearborn and H. A. Simon, "Selective Perception: A Note on the Departmental Identifications of Executives," *Journal of Sociometry,* 1958, 21, pp. 140–144.

responses that have been reinforced over time and that remove a cognitive or deliberate selectivity.

Perception and Attitude Formation

Perceptions affect judgments and subsequently behavior; in the process, they help reinforce old attitudes or form new ones. Attitude formation is associated very closely with the perceptual process. For instance, applicants who present themselves for employment possess very definite attitudes about the type of work they desire, about the circumstances surrounding their involuntary termination or resignation from their previous employer, and about the type of supervision under which they work best. These attitudes represent some of the stimuli the interviewer will perceive. By the same token, employment interviewers possess attitudes that affect their perception and influence the formation of attitudes about the applicant.

Let us now review the mechanisms by which attitudes are formed and the perceptual processes thereby affected. The circumstances surrounding the interview will determine to a greater or lesser degree whether the participants will rely on rational and objective criteria in their respective judgments or whether they will fall victim to perceptual and attitudinal misconceptions. When it is not possible for either applicant or interviewer to explore in detail all aspects of their respective interests, when the interviewer is under duress created either by a shortage of applicants in relation to openings or by the urgent need to fill an important position, and when the applicant or the interviewer is influenced by strong emotions, then applicant and interviewer may react mechanically and uncritically. In less pressured situations where time allows and where circumstances permit, the interview can be more studied, objective, and exploratory. If realistic alternatives are available, conclusions and judgments are naturally more rational, more critical, and less affected by personal prejudices and mechanical reactions and the perceptual distortions that result from them.

How Attitudes Affect Interviewing

Let us now concern ourselves with attitudes: how they function and how they can affect both interviewer and applicant. Attitude has been defined as the predisposition to evaluate some symbol, object, or aspect favorably or unfavorably. Although opinion is the verbal expression of an attitude, attitudes can also be expressed in nonverbal behavior. Thus attitudes express beliefs that, when organized, become a system of thought. However, employment interviewers should bear in mind that the expression of a feeling or belief on the part of the applicant may not necessarily be indicative of a system of thought or a hierarchy of attitudes. Some attitudes are quite complex and may be composed of numerous cognitive factors, whereas others may be simple and general in nature. The applicant who expresses shallow beliefs, which apparently are not part of an ingrained structure of thought, will be more likely to change or alter his attitude than a person who expresses intense beliefs that are part of a total system of thoughts and values. It can be seen, therefore, that attitudes that are part of, or are associated with, a person's value system are tied to his self-esteem and that attitudes related to the personality are difficult to alter. Obviously, some attitudes affect behavior more than others.

The same attitude can be implemented differently by different people. For example, an applicant may be strongly in favor of personal self-development and may have initiated appropriate action by attending night school or participating in programs that he feels enhanced his development. Another applicant who likewise expresses favorable attitudes toward self-development may have taken no action on his own and may do nothing until required to by some authority, such as an employer. There is, of course, a relationship between attitude and behavior, but what is of particular importance to the employment interviewer is the intensity of the attitude in terms of its power to compel action and influence overt behavior.

Let us look more closely at what we mean by "action-oriented." One applicant expresses an interest in action programs; he theorizes effectively and states his belief in the need for action plans; he understands the mechanism of organizational activity and the methods and procedures necessary to initiate movement and thought on the part of others. His record, however, indicates little if any evidence of action. Another applicant is less vocal and has formulated few theories, but he has a record that gives concrete evidence of action. The second applicant is action-oriented in our sense of the term.

Some applicants try to influence the thinking (and thus the perception and attitudes) of an employment interviewer by presenting themselves as the ideal applicant. They try to give the impression that they are exactly the person the interviewer and the company are seeking; they are selling an image. On the other hand, another applicant may attempt to influence the attitudes and judgments of the interviewer by impressing him with his management philosophy, his job skills, his experience, his interests, and any other ideas he feels will be in his favor. This applicant wants to reach the interviewer on the basis of specifics rather than effects.

It is not uncommon to find applicants who are quite skillful, shrewd, and beguiling in building their image. They seem able to "read" the company and its basic philosophy and to know the kind of person the company is most likely to seek out and hire. Then they create for themselves a kind of halo effect so that their comments and expressions are favorably received. On the other hand, the applicant who addresses himself to the "issues" risks running afoul of the company's or the interviewer's ideas on any of them.

In neither of these approaches is the applicant being honest with the interviewer, and the latter must guard against both. A line of questioning can be developed to break this type of attitude attack.

Perception and Attitudes

In attempting to understand the relationship between perceptual processes and attitudes and their effect on the interview process, it must be understood that the complexity of attitudes and their formation gives rise to a wide variety of motivational forces and that the same attitude does not produce the same motivation in all people. Attitudes serve many purposes. They may serve to determine goals or pitfalls. Attitudes linked to what a person feels is advantageous determine his behavior in a positive sense, just as attitudes people hold regarding harmful or undesirable elements in the environment will affect behavior in a different direction. Thus attitudes serve to determine behavior by helping the person adjust to his environment in a *utilitarian* manner. An applicant for employment may have a favorable attitude toward a former employer. He may have liked the fringe benefits, tuition refund programs, and salary scales. The former employer has, therefore, succeeded in gaining the goodwill of the employee to the extent that he regards the company as a good place to work. But the employee nevertheless wants to leave the company. It can be seen, therefore, that the applicant has generalized his attitude about his former employer. The company has failed to gain the applicant's goodwill toward his job. The attitude toward the job—unfavorable—is essentially personal; the attitude toward the company—favorable—is generalized. This applicant should not be thought of as contradictory or confused. His attitudes, in such an instance, are affected on two levels: the personalized and the generalized.

Interpretation of Attitudes

Attitudes can also buffer the environment as well as prevent a person from developing a clear understanding of himself. Attitudes, therefore, can assume the function of *ego defense.* An applicant who maintains high aspirations despite his inability to achieve them is shielding himself from reality and self-knowledge. Because the ego-defense mechanism is inflexible, it prevents the applicant from achieving what he might and subjects him to continuous frustration.

When an applicant is described in an employer reference as "argumentative" or "unable to get along with his supervisor," he may have conflict and stress that he relieves by emotional outbursts. Since the ego-defense function of attitudes does not allow a person to adapt easily to his environment, such tensions are to be expected. Defensive attitudes can sometimes obliterate reality and cause a person to fantasize about the world in which he lives. The applicant who finds difficulty in admitting that he is a poor worker may project his defensiveness by blaming a bungling supervisor, an inadequate on-the-job training program, equipment failure, or the like.

Value-Expressive Attitudes

Attitudes also provide us with a way of expressing our *values.* The applicant who considers himself to be—either now or potentially—a member of management may express values that he believes are consistent with his strivings. The clerical worker who considers himself, much like the production worker, to be the pawn of management and little more than an anonymous cog in the machinery of industry may express values that are consistent with many of these attitudes. In effect, expressing values is a way of striving for self-identification, self-assertion, and understanding. The high school or recent college graduate seeking employment who resists dressing or acting in a manner that a recruiter or an employment interviewer would consider appropriate for an interview may be trying to identify with people his own age and at the same time to assert his independence.

An applicant's ability to develop productive, social, work-oriented attitudes is naturally of concern to the employment interviewer. Certainly, the interviewer will look for evidences of this ability in the applicant's occupational history and will make every effort to determine how he will adjust to a new work environment. Such considerations are closely linked to the *value-expressive* nature of attitudes. If an applicant expresses dissatisfaction or unhappiness about a previous job, then the interviewer knows that he should pursue the matter in terms of the value attitudes that were not satisfied and that may or may not be satisfied in the new job. The work unit, work group, department, or company may project values that are not consistent with those of the applicant. For example, the applicant who has altruistic feelings about offering services to mankind would be dissatisfied if he were thrown into a work situation where the emphasis is profit. In terms of value-expressive functions, a work group may be very clear in its expectations and demands on group members. The prevailing code of conduct may not necessarily correspond to the employee's values. Production line workers typically experience this divergence with regard to attire, attitudes toward the union and management, and even life styles during off-duty hours. In the same way, managers may be aware of a divergence between their own and their company's value-expressive attitudes in respect to the way they perform their jobs and to their life styles.

The manner in which the work unit or group attempts to reach its objectives can be highly important in the scheme of value-expressive attitudes. A salesman who is accustomed to dealing with top-level executives and who has evolved his own sales approach might find it extremely difficult to function as a door-to-door salesman whose pitch is wholly determined by a local sales manager. This is an example of a situation in which the activities of the work group deny a person the opportunity to perform the way he would like. The ideal work environment is one in which the employee can be ego-involved because he is able to absorb and accept what the group stands for and feels is important. The ideal is exemplified by a situation in which a group member can apply his skills and at the same time take part in the decisions and actions of the group.

Attitudes and the Environment

It should be recognized, too, that attitudes help provide a kind of frame of reference, imperfect though it may be, together with a certain stability, and, if you will, insight. Attitudes help a person feel that he is in control of his environment—that he is less subject to unknown and mysterious contingencies that can affect his life. People rely on their attitudes in the belief that these attitudes reflect the way things are and the way the world is—they never realize that attitudes are learned.

Attitudes tend to correspond to the role assumed in life. Applicants for employment may experience changes in their self-image and in their values. A person moving into a management position or rising to a higher management level will adopt attitudes he feels are consistent with that goal or station. Production workers who are given the responsibility of stewardship in a plant become pro-union whereas workers who are given managerial responsibilities become more pro-management. There is every indication that as a person advances in status and as his new behavior is reinforced, his attitudes become more ingrained, more stable, and more consistent. This is an important point to employment interviewers who represent typically nonunion, white collar organizations.

Attitude Reinforcement

Employment interviewers and managers tend to be apprehensive about applicants for positions in a nonunion shop or a typical office environment when the applicant has had previous union involvement. The feeling is that the applicant may maintain his prounion attitudes, attempt to organize the workers, or be difficult to deal with because of antimanagement bias. There is a strong current of opinion, however, to the effect that this "attitude reversion" probably will not materialize if the employee is upwardly mobile and if his status does not fluctuate. A new job with greater responsibilities creates a new role for the employee, and there is every indication that a new role brings with it new attitudes that are appropriate and durable. This has broad implications for the employment interviewer. Tests designed to interpret and isolate specific attitudes toward work, supervision, authority, responsibility, leadership, and other factors, in combination with comments by the applicant regarding his attitudes toward previous employment, salaries, fringe benefits, and other circumstances of employment, may not measure this factor of adjustment.

The significance of the attitudes revealed is not so much in the attitudes themselves as in the circumstances that either reinforced them or helped create them. It is, therefore, essential that the employment interviewer try to determine the role in which the applicant saw himself in his previous job and the link between his role and his attitude. The key is the applicant's willingness and ability to accept the new role and to personalize it. Training, of course, is important, but it can sometimes produce a kind of exterior veneer of adjustment, simplifying the mechanical operations involved without imbuing the employee with the full sense of his new responsibilities. Thus the applicant must have a choice with regard to the new job. The wider the choice, the greater the chances that he will accept the full implications of his new responsibility. When choice is restricted, an employee may accept a position with reservations that may hamper—however subtly—his performance. Even then, however, there is the possibility that co-workers will act as a strong determinant in affecting attitudes. Certainly, the work unit or work group exercises such influences on the individual worker.

A change in attitude is not an absolute requirement every time an employee advances. Conformity of attitudes may produce a kind of paralysis and may dampen vitality, originality, self-expression, and initiative. It is important for employment interviewers and managers, in the light of prevailing company policy, to determine whether an attitude change will be necessary. On the other hand, if the employee fails to adopt group standards, he may feel frustrated and unhappy and may eventually leave the group. When group attitudes are consistent with the company's policies, then the employee becomes a part of the mainstream of the company's activities.

There are, however, situations in which group attitudes run contrary to company goals and objectives, and in fact may have been formed in opposition to them. For example, work groups may decide that the production schedules are too high and try to restrict production. But group standards imposed by management can be detrimental to the individual as well as to the group as a whole, causing loss of identity and self-image and retarding personalized job goals.

Attitude Change

As a matter of sound employment practice, the employment interviewer should not view divergent attitudes as a reason to eliminate the applicant from consideration. (*Divergent* in this sense means differing from the company's philosophy.) There is always the possibility of attitude reversals and changes if the conditions are properly structured. But simply stated, if the employee believes that he can satisfy his needs and reach certain goals or experience some degree of self-actualization as a result of an attitude change—in other words, when he believes there will be something in it for him—then it is likely that an attitude change will take place. If, however, the employee is relatively certain that his approach to problem solving is better for him than that of the group, he may resist changing his attitude.

There is an interesting relationship between what and how much a person knows—how aware he is—and his willingness to adopt attitudes prescribed or endorsed by the company. Typically, a person's level of competence increases as his work situation becomes better defined, and as he is faced with more and more alternative choices of behavior, he is likely to be less receptive to group norms and to rely on his own attitudes and perceptions.

Group Effects on Attitude Formation

The employment interviewer should pay close attention to the type of group in which an applicant worked in his former job. This is important in terms of the depth, strength, or intensity of his attitudes. It is generally expected that uniform, stable, or consistent attitudes will be formed in tightly knit, highly cohesive groups, whereas people who have only "loose" associations may exhibit varying attitudes. Therefore, in terms not only of previous work experience but also of possible placement situations, the cohesiveness of a group or the intensity of a shared central theme within a group can be quite important. Consider the applicant who has been in the habit of coming and going as he pleases, having lunch as he can, and working in an unstructured situation with respect to the allocation of time and the determination of work priorities. The employment interviewer may tend to feel that the applicant has developed habits that are not appropriate to his company because work routines, lunch schedules, and other conditions of employment are highly structured and specific. There is evidence to suggest that these habits are not ingrained and should not be held against the applicant. The results of a number of studies and research experiments suggest that a person will alter his behavior in keeping with rules and regulations. This does not necessarily mean that deep-seated attitudes can be easily altered, but there is every evidence that behavior can change and attitudes can be influenced, particularly when the new rules and regulations are a group norm.

Certain mechanisms must be understood so that we can develop insight regarding change in attitude and in behavior. Attitude is not necessarily reflected in behavior. An applicant whose behavior seems most favorable may be concealing undesirable attitudes simply because he wants to be thought of in a positive way by the interviewer and by his prospective supervisor. Later, however, the applicant may assimilate or "internalize" the desired attitude, embracing it as his own. This is particularly likely if the attitudes of the group are consistent with his self-image.

Changing Attitudes

The interviewer may be able to change the applicant's attitude (or have hopes of doing so) by giving the applicant certain facts that he feels would motivate change. Such information must relate to the important drives within the applicant. In other words, when the employment interviewer indicates that a rule, practice, or method exists within the company, he must be able to justify it in terms of work satisfaction or some other need of the applicant. To accomplish this, the employment interviewer must be completely conversant with the rules, regulations, methods, procedures, philosophies, and attitudes he talks about. If he is not, or cannot convey that he is, his chance of influencing attitudes is diminished.

After all that has been said, an employment interviewer who attempts to alter or influence attitudes may still not succeed with all applicants. Such factors as the applicant's prior experiences, his personality (open-minded or dogmatic), his ego-involved and value attitudes that screen the perceptual processes—all affect the willingness of the individual to be influenced. Another factor in the influencing of attitudes is the observed status of the interviewer. The status of the person imparting information can significantly affect persons of an authoritarian or dictatorial nature, whereas broad-minded, less dogmatic persons are less affected.

Situations may arise in the work environment to force an employee to seek a new job, but the reasons motivating the change may be obscure and even confusing to the employment interviewer. Here is an example. An applicant for employment declares, "I got along all right with my supervisor; I enjoyed my work, but I hated the people I worked with! Everybody was at each other's throats. It was like a great big contest." Any of a number of conclusions, favorable or unfavorable, could be drawn from these remarks; examples: The applicant cannot stand competition; the applicant is exaggerating; the applicant was the supervisor's "pet." The employment interviewer should begin by trying to find out what competitive factors in the applicant's former job seemed to create such tension among the employees. Obviously, something was motivating them to be "at each other's throats." Generally, for competition to reach this pitch performance records, performance appraisals, and quality control or production records must be kept and made the subject of group concern. The supervisor may encourage his people to improve their work performance and to be innovative in order to meet production schedules. When the employee is able to respond effectively to this pressure—

incidentally influencing his environment and realizing a measure of ego satisfaction—his relations with his supervisor are probably congenial. But he may be creating a veritable jungle of conflict and anxiety among employees, becoming, in the process, the object of resentment out of simple jealousy or for having altered performance standards.

In shaping the attitudes of the applicant toward the organization, the interviewer must not convey any hint of a threat. Categorical statements to the effect that, if X occurs, Y will follow, tend to make the applicant defensive and to pit him against the system. The result may be a reinforcing of old attitudes and even expressions of hostility, so that the interview becomes a shambles. The applicant, even if he is between jobs, likes to feel that he has a choice not only in the selection of a job but also in the manner in which he is to conduct himself in the new position. If the applicant chooses to make himself a part of a new system and to follow all its rules and regulations, his attitudes are more likely to develop in the direction the new employer desires. There will be less defensiveness since the work and what it demands are now a part of the applicant's motivation. Such an applicant may tolerate initially unfavorable conditions in the belief that they are temporary and that the long-range advantages of the situation make it worthwhile to be patient.

Attitude and Self-image

The attitude an applicant brings to the employment interview is, to a significant degree, determined by his self-image and his evaluation of his progress within his chosen field. Typically, workers measure their success not so much by what they have achieved in an absolute sense as by what they expected to achieve—in other words, their goals. They feel unsuccessful if they have not achieved these goals, and successful if they have met or surpassed them.

It may be considerably more difficult to effect change in a disappointed worker (disappointed in terms of his achievement levels) than in one who feels fulfilled. When an employment interviewer perceives undesirable attitudes—attitudes that the company tries to discourage—he must evaluate them in the light of the worker's success or failure. A disappointed individual must defend himself in some way from the burden of responsibility for his failures. His ego has become involved, and so he is likely to blame his job, his machinery, his training, or his supervisors. He is less likely to be interested in forming new attitudes and in behaving differently because he fears the risks involved; he tells himself that they probably outweigh the advantages. Such a person may feel that the environment is pressing in on him and that it will overcome and dominate him. As a result, he may entrench himself in his old ideas and attitudes with a stubborn ferocity. It is to be expected that changes in attitude will occur more readily when a person has insight into himself. Behavioral changes may be imposed for the sake of conformity with a work group or an employer, and various inducements, including rewards or outright bribes, may be offered, but the change in behavior will not necessarily be one of attitudes. If attitude is not affected, a conflict will arise within the worker. Considerable research has shown that the size of a reward directly affects a person's willingness to shift attitudes. In many cases, however, the larger the reward the less change there may be. In practice, it is difficult to predict just what the outcome will be.

Effects of Manpower Scarcity

Employment interviewers who deal with applicants for managerial positions sometimes allow the scarcity of high-potential managers in the job market and their reliance on management development programs to affect their judgment. All evidence points to the fact that management development programs have the potential to change attitudes, particularly when the change (and the change-producing courses of study) is tied to the employee's managerial goals and objectives. Subsequent studies have shown that long-lasting changes in attitude are possible when the employee voluntarily embraces the need for change, can actively participate in making the change, and understands himself, his motives, and the reason for the change (particularly when the reason is in keeping with his goals and motives). The change will also be long lasting if it is internalized and the new attitudes are reinforced by the employee's experience in his environment.

Perception and Reality

As the employment interviewer contemplates the significance and complexities of perception in attitude formation, he must realize that selectivity in perception and in the formation of attitudes is not a deliberate or conscious effort to form prejudices. People generally find it easiest to take little pieces of information and bunch them together into groups so that they perceive "reality" in terms of categories. Hence a "total impression" of a person (actually a kind of categorization) is a mosaic of smaller impressions. The behavior of an applicant in an interview sometimes reflects his attempt to convey a false total impression by means of poses: the boaster, the "buck passer," the belittler. The real purpose is to camouflage certain deficiencies in personality or abilities. The need to do this is often so desperate that the applicant persists even in the face of the realization that he is not deceiving the interviewer. Or the mechanism may be unconscious, the applicant unable to admit any defects that would flaw his self-image.

This does not mean that the applicant is unreliable or a lunatic. Defensive behavior can be an important element in maintaining emotional stability. Although it must be admitted that there are extremes, a man who is defensive is not necessarily unemployable. An employment interviewer must remember that he is not a psychoanalyst and that exposing the applicant's defensive mechanisms would only damage his ego and gain nothing.

When an applicant's work history appears to be marked by superior performance, the employment interviewer cannot assume that these high standards would be carried over automatically to the new job or, even if they are, that the applicant would be happy or accepted by his co-workers. Therefore his motivation and attitudes must be explored as with any other applicant. For example, if he boasts a history of rate busting he may come from a lower-middle-class family environment in which economic independence was prized. He is probably a loner, since rate busters usually are not well liked, and he will probably not participate in after-hours activities. This employee is highly achievement-oriented, will take advantage of company savings programs and stock purchases, and should react well to monetary incentives. But an applicant who wants to be a part of the employee ingroup, and to maintain close friendships with his co-workers, may restrict his output. He probably comes from a laboring-class family. This type of person may be relatively free with his money, not caring enough about it to make the effort to earn more.

In the light of these examples, it is apparent that the motivations and attitudes of these men will affect the image they project at the time of the interview. In order to make the interview more effective, stimulating, and productive, the interviewer must be prepared to look into the many dimensions of such people.

Cognitive Dissonance

It is important for the interviewer to realize that the certainty or consistency with which we perceive our environment is man-made and has meaning only in terms of an individual's behavior. What the interviewer perceives as true, factual, or real about an applicant stems from the interviewer's experiences, learned responses, motivations, frustrations and anxieties, hopes, strivings, and needs working in concert to produce what is, in psychological terminology, a "real life" situation. Attitude formation and attitude change are two totally different processes, but both are affected by the process of perception. In the process of forming attitudes, we call on predispositions, psychological sets, perceptual configurations, and influences that we feel and absorb over time. When it comes to the process of changing attitudes, however, we are more concerned with motivational processes and influences. When a predisposition or a cherished attitude is no longer workable, functional, or satisfying, then the desire to change or modify that attitude is aroused.

In what Festinger has called "cognitive dissonance," a person discovers that certain of his feelings, attitudes, or beliefs are in some way inconsistent with those of others.[5] The natural tendency is to try to reduce the inconsistency. There are several ways of doing this, some of which require discipline and control over our perceptions and attitudes while others require a kind of accommodation. We can, of course, change our opinion. This may be the easiest solution when those with whom we differ are formidable in number and in status, so that the advantage of being on their side is obvious. Or we may make an effort to change the opinion of others. Here we are in effect trying to change our environment. A third way of reacting to attitudes and beliefs different from ours is to discredit them, or those who hold them.

For an example of a "dissonant" situation imagine an applicant who recently resigned from Inconsequential Industries, Inc. because of poor supervision, low salary, and bad working conditions; imagine further that his interviewer regards Inconsequential Industries, Inc. as a fine place to work, paying top dollar and maintaining a staff of excellent supervisors. The interviewer may suspect that his original information, which came from management, is biased and consequently change his opinion. Or he might reject the opinion of the

[5] L. Festinger, *A Theory of Cognitive Dissonance* (Palo Alto, Calif.: Stanford University Press, 1957).

applicant, reinforcing this attitude by downgrading the total person as an unintelligent, unenlightened clod who probably would not recognize good management if he saw it. In this instance, the interviewer does not admit the possibility that he is wrong. By condemning the applicant's judgment, the interviewer avoids having to examine and possibly change his own beliefs. In effect, the interviewer blames the dissonance on the applicant, assuming that, if the latter were of a caliber equal to himself and therefore able to recognize the advantages of working for a company like Inconsequential Industries, Inc., the dissonance would not exist or, if it did, it would be slight.

There is another possibility. Suppose an applicant enjoyed working for Inconsequential Industries, Inc. but found that the satisfactory working conditions, good pay, and good supervision created technical and organizational problems that inhibited opportunities for advancement. In this case, there is less distance between the cognition of the interviewer and the attitude of the applicant, so that dissonance has been reduced.

Let us add another dimension. In these examples, two applicants have two different opinions of Inconsequential Industries, Inc. Let us assume that the first occupied an extremely low position with minimal responsibilities. Let us assume, further, that the second applicant was a middle manager, with a good deal of experience, who had worked in several other organizations prior to joining Inconsequential Industries, Inc. There is every reason to expect that the interviewer will respond more favorably to the middle manager than to the low-level worker.

Now let us suppose the circumstances are reversed and that it is the interviewer who has strong negative feelings about Inconsequential Industries, Inc., while the applicant with lower status indicates that the former employer was a good one. Further suppose that the interviewer works for a company very much like Inconsequential Industries, Inc. We can now see the perceptual and attitudinal problems confronting the interviewer in such circumstances. If working conditions, methods and procedures, and management philosophy in the interviewer's company are similar to those of the applicant's previous company, then the interviewer must decide whether the possibility that the applicant's attitudes will change justifies the risk of hiring him. If he decides to hire the applicant in the likelihood that he will change in time, the interviewer must understand that he may *not* change. He may become more firmly entrenched in his opinions, changing slightly and only when he feels threatened.

The interviewer should also be aware of the fact that some persons, primarily on the basis of their education and training, are not at all bothered by dissonance and are perfectly willing to live with it. Also, it may be assumed that in general higher-level executives, researchers, theoreticians, and certain others, whose work involves innovation, build up a tolerance of dissonance because they must frequently clash with existing modes.

It is not uncommon to find that employment interviewers distrust an applicant who speaks fondly of his former employer (who may be in direct competition with the interviewer's company). This loyalty should not be disturbing since the experience the applicant obtained, his feelings of satisfaction, and the personal or professional contacts he may have made can be worthwhile to the new employer. The fact that the applicant is looking for a new employer, although he liked the old one, does not mean that he is a spy for the competition. It is quite possible that an employee can have good feelings about a former employer and still want a new job elsewhere.

In sum, a person's perceptions of his environment do not necessarily reflect reality—they are essentially a medley of logical forces. The interaction between the perceptions of the parties to an interview imposes on the interviewer the need for controlled sensitivity in his job. During the interview he observes the applicant's behavior, reviews past behavior on the basis of applications, résumés, and life histories, and attempts to understand or reconstruct the situations that caused the behavior. The applicant's activities are then analyzed in terms of the observed relationship between the behavior and the circumstances that caused it. The interviewer can also help the applicant understand his own behavior and motivations so that perception becomes a controlled process and the interview becomes mutually beneficial for both applicant and interviewer.

3

Decision Making, Problem Solving, and Programming

THERE IS A DELIGHTFUL PASSAGE in Lewis Carroll's *Alice in Wonderland* that is apropos of decision making, problem solving, and programming. Alice asks the Cheshire Cat which way she ought to walk. "That depends a good deal on where you want to get to," said the Cat. "I don't much care where," said Alice. "Then it doesn't matter which way you go," said the Cat.

In the final analysis, where one wants to go becomes one of the most important questions in employment interviewing. The problem breaks down into a basic, deceptively simple, highly logical exercise. If a man plans a trip to California, he does not allow himself to end up in New York. That statement seems ludicrously simple, but the logic on which it is based is sometimes ignored in interviewing. The interview has a purpose, a process, and a goal. It also has a specific function in combination with all the other methods that are part of the total process of deciding whether to hire someone. Therefore, the employment interviewer must direct, control, and coordinate the interview rather than just let it happen as one might start a car, release the brake, and, without steering, allow the course of the road to determine the direction of the car. The interviewer must exert *selective* control over the information he seeks and gets—that is, he must determine whether the information is *prime* (necessary, pertinent, and therefore usable) or *nonprime* (unnecessary, irrelevant, and therefore unusable).

The primary task for the employment interviewer is to arrive at a decision about an applicant. In its most skeletal form, such a decision is the conclusion reached after all available alternatives have been considered, weighed, and selected. A series, almost a continuum, of steps in logical sequence leads to the ultimate decision. Each phase of the decision-making process must be well planned with investigation, analysis, imagination, inquiry, and diagnosis at each step. Thus there is a chain effect in the decision-making process. In the course of arriving at decisions, it is clear that the employment interviewer is problem solving.

In order to utilize fully the benefits from careful planning and programming, it is mandatory that three distinct areas of thought be clearly delineated in the interview process: (1) the structural components of decision-making behavior, (2) the mechanisms of problem solving, and (3) programming techniques.

Let us look at the fundamental differences between these three areas. Decision making is a process of choice in that the employment interviewer selects from among alternatives. The number of alternatives regarding the possibility of employing an applicant decreases as the interview progresses. At the outset, there are many alternatives because facts are few and assumptions are sketchy. But, as the number of uncertainties diminishes, so does the number of alternatives until the interviewer is faced with only two: to hire or not to hire.

Another cognitive process is problem solving; and, although it is closely linked to decision making, there are sufficient differences to warrant separate consideration. Problem solving implies the existence of an obstacle that must be hurdled. Typical of problem-solving activity is the calling up of remembrances and experiences and the reapplication of past problem-solving techniques, together with the use of each of these individually and collectively to overcome the obstacle. It is not, however, a mechanical or habitual reaction.

Programming the interview is a way of dealing with "input" information; that is, information (in the form of facts, perceptions, assumptions, and attitudes) is absorbed by the interviewer and must be dealt with effectively. Programming provides the mechanical means of selecting a useful course of action. It is the planning and preparation that precedes the interview and the guide that allows for midcourse corrections when needed. It determines the steps that must be taken to reach the desired goal or the decision-making state; it provides the means by which to control the intensity of the investigation or search and to weigh the applicant's responses as prime and nonprime. It also enables the employment interviewer to screen out nonprime data.

Our first concern, therefore, will be to understand the structural components, theory, and method of decision making since the interview is geared toward and designed for bringing the interviewer to the decision-making stage. Knowing the components of decision making and their function enables the interviewer to eliminate nonprime data. In the business world only decisions based on prime data can be accepted. Next we will take up problem solving, exploring the various approaches to it in order to provide the interviewer with enough insight to enable him to select the most effective for him from among several approaches. Thus we will view the problem-solving process in terms of the dynamics of solutions, method of problem definition, habitual problem solving, and cognitive elements involved in decision making. These considerations will lead us logically to construct the theoretical basis for the programming technique in the interview process and to derive a practical application.

General Theory of Decision Making

Decision making is a precarious business at best. The environment is a challenging, ever-changing, pressurizing flow of stimuli over which we have limited control. We cannot hope to know all that is taking place in the environment or to gain insights at every turn—we are simply not conditioned to respond in quite that way. When we receive stimuli from our environment, we exercise a certain degree of selectivity regarding what we react to. This selectivity is highly personal; rarely do two persons select things in the same way. Decision making, therefore, is an imperfect kind of thought resolution. When we make decisions, we draw on a wide spectrum of capabilities, some of which may be stronger than others. Psychological research has shown that, because people vary widely in their abilities and because they are selective in the stimuli to which they respond, it is difficult to generalize or make an overall analysis of the process. Each decision is the product of the decision maker's environmental stimuli and his individual pattern of responses. Of course, bad decision making is not always due to uncertain facts or inadequate information. It is generally conceded that people use only a small portion of their mental capacities; and, although these capacities can be trained and developed, a decision maker approaches his problem with self-limiting capabilities. Employment interviewers, as is true of all decision makers, may arrive at incorrect or bad decisions for a wide number of reasons. For example, one of the most insidious problems in decision making is what is referred to as mental set. Mental set tends to affect an otherwise sound decision by imposing biases on that decision. This, in effect, is a matter of perception because what the decision maker sees is affected by what he is conditioned to see and is a result of his experience, motivation, needs, environmental pressures, and personal preferences. When the decision maker recognizes or thinks he recognizes a familiar set of circumstances he dealt with successfully in the past, it is a simple matter for him to rely on his previous problem-solving and decision-making techniques to help him make the decision he is confronted with now. Mental set is a kind of crutch and a reference point that comes to the fore in times of pressure or stress. It can cause the decision maker to draw conclusions or make assumptions that may not be wholly valid for the situation at hand.

One of the reasons decision makers in business do not always guard against stereotyping, bias, and mental set is that people in the work milieu want fast action, recognition and satisfaction—there are production schedules to meet, fires to put out, and superiors to satisfy. Consequently they are unwilling to subject themselves to the tedium of methodized decision making with its selectivity of assumptions and careful bias control.

Alternatives in Decision Making

Sometimes a decision maker is uncertain of his facts; he seeks more information, checks and rechecks his data, grows more and more cautious to the point of immobility, and experiences emotional trauma when he must reach a final decision, which he is quite likely to delay. If the decision is bad, he will try to excuse it, pleading insufficient data. The decision maker is said to be suffering from inertia; that is, he is bogging down in defensive attitudes and self-protecting mechanisms by which he hopes to diminish the degree of risk involved in the decisions he makes. The decision maker's inertia could stem entirely from his own weakness. But unfortunately there are situations in which he would have some justification. Everyone wants his decisions to be right, but because they are right does not always mean that they will be accepted by superiors. Many have learned through hard experience that occasionally wrong or weak decisions gain broader acceptance in politically charged business organizations than a right, although unpopular, decision.

A manager attempting to arrive at a decision has three alternatives: (1) He can face his problem head-on, completely committing himself. If the decision is a successful one, then he too is successful; if the decision is unsuccessful, he is vulnerable. (2) He can decide not to take direct, positive action, so that the decision-making process becomes a prolonged analysis. Here again, if his analysis or his decision is correct, he is successful—but the consequences of being right or wrong are somewhat dampened. (3) The decision maker can delay action, postpone his decision, and then blame an ineffective research staff, inadequate information, or other circumstances for his procrastination. This is a dangerous approach because the decision may be needed now, so that a late decision, even if it might have been good earlier, could be a failure.

Obviously, the correctness or incorrectness of some decisions may be immediately apparent, whereas the outcome of others may not be known for years. To judge a decision without waiting for the outcome, it is necessary to rely on other criteria—style, action, movement, and thought.

Because there are no rules that can be applied in all cases to employment interviewing, an interviewer who tries to make decisions by following rigid standards or procedures will undoubtedly be trapped into making bad decisions. Hence the employment interviewer must rely heavily on logic. Logic is the thought process that enables people to reach conclusions from one or more assumptions. When an illogical decision is made, it is because there is a fallacy or specious error, usually in the original assumptions, occasionally in the method by which the conclusions are drawn. Note, however, that flawless logic will still lead to an incorrect decision if the facts on which the assumptions were based are wrong.

Common Fallacies

Let us analyze a number of common fallacies. First we have the *fallacy of composition*—assuming that what is true in one special situation is true for all situations. This leads to overgeneralization or jumping to conclusions. Let us take a ludicrously simple example. An employment interviewer may have had one or two female clerical applicants who were exceptionally fine typists, in fact better than most other typists—and these ladies had blue eyes. The employment interviewer then infers: "*All* female clerical typists with blue eyes are fast typists." What he really should infer is: "*Some* female cleri- cal workers with blue eyes are fast typists." Obviously, he could not possibly know all blue-eyed female typists, and so his judgment must be based on the *some* rather than the *all*.

There is another kind of overgeneralization, this one involving prediction. An employment interviewer insists that the only way to make sure of getting good applicants is to test them. Actually, what he is saying is that a test score is the only valid criterion of accepta- bility. This is untrue; other methods of screening are also valid.

The fallacy known as *after, therefore because of* is another that can create unnecessary problems for the employment interviewer. In this kind of fallacy, if event A precedes event B, then event B is somehow the result of event A. For example: An employee receives a raise and his productivity thereupon drops. The fall in productivity is assumed to be the result of the raise. A close relative of this fallacy is the *fallacy of false cause*. The employment interviewer re- views a résumé and makes an inference: "I see from your application that you were fired from your last job after you finished your training at the trade school. Couldn't you apply what you had learned?" A variant of this fallacy is the basis of what is known as guilt by asso- ciation. This mistake, from which employment interviewers are not immune, is exemplified by such comments as: "I wouldn't hire that girl for anything. She's a close friend of that girl we had to fire a month ago."

False Analogies

Employment interviewers are also vulnerable to false analogies. In a false analogy two different situations are held to be the same when in fact they are not. For example, an employment interviewer com- ments, "I remember that little redhead who was here about a year ago. She claimed that she did not plan to quit work and get married. This is exactly the same situation." The facts may appear to be the same, but they are not necessarily so, because these are two different occurrences. Although it is possible that the situations are similar, it should not be assumed that they are the same until all the facts are uncovered.

False analogies are frequently combined with appeals to authority. Thus our interviewer might add to his comment, "I can recall Mr. Brodie saying, 'Let's never get into that situation again.'" The refer- ence to Mr. Brodie, which is a kind of appeal to his authority, implies that Mr. Brodie cannot possibly be wrong and that the course of action he charts is to be followed regardless of the circumstances. Sometimes the authority cited is statistical. Interviewers have been stunned by managers who reject applicants with explanations like this: "I *know* your applicant cannot possibly be successful. I read once that according to statistics 79.53 percent of all left-handed people are unsuccessful as lathe operators." An appeal to personal authority may be combined with an appeal to statistics and to group opinions. Example: "We should definitely hire only those employees with 20/20 vision because 46 percent of our work stoppages are caused by on-the-job accidents. The executive vice-president agrees with me on this and so do a number of supervisors."

Guilford describes the decision-making process as an intellectual exercise comprising memory and thinking.[1] He indicates that thinking operates on three levels. At the *cognitive level* we unearth, investigate, and discover or rediscover bits of information. At the *productive level* we use this information to build, sometimes creatively, on the facts and data already known. (Productive thinking may be divergent, moving off on a tangent of its own, or it can be convergent—strictly applicable to the problem.) At the *evaluative level* we determine the applicability of the facts from the cognitive level and the constructs from the productive level.

Decision Theory Versus Decision Making

At this point, we must differentiate between decision-making theory and decision making. When a person makes a decision, he is, in effect, making a final choice based on a sequence of alternatives in a thought process. The making of the decision (for example, as to whether one applicant is more suitable for employment than another) is the end point of the thought process; it is a single act that is the result of all the steps, factors, and interrelationships distinguished by decision-making theory. It should be pointed out, however, that decision-making theory is not fully developed. Decision-making mechanisms are closely linked to psychological processes, about which much is yet unknown.

Obviously, the chain of thoughts that result in a decision is composed of many complex variables. Economists, mathematical theorists and statisticians, manpower planners, corporate planners, and the like construct payoff matrices in order to establish mathematical

[1] J. P. Guilford, *Personality* (New York: McGraw-Hill Book Co., 1959), p. 360.

models by which these variables can be more precisely understood and, perhaps, controlled. In this way they hope to reduce the element of chance in the decision-making process. Although economists have led the field in decision-making theory, psychologists have attempted to construct models as well. The subjectively expected utility (SEU) maximation model is one example.[2] The SEU model approaches decision making on the basis of objective values and subjective, or utilitarian, values as well as objective and subjective probabilities. The word *utilitarian* (subjective) refers to the value an individual personalizes, one that he feels or believes is important. This is in contrast to objective value, which refers to real value measurable in dollars.

Current theory holds that a person will select what he feels will fulfill his subjective values. Experimentation with the SEU decision-making theory model gives rise to evidence that decisions are largely based on and affected by the problem solver's personal view about the probability of obtaining the "right" or valued outcome. And the person's judgment about probability is overshadowed by the value he places on the possible outcome or payoff of the course of action he chooses. People generally expect a desirable outcome to result from their decisions, and they typically underestimate the possibility that their decisions will produce undesirable results. It has been further suggested that people place higher value on successful decisions when the probability of success is believed low than when the probability is believed high.

Decision Making and Motivation

Major influences on decision making are achievement orientation and the desire to avoid failure. The decision-making process is affected by the decision maker's motivations. For example, if a person perceives that the result of his decision will succeed or fail in accordance with his abilities and skills, then his decision will be determined by, and somewhat controlled by, his own confidence and self-esteem. Certainly, there are sufficient theoretical and experimental data to indicate that "the impossible dream" motivates people to make risk decisions. Improbable achievements (such as a winning bet on a long shot) have a certain glamour because of psychological and sociological conditioning rather than because the person innately believes the value of the outcome justifies the risk.

[2] W. Edwards, "Utility, Subjective Probability, Their Interaction and Variance Preferences," *Journal of Conflict Resolution,* 1962, 6, pp. 42–51.

An employment interviewer cannot avoid violating several basic tenets of decision theory. This contradiction is an inevitable consequence of the pressures of his environment and the circumstances in which he must make his decisions. For example, decision theory assumes that the decision maker is rational and, if possible, uses logic and probability data. In a typical business environment, particularly in the screening and preemployment stages, the employment interviewer cannot be totally rational, nor can he have sufficient insight into all aspects of the applicant. He is limited by the availability of pertinent information and its appropriateness. The interviewer is further handicapped by the limitations of his perceptual capacities and by his psychological involvement in the interview process.

Need for Data in Decision Making

Some writers argue that the ability to obtain data plays a significant role in decision making and must, therefore, be considered a factor in decision theory along with, and perhaps equal in importance to, logic and probability factors. They hold the position that techniques used in electronic data processing can be applied to decision theory. For example, there are programs for arriving at certain kinds of decisions, and specific rules, guidelines, or contingency factors can be laid down to direct the decision maker from one decision-making step or program to another. Computer programs are tested, cleared of error, and, with mechanical precision, perform each time as expected in exactly the same way. It is, obviously, less likely that the same type of programming can be carried out where people are concerned; and the proponents of programmed decision making do not expect perfect repetition. One writer maintains that nonprogrammed decision-making techniques are those to which people are most subject because they deal with nonrepetitive, uncertain (confused by the psychological set of the decision maker), ill-defined, or otherwise complex decision-making demands.[3] This is in contrast to programmed electronic data processing decision making, which, although supremely complex, is routinized, predictable, and contingent on the accuracy and ability of the programmer. The computer's ability to "make decisions" is restricted by the program under which it operates no matter how vast and complex the program may be. But it is not weakened by the multidimensional nature of human thought, which can be divergent or convergent at any given time.

[3] H. A. Simon, *The New Science of Management Decision* (New York: Harper & Row, Publishers, 1960).

Although complex electronic computers now make decisions that were once made by people, the manager (and the employment interviewer) will not disappear from the scene. According to a *Harvard Business Review* article:

> It [the new decision technology brought about by electronic devices] can . . . relieve management of that part of his assignment which makes the smallest demands of management talent, but claims the largest, most immediate share of management attention. Freed of this time-consuming, energy-draining burden, managers are in a better position to work on the unstructured decisions that often are not competently handled.[4]

Interviewing and Goal Orientation

The employment interviewer who is involved with the problems of decision-making theory must have some acquaintance with the concept of purposive effort. This means that the decision the employment interviewer arrives at must serve a purpose and, in effect, be directed toward a predetermined goal. In its most fundamental form, the concept involves making a choice between two types of applicant: one who can do the job extremely well now but has limited future potential or one who shows growth and development possibilities for the future but limited skills now.

But in its broadest implications purposive effort requires the interviewer to think of his function not in terms of his *immediate* job responsibility or of his need to fill an available job vacancy but in terms of the comprehensive applicability and relationship of his job to other jobs within the personnel department and to other departments that act synergistically to achieve shared goals. Thus we begin to evolve a decision-making process that takes into account the fact that every decision, both large and small, made by an employment interviewer during and immediately following the interview will have a cause-and-effect relationship with (1) the entire employment process, (2) the total personnel function, (3) the operation of the departments, and (4) the ability of the organization to reach its goals and objectives in terms of manpower replacement and the development—occupational, personal, and psychological—of its employees.

Purposive effort is a difficult concept. However, it does not always

[4] M. Anshen, "The Manager and the Black Box," *Harvard Business Review,* November–December 1960, p. 90.

require explicit attention because it is implicit in the very nature of employment interviewing.

Task Delineation and Solution Finding

This leads us to consider task delineation as it relates to the decision process. Task delineation refers to the number of steps that must be taken before a problem is solved.

The problem to the employment interviewer is the vacancy; the solution is the filling of the vacancy. To fill the vacancy properly the interviewer must get the right person for the job. This means that he must make certain decisions regarding the educational and occupational prerequisites for the job. It also means that he must recognize and deal effectively with the needs of the applicant, weighing these against the environmental circumstances of the work situation. A job requiring highly technical experience and education, for example, limits task delineation; that is, fewer steps are necessary to determine the prerequisites. A nontechnical position broadens task delineation; the choices the interviewer can make regarding applicants' backgrounds are multiplied, so that the final decision may be based on many large and small contingent decisions within the decision process.

The decision maker begins, then, by purpose setting—determining the basic problem, and what in broad terms, needs to be done. He now has an established purpose and an awareness that he must take action to achieve it, but he has not yet defined the task in operational terms. He now has to decide what path to follow to the final decision and solution. Suppose that the turnover rate were high and the proposed solution were more stable employees. This is a problem of task delineation since the purpose and objective are clear. When more stable employees are acquired, the solution follows. On the other hand, an interviewer may be faced with the problem of hiring more managers with graduate degrees. Here too the purpose seems to be clear— in that definite goals have been set—but the task has already been delineated and defined, so that the interviewer is faced with solution finding.

The critical stage in solution finding is the task of selecting from among several solutions. This means that there must be an evaluation period during which the weighing and selecting are carried out. In many cases the decision maker is not confined to one choice. He may be able to combine several choices to form a supersolution. It is reasonable to expect that, if a rational approach has been taken throughout the decision-making process, the choices will often have elements within them that, if they could be combined, would produce a better solution.

Prediction

Part of this selection process concerns prediction. One of the methods for determining the best solution is to develop a relative value scale with which to analyze each alternative. Let us say that the employment interviewer has to fill a job vacancy. He may select two, three, or perhaps four applicants out of ten or twenty. Solution finding involves narrowing this choice to the best qualified. After he has compiled all the necessary information, he may follow a conceptual or theoretical plan in order to make his differentiation. One applicant may require little training time after employment; he may be more productive and surpass expectations because of past training or experience. Another applicant, on the other hand, shows no promise of surpassing quotas and will probably need more immediate on-the-job training. Yet his educational background and career goals indicate that he may in the long run develop beyond the capabilities of the first applicant. A third applicant may be more personable than the first two. It might be helpful if the interviewer developed a value scale of what is important to him, the operating department, and the company. He could even construct a payoff matrix. However, it is not always possible to affix monetary values to such intangibles as personableness or the possible result of long-range projections.

When the consequences of a decision seem reasonably certain, then selecting the right alternative is a rather simple process. But, in an ill-defined situation in which consequences are unknown, there is little basis for selection. So the interviewer may find himself reverting to intuition. Yet we seek something better than intuition, and the advocates of probability theory tell us that it holds the greatest promise of filling the void. Certainly, probability theory is applicable in terms of statistical considerations and those factors that can be broken down into component parts, isolated, weighed, measured, and valued and that are not subject to human interpretation. By its nature probability theory applies directly to actions that may have a number of different consequences. Therefore, it can be applied to determine the probability of the consequences of an action. Theoretically, if the sum total of all of the probabilities is one, then the probability of each individual outcome will be a number between zero and one.

Probability

When we think of probability theory, we often think of the classic example of flipping a coin or throwing dice. These are games of chance, and probability theory, in fact, concerns itself with chance occurrences. A typical employment interviewer is familiar with the relative-frequency theory of probability—of which random sampling is an example—because his entire interview approach, analysis, and decision making may be governed by it. But it is subjective probability that for the most part guides the employment interviewer in his conduct of the interview, his methods of analysis, and his decision making. This is intuitive theorizing about events in an individual's experience, background, and potential. And it presents numerous alternatives about which judgments must be made, not about individual facts but about the cumulative effect of all the pertinent facts. The reliance on subjective probabilities is, in effect, a measure of self-confidence, of belief in one's own judgment.

This is called the Bayesian approach, and any employment interviewer who screens more than one applicant for a job vacancy uses it. The Bayesian approach is based on intuition or methodized analysis by interviewers who claim expertise in dealing with probabilities. The process, simply stated, is as follows: Applicant A is screened and interviewed, and a decision is made. The decision is a projection of the probability of the applicant's success or failure on the job. Applicant B then presents himself, and a decision is made about him. The presence of Applicant B causes the decision made about Applicant A to be reviewed and reconsidered, and the interviewer may want to revise his original decision. He may then find that it is worthwhile to postpone a decision regarding either Applicant A or Applicant B until he has interviewed Applicant C. The presence of Applicant C forces the same type of revision as Applicant B. With the advent of each applicant after the first, consideration of prior applicants is reopened. The employment interviewer must project the probability of success or failure on the job for each applicant.

It can be seen that for the employment interviewer decision making, in which he focuses his knowledge and skill on the solution of a problem, can readily become an applied science. Each time he makes a decision about an applicant he is asserting that there is a strong probability of the applicant's success. And the results will certainly be better if the interviewer relies on method rather than on guesswork or pure chance.

Problem Solving

Problem solving has as its goal the circumvention of a problem or an obstacle; therefore, problem solving is goal-oriented. It differs fundamentally from decision making in that decision making is a process of choice—the selection of alternatives. Obviously, decision making and problem solving are interwoven, and they cannot be considered independently, nor are they exclusive of each other. Instead, decision making is seen as a part of the more generalized problem-solving function; most frequently it is the end result of the problem-solving continuum. Decision making is discussed before problem solving because of the theoretical nature of decision making and because decision theory is an interdisciplinary problem that involves mathematical formulation and empirical study.

When a person is confronted with a problem that has to be solved, he enters a prereflective phase, which is the stage at which the problem is defined. If the problem is moderately complex, the person has doubts and uncertainties that he knows must be resolved. His immediate impulse is to seek the simplest, most efficient, and quickest solution possible. Therefore, once the problem has been recognized and reflected on, the individual must give thought to all possible solutions.

Thus, in the problem-solving process, it is useful to formulate hypotheses to help guide observations and to insure that reasoning and discrimination are applied to the problem. Of course, the sequence may vary. It is not always clear, for example, at what point in the problem-solving process the formulation of the hypotheses begins. In fact it is difficult to know at what point in the interview the employment interviewer becomes aware that he is facing a serious problem. The applicant is constantly supplying new information that alters the attitudes of the interviewer.

Stages of Creative Thought

There are four stages of creative thought: preparation, incubation, illumination, and verification. These stages are loose guidelines for problem solving and will not in themselves produce an easy solution because every task, motivation, person, and work environment is different from every other. This does not mean that the interviewer eliminates these four stages in the process of making a decision. He may employ any or all of them at any time during the interview, particularly at critical junctures when he must make decisions about which path to take, which hunches to follow, and which areas of concern to deal with.

In the preparation stage, the problem solver becomes aware of his problem and makes every effort to accumulate information about it so that he can find a satisfactory solution. When he has difficulty in finding a solution, the problem should be set aside to be considered at another time when pressures, environmental circumstances, and the like are more favorable. This is not always possible. But, during such an incubation period, new insights and information about an applicant may come to the surface and provide the solution that previously seemed beyond reach. This is not to suggest that something magical is brought about by simply setting the problem aside and coming back to it later. The value of the incubation period is in direct proportion to the quality of the preparation. With each new applicant applying for a given job, decisions regarding prior applicants for the same job are constantly being tested and compared. In the course of the interview, new facts are supplied that contribute not only to understanding the problem but also to its solution. Yet each individual fact is completely inadequate in itself. Facts are valuable only in conjunction with other facts, and when they serve as the basis for new information. For example, a single fact, the decision of management to hire an experienced corporate planner, could have many implications. It is reasonable to infer that there is a need for the services of this specialist —although his prestige value may be an additional impetus. But the decision to bring a man in from outside could stem from many causes. The company may lack a training program to develop someone from its own ranks; the need for the planner might be too urgent to allow for setting up a program; it might be thought desirable to have a fresh point of view. Finally, the prestige factor might be significant in the choice of a man with an established reputation. Thus understanding the circumstances of each situation helps establish the value of the information at the interviewer's disposal.

Classifying Possible Solutions

A useful technique in problem solving is the classification of possible solutions. Assume that we have three applicants for the job of campus recruiter. Applicant A has a good deal of experience, so that with a minimum of training he can be productive; Applicant B lacks practical experience but has the education, career goals, life style, motivations, needs, and attitudes that imply that long-range development would be profitable and worthwhile; Applicant C is highly personable and has the tenacity, aggressiveness, mental ability, and social adaptability required but lacks the experience of Applicant A and the theoretical background and potential of Applicant B. In analyzing the problem from the point of view of classification, it is necessary to evaluate abstractions, grouping many alternatives into a few generalized categories. In this very limited example, the natural classification is the area of experience. Applicant A could be placed in a broad category labeled "Experience—Immediately Productive," whereas applicants B and C could be labeled "Developmental." In this way it is possible to deal with alternatives effectively.

It is not uncommon for an interviewer to have the solution to his problem and not know it. He may be working his way through the ninth applicant for a particular job opening and simply not realize that Applicant 2 was the right choice. When he finally does realize that the second applicant was the right man for the job, he can either search for another applicant like Applicant 2 or, out of frustration, settle for second best. Hence the question the interviewer must ask himself is: How do I know when I have the right applicant? In other words, how do I know when I have arrived at the proper solution? The interviewer's decision must not be based on emotional, physical, educational, or occupational values but on what have been referred to as functional values. For example, gasoline placed in a power mower will cut grass, but the relationship between gasoline and cut grass in itself is not clearly defined. Actually the gasoline has a functional relationship to the cutting of the grass, but the relationship is only established by the intermediacy of the motor. In the case of our three applicants, the reasons for hiring Applicant C instead of Applicant A, who has immediately applicable job experience, and Applicant B, who is well grounded in theory and has potential, may not be immediately clear. But, if there is a scarcity of manpower and a need to accelerate college campus recruitment, then the reasons for hiring Applicant C are apparent. He is personable and outgoing and, with the proper training, could become an ideal campus recruiter. Like the relationship between gasoline and cut grass, the applicability of Applicant C's talents was initially obscure. But when the relevant factors are considered, Applicant A holds promise of immediate productivity, but may not turn out to be a good recruiter; Applicant B promises neither immediate productivity nor recruitment ability—but only long-range potential; Applicant C is the most personable and, after he has had operational experience, his capabilities in campus recruiting, customer relations, public relations, and other public contact may be of more *strategic* importance to the company than any *operational* benefits. Although it may be true that there are immediate production needs in a department and that manpower planning forecasts indicate that the potential capabilities of Applicant B are needed, the functional needs of the business, which can be clarified only by careful analysis of the problem, may prove Applicant C to be the best candidate for the job.

Habitual Behavior

It is important for the employment interviewer to understand the distinction between habitual behavior, genuine decision making, and problem solving. When problem solving is the result of associative learning and habit formation, the interviewer's response is largely conditioned by how recently and how often he has faced similar problems and by how well he has succeeded in coping with them. The relationship between associative learning and habit formation can perhaps best be characterized by the statement: As you have done, so you will do. And, conversely: As you do now, so you have probably done before. Thus we get a picture of inflexible, slow-to-change, mechanical behavior in response to problem stimuli. This kind of behavior aims at minimizing risk; one relies on previous successful experiences, relates these uncritically to the current situation, and feels secure in the thought that once successful, twice successful. The pitfall is that the prior situation was probably different from the present one. It may be useful to refer to, but only if the differences are properly understood and allowed for. Employment interviewers might well feel uncomfortable when reading this. Too often what they refer to proudly as their knowledge of people is based on associative learning and habit formation.

Genuine Problem Solving

Genuine problem-solving behavior should be deliberative, directed, goal-oriented, selective, discriminating, and even creative. It implies the careful weighing and analysis of alternatives—their consequences and advantages. It does not necessarily assume that each new problem-solving situation is new, nor does it require the problem solver to reject previous experience, impressions, perceptions, or memories of achievement and failure. In a creative sense, it does require that each factor or component of a new problem be examined with the insight gained from previous experience. In short, each problem should be treated as unique.

Genuine problem solving is more likely to result in clear-cut, easily discernible, and dramatic decisions than habitual behavior is. Contrast the decision to halt the hiring of persons without college degrees for management-level positions with the decision gradually to phase out nongraduates over time, or the decision to test all applicants from a certain date forward with the decision to test some and not others or to test a small percentage and gradually increase it to include all applicants.

Concept Formation

Habit formation and habitual problem solving are closely tied to concept formation. The employment interviewer who observed that very young applicants, married female applicants whose husbands work with a large company, applicants for part-time employment or those who seek summer work, and retirees whose earnings must be controlled are rarely interested in the company's pension program furnishes an example of concept formation. He has grouped together dissimilar people and labeled them the not-interested-in-pension-program group. It has been suggested that the formation of concepts is the application of a common response to dissimilar stimuli. Concept formation may be a fundamental, stimulus-response reaction on a one-to-one basis. For example, the employment or personnel department may decide that not all typists should receive the same salary and that, in fact, each typing applicant should be treated differently with respect to salary. An employment policy could be established that would divide typists into two groups: those who type more than 70 words a minute and those who type fewer than 70 words a minute. Thus a concept—typing speed—becomes the basis for categorizing the typists. But is this kind of categorization valid? Should salaries in fact be based on typing speed? Suppose that some applicants are statistical typists and others are legal typists. Or suppose that college graduates are slower typists than high school graduates. In these cases, the categorization on the basis of typing speed would be difficult to justify.

The imperfections of conceptualization have given rise to attempts to find a mediating element or middle ground between the problem (stimulus) and the conceptualization (response). Strategy can be used for this purpose. For example, Department A indicates that an open requisition for personnel has been unfilled for the past two months, Department B is frantic with the need for new people, and Department C is almost immobile. In addition, Department D is anticipating a retirement, a military leave of absence, and a transfer. It has begun a training program to fill the positions by promotion, but cannot inaugurate the program until those who are to be promoted can be replaced with new hires.

Categories of Facts

The employment interviewer (and certainly others in the employment-personnel function) reports that applicants are scarce and reverts to the stimulus response (one-to-one reaction) by explaining that conditions in the job market are bad. Now let us assume that a competitor, whom we shall call Minutia, Inc., operating in the same geographical area or even the same city and therefore drawing on the same job market, seems to have little trouble attracting applicants. Notice that we are beginning to build contingent categories of information to apply to the problem. We begin to see that the problem may not lie in the job market but rather in the company. Perhaps pay scales are low, the company image is bad, or recruitment is not energetic. As the problem is further delineated, the pertinent facts can be categorized.

Group I facts. Departments within the organization lack employees. Each department requires different skills, educational background, and experience. If all or most departments needed a comparable skill, there might be justification for the conclusion that the specific skill is rare on the job market, but the skills are of such a wide variety that this claim does not seem to be valid. Therefore, there seems to be a generalized inability to bring applicants into the organization.

Group II facts. Competitors in the same geographical area, with about the same requirement for skills, seem to have no trouble finding applicants. This delineation serves as the basis for the strategy, which mediates between the stimuli created when the problem is recognized and the conceptualization of the problem.

Now let us consider the employment interviewer who comments, "I know we are in trouble on this open job order, but the way engineers are these days, we simply cannot find the right person." The comment implies that engineers are not what they used to be. Certainly this can be taken as a reference to professional competence. Furthermore, the phrase "right person" leaves the door open to the inference that personality, character, and desired behavior are also lacking. The interviewer has conceptualized his problem without a mediating strategy based on careful factual delineation. His solution may be to continue searching, interviewing, and rejecting until somehow he finds the one "Mr. Right." In other words, he will revert to behavior that requires him to reapply with greater intensity the wrong approach.

If he had employed strategy, he might have concluded that what is wrong is not the times or the personalities, character, or behavior of the engineering applicants but rather the hypothetical construct the employment interviewer has allowed himself to build regarding the right kind of person for the organization. This is not to say that scarcities in the job market is necessarily an invalid concept by which to approach such a problem, nor does it negate the fact that certain personality types may be preferred in a particular job situation in certain circumstances. However, the point is that unless the problem is properly conceptualized there will be a reversion to habitual behavior, which in turn may result in an ineffective, unworkable, or downright wrong decision. Obviously, in the example of the engineering vacancy, the problem stimulus may not be instant; that is, the problem reveals itself gradually in a sequence of events. Some of the problem stimuli, of course, must be rejected as irrelevant, whereas others lend themselves to the formation of concepts and the development of problem-solving strategies. It may be that for some problems a one-to-one relationship—stimulus and response—is sufficient for solution. On the other hand, certain problems call for a complex strategy and a highly sophisticated conceptualization requiring considerable maneuvering and even risk.

The amount of risk an individual is willing to take may be a factor in the strategy chosen. There must be a reasonable relationship between risk and consequence; risk should be proportionate to the gain. Therefore, in the narrowing down of the number of alternative solutions as part of the problem-solving process, the degree of allowable risk must be considered.

Interviewer Ineptitude

The fact that problems vary in difficulty—that is, that some are easier to solve than others—is attributable to differences in people. In accordance with the nature of the employment interviewer, the decision to accept or reject an applicant, refer him to management for further review, or put him off with "Don't call us, we'll call you" may be easily arrived at, or it may require considerable time and thought. Unquestionably the inabilities or ineptitudes of the problem solver can make the solution of a problem more difficult than it might otherwise be. In a highly pressured environmental situation an emotional state may be engendered that affects attitudes and perceptions and interferes with contemplative problem solving. This is by no means uncommon with employment interviewers. On the other hand, the interviewer may be facing each applicant with a mental set that is unreasonable in terms of the actual needs of the organization and the capability of the job market to produce the kind of applicant desired. He may have attitudes and biases that distort his judgment.

The ability of a problem solver to deal with information or input data about a current problem by calling on experience and maturing skills may be inhibited and thwarted because of certain internal or external conditions that prevent the problem solver from applying what he has already learned. The internal conditions are within the psychological makeup of the problem solver; the external are in the environment. In effect, problem-solving experiences are so completely tied to past emotional experiences that the former cannot be freed for reapplication in a more successful and creative way. The problem solver may be repeating errors or fallacies in thought and logic, habitually interpreting, analyzing, and dealing with facts in a way that he realizes is unproductive because it seems never to completely resolve the problem and constantly engenders the same unsuccessful outcome. But freedom from this cycle seems beyond the problem solver's reach. This, in too many instances, characterizes the behavior of employment interviewers. Either through environmental pressures or through synergism of the effects of the pressure-charged environment and the psychological weaknesses of the problem solver, flexibility and creative application of experience are inhibited.

Misuse of Information

Another factor that hampers problem solving is the misuse of information. The failure to evaluate or to apply information correctly may stem from the inability to crystallize the problem, to understand it fully, to grasp its subtleties, or even to define it properly—for within the definition of the problem lies the direction toward which the solution should point. One answer is training. Employment interviewers can train themselves to handle the problem of filling job vacancies in terms of individual short-range decisions for which they must process each bit of information about an applicant. True, there will always be individual differences with respect to intelligence, analytical ability, technical know-how, application of prior experience and learning, and work milieu where the problem is to be solved, but training remains indispensable. Although it may seem to be a simplification, it is nonetheless important that the employment interviewer's professional image of himself incorporate unending theoretical and practical training and continuous growth in capability as well as the developmental attributes of flexibility, perseverance, and patience.

The employment interviewer's technical and intellectual ability to solve problems is potentiated when the entire interview process is geared toward a problem that has practical application to the entire organization. The interview is then directed toward a specific goal; and the interview technique, sequence of questions, and resulting intermediary and final decisions make the goal attainable. On the basis of what we know about problem solving and decision making, programming an interview, which deals with the data collection and retrieval and inputs, becomes a highly significant mechanism to the employment interviewer, a kind of vehicle by which to accommodate his problem-solving and decision-making requirements.

Programming the Interview

A program is a way of performing a task, a kind of control on the course of affairs. Programming the interview means applying organized thought to the interview process. With programming, the problem remains the same, the goals are unchanged, but the behavioral responses to the problem may be altered. The interview program offers the means by which information can be controlled and, once controlled, dealt with.

The program that the employment interviewer constructs is a kind of road map, a route the interviewer must travel to reach his objective. The purpose of the program is to obtain information from the applicant in an orderly way, thus providing the means by which to sort the information into prime and nonprime categories. (Pursuit of nonprime factors is a waste of time at best and can result in a faulty choice.) The employment interviewer will define the qualifications for prime and nonprime factors when he forms his conception of the kind of applicant who best suits the job.

Definitions and Methodology

The interviewer begins by familiarizing himself with a few basic definitions that will serve as the operating vocabulary of interview programming. *Base* refers to basic subject matter, the starting point or the purpose of any line of questioning. For example, when the interview begins, there is the need to establish that the applicant standing before the interviewer is, in fact, the applicant whose name appears on the application; there is also the need, perhaps, to clarify the pronunciation or spelling of the applicant's name. Therefore, base 1 is name; base 2 may be address. Later on in the interview, base 300 may be a question concerning a previous employer. *Pursuit* refers to the questions that ensue after the base has been established in the interviewer's mind. Pursuit does not refer to mental processes but to the visible route the interviewer follows—a route obvious to the applicant as well as to the interviewer. The interviewer establishes base 1 as the name base. He asks the applicant his name and receives a reply. The pursuit might lie in name clarification: "Mr. Holnich? Is it Holni*k*? or Holni*tch*?" The answer received is the terminal point of pursuit 1, so that pursuit 1 leads from base 1 to the first answer. This is diagrammed in Figure 1.

The applicant's answer to the pursuit is evaluated as prime or nonprime. If the answer is nonprime (NPR) the interviewer must establish a new base, thereby terminating this line of inquiry or pursuit path. If the answer is prime (PR), it becomes prime 1, and the interviewer has a choice. He may decide that prime 1 is sufficient for his purpose and drop the matter; that is, terminate the pursuit path. Or he may decide that prime 1 has raised further questions that he feels are pertinent. If so, he will continue the pursuit either by establishing a derivative base in the same path (base 2 an outgrowth of prime 1), or simply by asking another question (pursuit 2). If the reply is prime, he has the same choice—(derivative) base 3, another question (pursuit 3), or termination of the path. If the reply is nonprime, the interviewer has only the third course, termination and the establishment of a new base. When he ends a pursuit path, the interviewer moves to a new base unless of course he ends the interview. If the interview program were actually drawn, it would be possible to locate any prime or nonprime response by simply identifying the base number, pursuit, and prime designations. Figure 2 illustrates the basic programming circuitry.

Branching

When a prime response initiates the need for questions to further illuminate the point, but that are not directly enough associated with the subject of base to remain on the same linear pursuit path, the path may branch. Branching is accomplished by establishing a derivative base at right angles to the first pursuit path. For example, consider a

FIGURE 1

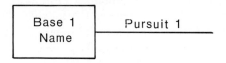

FIGURE 2

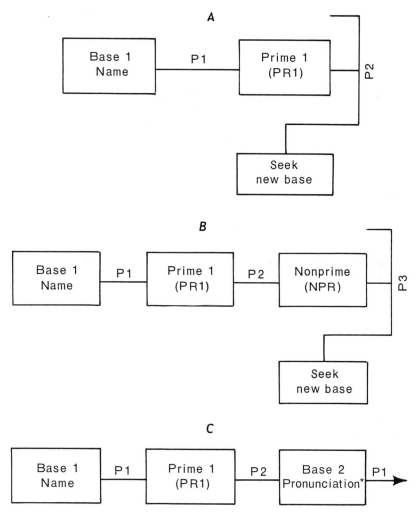

* The matter of pronunciation is directly enough associated with Base 1 to remain on the same linear pursuit path.

pursuit path regarding a former employer (Figure 3a). Base 210 may request information about the specific job function the applicant performed. The pursuit (P1) charts a path intending to elicit a response. The response, if understood by the applicant and pertinent, is prime 1. If the pursuit is unclear to the applicant, the response may still be classed prime if the applicant, in the interviewer's opinion, should have known the answer or should have understood the question sufficiently to make a response. If the response is prime, the interviewer may wish to restate his base 210 question but in a somewhat different manner. In this case he would branch from the pursuit path initiated at base 210 (Figure 3b).

Notice in Figure 3b that when a branch base is created the next consecutive number is used exactly as if the extension were linear. Notice, too, that the title of base 211 is "Job Function—Restate." Insofar as consecutive numbers are concerned, codes may be substituted for numbers, or a subnumbering (decimal, for example as shown in Figure 4), or sublettering system used as the number of branched bases increases.

Notice, too, in Figure 3a that the pursuit path leading from the terminal point and toward a new base is numbered consecutively in keeping with the prior pursuit numbers along the same pursuit path. When a pursuit path seeking a new base is sought, the new base is linked with the "seek new base" box and there will be a pursuit line to the new base. This is illustrated in Figure 5. You will note that in Figure 5 it was not necessary to establish a terminal point before a new base was pursued.

In Figure 6 the employment interviewer may want to pursue base 211 and obtain a subsequent prime response before returning to the pursuit path emanating from base 210. As a matter of fact, he may wish to pursue base 212 before returning to the linear path emanating from base 210. Notice that base 211 refers to specific job duties and that base 212 refers to a single specific job duty. Probably prime 1, base 211, highlighted one of several job duties that the interviewer wanted to pursue. Base 212 does not qualify to be in the horizontal pursuit path emanating from base 211, but does qualify for branch treatment.

There are also situations in which the information may not be readily available; for example, references might need checking, or verification that cannot be produced at the time of the interview might be necessary. The interviewer may create a terminal point and go to a new base (which would not be the most desirable choice), or he may simply note why there is not a terminal point and continue the pursuit

FIGURE 3

A

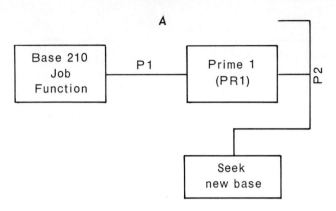

B

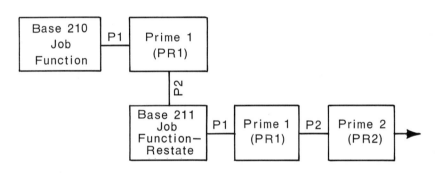

FIGURE 4

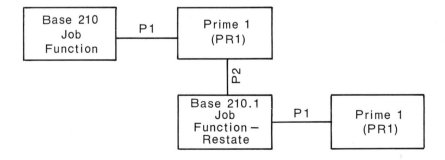

FIGURE 5

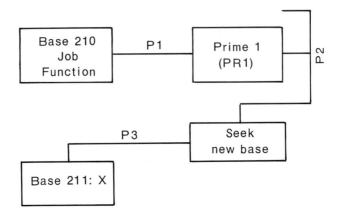

FIGURE 6

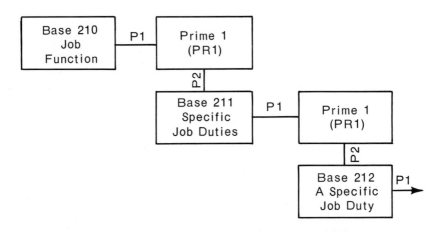

FIGURE 7

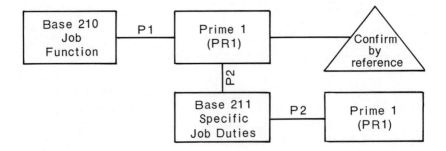

of bases emanating from that specific subject, thus building additional and needed peripheral input data, or he may establish a new base. An example of this delayed prime pursuit with notation is shown in Figure 7.

Prime Response

It should be kept in mind that a prime response is a pertinent and usable response and one that advances the understanding of the interviewer. It need not, however, work in the applicant's favor. For example, an applicant for an employee relations position who is asked about his experience with labor relations and union contracts and indicates that he has had none delivers a prime response—but hardly one that will advance his cause.

When a prime response initiates the need for new bases specifically linked to it, multiple branching results. This is shown in Figure 8. Notice in Figure 8 that the multiple bases 212, 213, and 214 are consecutively numbered (although their respective pursuit paths are all numbered P1) and that they all deal with subject matter associated with a specific job duty, yet do not in themselves deal with job duties. They are not different enough to form a new base but not qualified to be a part of the linear pursuit path. A pursuit path leading horizontally from base 211 (beginning P2) would have to be concerned strictly with job duties.

Certain refinements are brought out in Figure 8. Notice that terminal points at the conclusion of pursuit paths from the multiple bases do not direct the seeking of new bases. If they did—at least if they did in the cases of 212 and 213—they would direct the interviewer to bypass the succeeding multiple base or bases from prime 1, base 211. Actually the interviewer should return to the linear pursuit path leading from base 211 after the pursuits from the multiple bases 212 and 213 are satisfied. Logically, we might expect that an instruction to return to prime 1, base 211, and then pursue base 213 would appear at the terminal point of the linear pursuit path from base 212. While not shown in Figure 8, this circuitry must be understood. A new base might have been established from prime 1, base 214, but this was not directed. Moreover, there is no termination sign at prime 1, base 211, an omission that indicates an intention to continue the pursuit path from there. Clusters such as that emanating from prime 1, base 211, can appear throughout an interview program.

This type of interview programming, if actually committed to writing, enables interviewers subsequently to monitor their performance

FIGURE 8

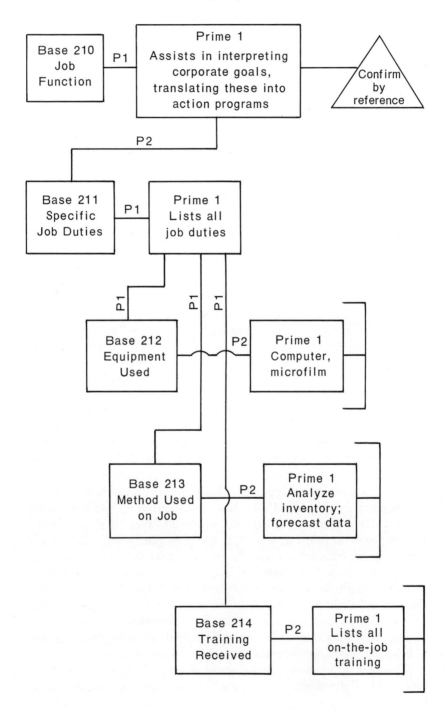

in terms of their ability to logically develop sequences of thought and select prime subject matter. Thus it permits a kind of performance appraisal, revealing qualitatively and quantitatively the ability of the employment interviewer to guide the interview along the most productive line while effectively communicating with the applicant. Obviously, unless the program indicates specific questions and answers, the qualitative conduct of the interview cannot be estimated. Restate paths (see Figure 3b) are not necessarily a reflection on the ability of the interviewer to make himself clear. They may reflect on the applicant, and, when they do, can be classified as prime or nonprime.

The development of either a written interview program or a nonwritten program as a guide to the employment interviewer is not an attempt to automate, mechanize, or otherwise "technolize" that most human activity, interviewing. However, the interview program, much like the computer program, is a schematic expression of the paths followed. Programming the interview minimizes predetermined judgments. It does not negate the use of prior experience, training, and behavioral responses; it enables the interviewer to apply them in a more disciplined and creative manner. In this respect, and in only this respect, the interviewer responds as a computer might—in a manner conditional on the results of its processes.

Perhaps in the final analysis, the significance of an interview program lies in its ability to help explain the behavior of both the employment interviewer and the applicant at the time of the interview. The symbols that constitute the interview program are simply mechanisms to show direction. Obviously, it is not possible, until responses are made, to program the prime responses or pursuit paths. In addition, it is not always possible to program all the bases. Yet the interviewer knows the most fundamental bases from experience even before the applicant reaches his attention. His notations at the time of the interview, whether made directly on the application, on an interview checklist, or on the résumé, could record his reaction to the information he receives.

The employment interviewer can make highly effective use of completed application forms, résumés, or test scores before the interview by using these as the basis for constructing an interview program. An interview program that is drawn up before an interview may be used as a guide, a checklist, or an actual method of notating responses to interview questions. For interviews that seem routine and are not highly complex, it may be that a mentally programmed interview is sufficient. Yet even here proper preparation can be useful.

Programming for Interviewing Managers and Technicians

Interviews for management positions or technical jobs or in which sensitive, detailed, complex, or otherwise nonroutine avenues of inquiry must be followed are especially well suited to prior preparation. In the review of the application and résumé, a considerable number of bases becomes obvious. These bases can be programmed through at least one pursuit path or a terminal point; in some cases several pursuit paths can be programmed on the basis of available information. This preinterview programming provides three major advantages: (1) It familiarizes the interviewer with personal, educational, and occupational background experiences of the applicant; (2) it provides an efficient method of saving time by eliminating the need for reviewing items that already have prime value or are evident on the basis of the material already in the interviewer's possession and are therefore not likely to render further prime factors; (3) it enables the employment interviewer to predetermine a certain number of bases about which he has no prime information and thus to narrow the focus of the interview earlier than would have otherwise been possible.

Let us now examine some program possibilities, evaluate the level of penetration the pursuit paths achieve, and note some subtleties in the development of prime and nonprime configurations.

In Figure 9 some facts are programmed prior to the interview. As the interviewer confirms the data, new base points are suggested. Prior to the interview, base 1 ("Name") was programmed and prime 1 confirmed on the basis of the application or the résumé.

INTERVIEWER: Let me see, your name is pronounced Hol-brine?
APPLICANT: Holbrine or Holbrin, either one. It's just as hard to get people to pronounce my present married name as it was my last one.

There is no indication on the application or the résumé of a previous marriage. This creates a new branch and base point for "Previous Married Name," as shown in Figure 10.

INTERVIEWER: What was your previous married name?
APPLICANT: *Anslemp.* The *p* was silent. Oh, it was terrible; some people called me "Anslep"; some called me "Anslem"; and some even pronounced my name "Anslempt." Well, that was just one of the problems I had with that little fiasco. I guess it was like the rest of the marriage—just one big confusion, trouble from the very start. I probably should have done something about it

FIGURE 9

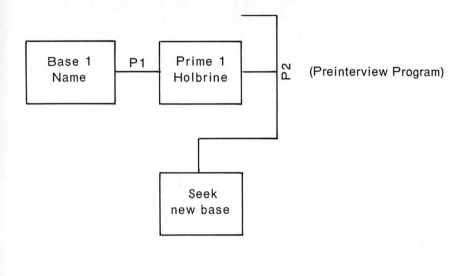

FIGURE 10

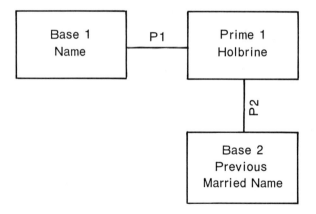

> sooner, before three years had gone by, but I thought I would give it every chance. The breaking point was when he started staying out late and——

The information that the applicant's name in a prior marriage was Anslemp is programmed as prime 1 on pursuit path 1 from base 2. That the first marriage lasted three years is programmed as a new base, base 3, "Duration of Prior Marriage," from which a pursuit path is charted with prime 1 information. Note, however, that the interviewer branches from this last prime 1 response and programs a new base, 4, which he captions "Lacks Discretion."

The interviewer considered that the applicant's remarks were inappropriate and concluded that she lacked discretion. Lack of discretion may indicate emotional difficulties. These can give rise to talkative or distracting behavior on the job and can even render the employee wholly ineffective in certain jobs. While the comments of the applicant are nonprime in terms of content, they are considered to be prime because of their behavioristic significance. Figure 11 is a representation of this new configuration. The creation of a base for lack of discretion is a refinement of the programming technique. The item is obviously not a typical base point in terms of broad data input that may be available. And yet, depending on the type of job for which the applicant is applying or the significant impression that is being made, such a base as "lacks discretion" could appear numerous times through the total program. It is even possible to program such a base in advance when a résumé or an application contains material the interviewer feels is inappropriate. Comments about problems on a previous job or office intrigue, gossip, and information that would normally be considered confidential, such as trade secrets, often fall under this heading.

Value Scale

It is also possible in programming the interview to establish a scale of values for prime responses. For a favorable reply a plus sign or number 1 could be used; for a neutral response, a plus-and-minus sign or number 2; and for an unfavorable response, a minus sign or number 3. For example, in Figure 11 the prime 1 response emanating from the base 4, "lacks discretion," might contain the number 3 or even a minus sign to indicate the interviewer's evaluation of the response. An applicant who is educationally overqualified (or at the other extreme, underqualified) could rate a number 3 or a minus symbol in the prime response box. (See Figure 12.)

FIGURE 11

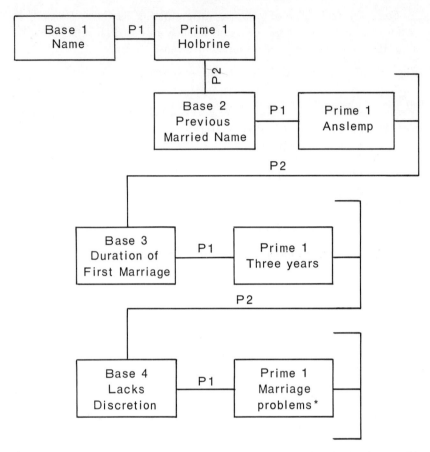

* Interviewer may seek a new base or pursue Base 4 if he feels it will
provide prime data about the applicant.

FIGURE 12

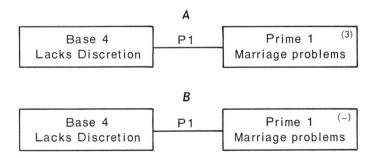

Once the technique of physical programming has been learned, it is possible to represent the program linearly rather than schematically as in the following sequence, based on Figures 9–12.

Fig. 9 B1 Name → P1 PR1 Holbrine → Seek new base

Fig. 10 B1 Name → P1 PR1 Holbrine → P2 B2 Previous married name

Fig. 11 B1 Name → P1 PR1 Holbrine → P2 B2 Previous married name → P1 PR1 Anslemp → P2 B3 Duration of first marriage → P1 PR3 Three years → P2 B4 Lacks discretion → P1 PR1 Marriage problems.

Fig. 12 B4 Lacks discretion → P1 PR1 Marriage problems (3)

or

B4 Lacks discretion → P1 PR1 Marriage problems (−)

The use of a base to indicate a factor such as lack of discretion (see Figure 11) suggests the possibility of a similar use of bases for pursuit paths leading to such qualities as sense of humor, general knowledge or awareness (beyond test score results), social adaptability, emotional quality at the time of the interview (with projections for pressure situations in which the applicant might find himself if employed), and other such intangibles, which may be significant to the interviewer. For certain positions, particularly in the management and sales areas, the individual's ability to make small talk, a possible reflection of personality, social adaptability, and other such related factors, may be considered relevant. Even the opening remark by the employment interviewer, "How are you today? I hope you didn't have much difficulty finding our office," could elicit a significant response from the applicant. If the interviewer finds that such points are critical or may be critical in his total evaluation of the applicant, then he should program the base points accordingly. A response may be classified prime because it is humorous even if the content of the response is nonprime. The way the response was made could imply significant insight or open a field of inquiry or a path of pursuit that, although it could not have been anticipated, the interviewer feels is significant.

Goals and Unproductive Paths

It is possible that during this kind of byplay the interviewer could be caught off balance and allow the interview to take an unproductive path or wander in directions that may not yield prime responses. Therefore, in this situation programming the interview is highly important. By following a programmed pursuit path mentally or on paper, the interviewer can make the most out of the byplay without disturbing the overall direction of the interview. He can also record his impressions and the points at which such impressions seem to be repeated. In diagramming an interview in progress, he may find a pattern in the prime responses. For example, in pursuing subjects he feels are critically important and have considerable weight in the overall problem-solving and decision-making process, the interviewer may find himself continually having to branch from prime responses to a base point that reflects the applicant's humorous approach. This continual reversion to humor may be the applicant's way of relieving his tension, a trait presumably manifest during periods of nervousness. On the other hand, it may be a reflection of his approach to serious situations—which does not necessarily mean that the applicant is flighty, immature, or lacking in perspective. When such factors are evaluated in terms of a total interview, they may have significance. It is quite possible that the interviewer may not be able to affix a quantitative value or weighting to a prime response such as humor until he has completed the interview and evaluates his impressions in retrospect, when he is able to consider the significance of a humorous response in the light of the pursuit path at which it occurred.

In our discussion of problem solving, decision making, and programming the underlying theme has been one of organization—organizing thoughts, disciplining perceptions, understanding the mechanisms of problem solving, decision theory, and decision-making practices in order to better control input and thus maximize the objectivity and rationale of a decision. Organizing or attempting to organize input data and thus control environmental stimuli (which in our discussion refers to the information supplied by the applicant in terms of the total context of the job vacancy) does not necessarily eliminate all the problems or reduce distortions in the perceptual process leading to problem solving, communication, and thought. One of the very basic behavioral responses to stimuli is the tendency to organize them (in the form of information or input data) into categories. In so doing, there may be distortion. Interview programming attempts to guard against the wholesale categorization of data by breaking down each step of the interview process and at the same time delineating the process along pursuit paths that may be branched, and repeating or reiterating it when necessary so that the interview becomes a more organic, more systematic experience.

As one industrial psychologist says, "The environment presents . . . ambiguous stimuli. We must make sense of the environment in order to strive for the attainment of goals. All behavior is based on the world as it is seen by the behaving individual, and each of us becomes emotionally attached to his organizations of the world and is reluctant to give them up." [5] The employment interviewer who understands decision theory and problem-solving mechanisms and who masters interview programming makes an effort to challenge his internalized perceptual organization and by subjecting his perception to more objective analysis moves toward clarification of ambiguous stimuli (applicant responses).

[5] M. Haire, *Psychology in Management* (2nd edition) (New York: McGraw-Hill Book Company, 1964), p. 60.

4

Breaking
the Semantics Barrier

Employment interviewing is a communications process. Applicant and interviewer exchange words and each hopes that, from this exchange, understanding will emanate. Sometimes it does and sometimes it does not, and when it does not we say that a misunderstanding or breach of communication has occurred. For the employment interviewer, words are symbolic of the great events in people's lives. Words convey personal histories and occupational experiences and they can reveal the central theme in a human being's behavioral processes. In short, words transmit meaning, and the semantics problems with which employment interviewers deal involve the constancy of meaning.

It is almost miraculous that words accomplish such a monumental task, for, after all, words are not things. They are symbols, often standing for abstractions, and they are themselves defined by words that are symbols. A word may have more than a single meaning and, because each person's experiences and psychological readiness to understand may be different, the speaker's intended meaning may be missed, so that the speaker is not understood.

The matter of communication is a growing concern to business because a high level of communication is necessary if modern business organizations are to maintain and increase productivity, morale, and sensitivity to the business environment and flexibility in reacting to it. But effective communication does not just happen. To be effective, communication must be precise and free of ambiguity. Likewise, the employment interviewer's questions must be precise; his probing of the applicant must be specific and never unsure or wandering. His expression of job and company expectations must be clear and understood. In order to accomplish this, he must use words properly.

Before examining the semantics barrier employment interviewers must overcome, it is necessary to establish certain characteristics basic to the concept of communication. First of all, communicating is not a haphazard process. It is systematic in that its elements—words, meanings, human responses and reactions—are interrelated. Second, communication fills a human need. Finally, communication deals with the symbolic representation of reality. In respect to this last characteristic, the matter of semantics is important.

When we speak of the semantics barrier, we refer to any disruption or blockage in the exchange of meaning between one person and another. From a behavioral standpoint this is critical because the meaning of words produces a reaction attributable to the form of communication or the linking of one word to another.

Connotative and Denotative Words

The employment interviewer should be familiar with the two basic categories of word meaning. Fundamentally, words are connotative or they are denotative. If words are connotative, they encompass a wide range of meaning; they are broad, often difficult to define except in the context of their use. They are easily misunderstood. These words can influence people because they are nondirective in relation to a specific point of reference. Responses to such words differ depending on the sophistication of the listener. For example, such connotative words as "effective," "hierarchical," and "organization" have wide connotations and to the experienced, seasoned businessman may have more meaning than to a novice. Yet even to the businessman they can be confusing. To put it another way, a person whose verbal communication is heavily loaded down with connotative words is terribly hard to pin down.

Denotative words are just the opposite. These words are specific and clear and have only one meaning. These words point to a single object and to no other. They are precise and free of ambiguity.

Whether a word is connotative or denotative, it has dimension in terms of the human response to it. For example, a word can have connotative *value*. It can, therefore, convey the pleasant or the unpleasant, good or evil. It can be a powerful word with much emotional impact or a very weak word. It can be active or passive. Words, obviously, can be rated for effect. The most singular problem in using language, and this is underscored for the employment interviewer, is to respond to word meanings as if words were actually the things they represent. Words are not reality; they are symbols or representations, and at best incomplete and inaccurate representations of reality. Furthermore, even the simplest words are riddled with ambiguity. For example, the word "and" is supposed to link ideas, and the word is generally understood to indicate an interacting and reciprocal association between them. In fact, this may not be true. The "and" may be intended to be taken in a purely conjunctive sense.

The applicant, in his desire to enhance his image in the mind of the interviewer, may emphasize connotative words. The interviewer should reject these words in applicant responses and demand (by rephrasing and repeating questions) denotative words, thereby communicating the need for precise answers to specific questions.

Problems in Word Dynamics

In the dynamics of words, therefore, there are several problems that become critical to the employment interviewer. The transmittal of a meaning from one person to another is one. Effect is another. Words have emotional effects on the user and on the listener or reader. The effect may be the same or it may be different, and it may be totally unexpected. Another problem lies in the difficulty of analyzing the values that words convey, or judgmental approvals. Certain words may elevate the user in his own mind or in that of the listener or reader; others seem to grade or devalue him. Thus the value attached to the words may depend on the point of view of the listener or reader. A fourth problem, and a major one for the employment interviewer, lies in the inability of words as symbols to fully convey facts. This problem will be considered first because it underlies the other three.

The power of words to convey facts is limited. Words may be thought of as containers capable of holding meaning but for the most part impossible to fill. Even if we were capable of selecting the proper "containers," we would not be able to fill all of them; that is, to express the totality of our thoughts and experiences. There are an infinite number of possible combinations of facts in the real world. Likewise, there is an infinite number of possible perceptual realities, each peculiar to the psychology of the observer. But language does not allow for this infinity of possibilities. In other words, there are more conditions and relationships of reality than words to express them. Our language is primarily a two-value method of expression. Things *are* or they are *not;* we see two sides of a question; investigation pursues on an either-or alternative. There is a third value, but it is for the most part dysfunctional. This is a negative quality, which in almost all instances defies the excluded middle. There is not, for example, a socially acceptable middle point between success and failure, or good and bad, or beautiful and grotesque, or adjusted and maladjusted, or employable and nonemployable.

Language Structure

The mastery of language requires a feeling for language structure, or the proper combination of words. It is through this combination that first-order facts are isolated from an infinity of abstraction. First-order facts do not, of course, materialize when needed for observation and measurement. Similarly, words are not internalized or physically felt, but they become tantamount to first-order facts because the structural linking of words, even the most abstract, calls up a principle, a universal truth, or a reality well above the level of recitation of what anyone can observe.

The task of structuring words is a most difficult one because a fact, once isolated, is almost always unique. It is rare to find two distinct facts that cannot be shown to differ in some respect. Furthermore, in human relations (and insofar as the physical world is concerned) few things remain exactly and indefinitely the same. In other words, reality as perceived or as measured changes either through natural phenomena or as a result of perceptual differences. But, although words may have different meanings, language has little flexibility. There is not a single word that conveys only one, precise, narrow experience or fact and is used for no other. The use to which words are put and especially the multiple uses of words in the abstract give rise to misunderstanding. Thus a gap between words and reality is created.

The listener or reader will take in words. When he is convinced that all or most of the words presented to him form a pattern of meaning he considers to be in keeping with his own attitudes, understandings, and expectations and so, when he feels he has confirmed the words either by logic or on the basis of other information, he considers that they constitute a fact. Thus there are so many variables that it is quite conceivable that what the speaker or writer considers to be a fact may seem to the listener or reader to be a nonfact.

Human Awareness and Understanding

Part of the problem may be one of point of view. Circumstances and conditions of the past do not change. They have occurred and cannot be undone. The memory of an on-the-job experience may dull over time and the factual details may be lost, but the emotional impression, the psychological experience, is locked in regardless of time and does not change in the mind of the individual even though his interpretation of the event and the circumstances surrounding it may have changed radically with maturity, experience, and insight. But regardless of whether interpretations change, the exact nature of the experience will never be completely known or totally understood because no one can know or express the *all* of a fact. What is expressed or communicated and what is agreed to as fact are fragments of what has been either observed, perceived, or broadly understood or assumed by an individual. It becomes a rather personal matter and as such is limited to an individual's ability or capacity to observe, understand, perceive, and express. This is one of the reasons that more than one witness to an event is usually desirable in a court of law. The greater the impact of the event on emotions, the more witnesses that are usually necessary to establish even a single fact.

Obviously, some patterns of impression, insight, and understanding are more reliable than others. In fact, they are reliable to the point where some experiences can be measured. The reliability factor is the degree to which the observer agrees with other observers. But what of facts pertaining to human experiences? How are these conveyed? By words that express the essence of these experiences, by words that also express attitude, perception, and motives. Because of similarities in human activity, common experiences, and shared values, there is an element of commonality in human understanding. This accounts for the acceptance of the possibility that certain events have occurred or will occur. When a person denies such a possibility, he finds the events described to him to be in conflict with what he understands to be possible. Because he cannot measure or directly observe the event, he has no alternative but to consider accounts of it unreliable or purposely falsified.

Levels of Abstraction

In order to be understood or to communicate, it is necessary to differentiate between what is reality and what is abstraction or what is symbolic and what is tangible. A symbol is not reality but a representation of it. If a person states that an applicant is qualified, the word "qualified" is a symbol or an abstraction to convey reality. The word may mean "employable" or it can stand for the parts of which "qualified" is composed. When the interviewer begins to break down the symbol "qualified" into higher abstractions or lower abstractions, he is then able to understand more or, at least, something else about these parts. Moreover "qualified" indicates a state of being, a quality inherent in the applicant. It lacks, of course, the element of time. The statement indicates that the applicant, today, *right now*, is qualified. But the fact of being qualified may not have been true of him last year and may not be true of him next year. Words of this sort have many levels of abstraction and are a constant source of confusion because they may be understood at a different level from that at which they are used.

But, even if a reader or listener—in this instance an employment interviewer—is willing to accept words as being representative of facts, he cannot know the fact in its totality. Certain deeper levels of meaning must be inferred, just as the reality of a fact beyond our abilities to observe it directly must be inferred. The rationale for hiring is not based on facts—even when these are measurable or observed firsthand. The rationale is drawn from inferences and assumptions that are highly abstract at best. At this level of abstraction, theoretical or scientifically oriented constructs can be formed; in other words, at this stage we are in a better position to begin explaining or accounting for the behavior that has taken place in the past and to venture educated guesses or predictions about the future. It is at this level that the employment interviewer attains the confidence to assume first A, then B. And even this may be presumptuous, for in effect the interviewer is confident that he will be able to dig deeper into the subject, to discover the stuff of which his first-order facts are made, and then to grapple with the inferred abstractions.

The employment interviewer should rarely be satisfied with the gross acceptance of words as facts, or with the observations, measurements, and intuitive understanding of events that give credence to words and make them seem facts. He must search for a deeper level of abstraction or inference. We may think of this process as something like walking down the stairs of an office building from the top floor to the subbasement. At the pinnacle of the building there may be a clock or a beacon turning at set intervals at night perhaps to warn low-flying aircraft. At this point, the interviewer makes certain observations, which are gross and general. As the interviewer descends through the building, he begins to learn more about its internal workings. The deeper into the internal structure he goes, the more he sees because the level of abstraction is different than if he stood on the sidewalk looking up at the building and made assumptions about it. Therefore, the process of abstracting becomes a test of validity.

Expression of Values

A major point for the interviewer to understand is that what has been referred to here as abstractions cannot be expressed in words. What is expressed verbally is a value, an attribute, or a physical or social relationship. One cannot speak of pain and expect the listener to feel the pain. One cannot discuss his career objectives and expect the interviewer to feel and experience the same sense of optimism or pessimism, fear, or excitement as the speaker. There probably was no truer statement spoken than that of the applicant who said to the interviewer, "You can't imagine how angry and frustrated I was when Mr. Pompous bawled me out in front of all the girls in the office." This statement should be viewed as analogous to the office building. The interviewer delves into it just as he worked down the steps of the building from the pinnacle to the subbasement. The gross words and superficial understandings are only the observable portion of the iceberg, only a fraction of its bulk. Below the surface are the inferences and smaller particles of abstractions that serve to help us better understand, explain, and predict something about the portion above the surface.

Functions of Abstraction

The process of abstraction is unlimited in that the number of details or particles of fact can be increased indefinitely. Abstraction is affected by the individual's psychology. The applicant who describes a previous work situation cannot reasonably do so, in terms of the proper use of the language, unless he describes himself in the actuation. This is a kind of reflexiveness. For example, when an applicant describes a previous work duty or circumstance of employment, he describes what he saw and did, not the duties or the circumstances themselves. In short, the interviewer must make an observation about an observation or an abstraction about an abstraction. The interviewer who cannot allow for this reflexiveness makes mistakes in judgment.

In the context of the interview, the factor of reflexiveness is highly significant because of the relationship of word meanings to abstractions. A word has multiple meanings depending on the context or how it is used or what level of abstraction is applied. An interviewer may say that college graduates make effective managers. This statement may be true or not and, in attributing truth or fallacy to it, we in turn make a statement about it. Another example: The interviewer may make a statement to the effect that studies indicate college graduates make effective managers. If we were to penetrate to the next level of abstraction, we would investigate what studies are revealed, how those studies were validated, and so forth. Each successive layer of abstraction is a statement about the preceding. Inevitably certain words will occur in more than one layer. Yet, depending on the level or degree of abstraction, a particular word may have a different meaning. We are faced with multiple meanings, a factor that increases the possibility of confusion and misunderstanding. Thus the employment interviewer cannot accept a statement unless he is sure that he understands it at the applicant's level of abstraction. The emphasis, therefore, should not be on understanding word meanings so much as clarifying context.

For the employment interviewer, abstractions are not as self-corrective as they are in, for example, the physical sciences. The interviewer cannot collect a sampling of the applicant, take it to a laboratory, and measure and test it. It is most difficult for an interviewer to test his assumptions or conclusions in a measurable, scientific way. The interviewer's sole defense against this immeasurability is the knowledge that his assumptions and inferences will not be challenged. Therefore, he may allow these to remain unchanged. He may even be unaware of the role of reflexiveness, abstraction, multiple word use, and perceptual influence in forming those conclusions.

The Communications Process

But, once abstractions are made and inferences drawn and tested for validity in terms of contextual relevance, a communications process begins. The interviewer communicates not only with others but with himself as well, and his resultant behavior may be more in keeping with this internalized communication than with the communication between himself and the other party. In this frame of reference, the total transfer of ideas has not taken place, and communication breaks down. This breakdown in communication can take place at any point in the interview. The interviewer may misunderstand the hiring need; he may misread qualifications or make a poor presentation. In the latter case, the interviewer's understanding of the specific occupational skill needed and his evaluation of the company's capacity to satisfy the needs of the applicant may be correct and his selection of a candidate may be perfect. But more than likely, in his presentation he did not set the stage for a given level of abstraction where his listener was concerned. Consequently the listener understood his words on a different level of abstraction than he intended, and his assumptions and inferences were not properly communicated. By indicating the level of abstraction, the interviewer establishes ground rules of conversation that prepare the applicant to understand interview questions and respond appropriately.

The employment interviewer is constantly striving to relate an applicant's past performance and attitudes to potential performance in future-oriented job demands or to estimate the applicant's effectiveness on the basis of his so-called track record. When positive relationships are "discovered," either by the applicant (who will be eager to communicate this) or by the interviewer (who may probe further to see if he is right or may arrive at a conclusion), what has happened is that either quantitative or qualitative differences were reduced and similarities increased. The fact is that, as more and more details are ignored, more similarities emerge. This becomes a function of abstraction. The applicant's background can be summarized in a broad, sweeping connotative way. Similarities pop out everywhere. Change the level of abstraction and the differences may be readily revealed.

In such instances, the semantics law of nonidentity must be recalled. Essentially, this law states that A is not necessarily A; words are not reality; Joe Doe today is not the Joe Doe of yesterday and neither will he be the Joe Doe of tomorrow. In interviewing, what comes first in the applicant's response to the question is the recollection of the experience and, then, the description. But the description is not the experience itself; it is word symbolism. Furthermore it is a description of words describing the experience on another level of abstraction. Neither is the (A) description the (A) experience. In this case, A is not A. The level of abstraction used in A (relating the experience) may be quite different from the level of abstraction used to convey the description.

Nonidentity

Joe Doe (A), supervisor at ABC manufacturing company, is not Joe Doe (A), supervisor at XYZ manufacturing company, in this case the prospective employer. In this example A is not A. On a higher abstract plan, certainly A is A, but connotative context must prevail. The interviewer must be prepared constantly to recognize nonidentity (A is not A). Only in this way can he examine the conditions that create the difference.

From the point of view of the law of nonidentity, the statement that Joe Doe was a poor employee is invalid. Suppose he had three jobs; the first with the Allness Company, the second with the Noneness Company, and the third with the Someness Company. Joe Doe with the Allness Company is not Joe Doe with the Noneness Company, nor is he Joe Doe with the Someness Company. Joe Doe one is not Joe Doe two and so forth. Joe Doe is not Joe Doe; he is Joe Doe at a particular time, place, and circumstance. The interviewer who is prepared to recognize nonidentity is not ready to reject Joe Doe out of hand. The law of identity (A is A) is subject to the degree of differences that the law of nonidentity (A is not A) will allow, and this is subject to the level of abstraction.

After all, abstraction is a way of leaving out details. The leaving out may not be intentional. Our efforts to reach allness may be restricted by a lack of technology, as in understanding the all of human behavior. The interviewer will never know the all of an applicant. Interviewers fail to make valid decisions about applicants when they begin to think of an abstract as if it were not an abstract, as if their theory about the individual were the same as the individual. This principle of nonallness has a safety valve for the interviewer, for it deters him from acting as if he had complete and total knowledge of the applicant. Thus the employment interviewer comes up against the probability factor of meaning, which prohibits absolutes since words are not concrete objects. And, because experience influences our sense of the probable, it once led Will Rogers to comment, "When you get down under the gravy, it has to be either meat or potatoes."

Certain words can trigger emotions and physical responses. These are the signal words. We expect to hear "you're welcome" to our "thank you"; we blush when vulgarities are spoken at the wrong time and place. We say "democracy" and there is the reaction of approval; "communism" and there is the reaction of disapproval; "Kelly passed on" and heads are bowed. These words signal learned behavioral responses. They have immediate effects; they make behavioral demands. And, in terms of the language, they are full-impact, rigid, no-holds-barred words. The speaker who communicates in signal words (and politicians do it well) can emotionally exhaust the listener if not tetanize him. On the other hand, symbol words are less taxing, usually require no immediate emotional response, allow a delayed reaction, are less rigid and nonspecific, and do not create emotional tenseness or physical hyperreactivity. The interviewer should strike a balance between symbol and signal words (and phrases).

Extensional Orientation

The matter of extensional orientation is another critical aspect of semantics about which the employment interviewer must be aware. Simply stated, external word meanings (generally adjectives used to describe people) are not used to indicate an absolute degree of a quality but rather to point up either similarities *or* differences. It is, of course, possible to indicate in what ways people are alike and in what ways different at the same time, but with our two-value language, it can rarely be done briefly or easily. There is not, for example, a word midway between good and bad that has impact equal to either of these two words. To say that an applicant has potential is to say that he is like every other individual who has potential. By the same token, we imply that all people possessed of "nonpotential" are also alike. In other words, our language does not easily allow for the expression of uniqueness. Yet for the interviewer, to express similarity *and* difference is a *must*.

Furthermore, an expression like "has potential," while a connotative abstract of a denotative abstract, implies the possession of potential as a matter of the applicant's being rather than indicating that (a) potential is a characteristic or an identifiable fact or a possibility, (b) Mr. Applicant's potential is unique in terms of Mr. Applicant only, and (c) we are referring to Mr. Applicant today and now. This latter point is important because if it is ignored the positive and negative aspects of Mr. Applicant may be seen as unalterable or unchanging, and this would affect estimates of his developmental possibilities and opportunities after employment.

Many people would feel more comfortable and secure in a world in which word meanings never change and in which there are no *levels* of abstraction but only one common understanding of word. meanings. This of course is no more likely than a cessation of change in the world. But difficulties do arise when our language does not change quickly enough to keep pace with other changes.

Semantics barriers can of course be minimized if the employment interviewer avoids technical, fancy, or archaic words and sticks to the most familiar—familiar not only to himself but also to the listener or applicant. In so doing, he should favor concrete over abstract words. He should use the shorter word in preference to the elaborate, descriptive, picturesque, or romantic. And he should be sparing in his use of concept linkage—stringing supposedly interrelated concepts together in single expressions—even with the more sophisticated applicant who may understand or may think he understands them. Examples are deferred executive compensation, interdepartmental functional relationships, and job-related training. If it is necessary to use concept-linked expressions, they should first be defined.

Communication is not easy. It is, indeed, an art to understand what the speaker means, not just what he says. Therefore the effective employment interviewer is a good listener, a quality that presupposes a certain amount of humility. He never pressures an applicant in the desire to elicit critical responses before the applicant becomes too exhausted to respond properly (applicants treated in this fashion often become unnerved and overcommunicative). He neither races ahead of the speaker in an effort to beat him to the conclusion nor draws conclusions about the nature or applicability of his remarks until all the facts are in. And he does not ignore what the speaker is saying on the assumption that he knows what the speaker *really* means. Interviewers who operate in this way may unconsciously fear hearing what the applicant has to say because these remarks may negate the interviewer's first impressions and throw his sacred theories about people into a cocked hat.

Closed-Mind Syndromes

The interviewer must avoid such communication traps as selective listening and the plural-inference and closed-mind syndromes. Selective listening is listening only to what reinforces prejudgment. The interviewer may have jumped to an unjustified conclusion, and if he listens selectively he may impose his own ideas on the words of the applicant. Selective listening is a major cause of confusion about what the applicant said as opposed to what he meant. The plural-inference syndrome is an unwarranted assumption by each party that the other agrees with him. The applicant, for example, may assume that the interviewer agrees that his reasons for walking off the last job were justified. In the same category is the tendency to take it for granted that certain facts are common knowledge, certain beliefs universal, and that "as we do, so do all."

The closed-mind syndrome is in many respects similar to the plural-inference syndrome. It differs only in that the listener believes he has arrived at a correct conclusion whether the speaker shares his opinion or not. From that point forward, the listener has stopped listening except in a highly selective way, extracting only those parts of the response that support his opinion. The employment interviewer who is guilty of this may respond to an applicant's statement in a completely irrelevant manner and throw the interview into chaos.

It has not been the purpose of this chapter to exhaust the highly complex subject of semantics. The purpose has been, first, to examine the essence of communication and, second, to isolate the factors of semantics that are most relevant to the employment interviewer. The employment interviewer is as guilty of semantics fallacies as anyone, but he may pay a much higher price for his mistakes. By the very nature of his role, the interviewer can no more afford to be uninvolved in the relevant mechanics of semantics than an artist can afford to be indifferent to the functions of color and form.

5

Evaluating
Success and Failure

CLEAR EVIDENCE of an individual's past success or failure on the job is both dramatic and disturbing. It is dramatic because it is significant and because it is exceptional. It is disturbing because of the challenge of projecting it to the requirements of the job applied for. The complexities and technological processes of the modern business organizational structure tend to make a clear determination of success or failure difficult. The employment interviewer may rely on direct questions or may attempt to deduce previous success or failure from such indicators as successive salary levels or job titles. The way in which the applicant arrived at his conclusions, the nature of the work environment, the applicant's criteria of judgment and his perception—all enter into the determination. In addition, the level of accountability, the size of the business organization, and the technological sophistication of the work milieu can make it difficult for an outside observer to identify job success or failure. In fact, it may be equally difficult for the insider; that is, the person directly involved, other employees in the same organization, or someone professionally concerned with a company's business environment. Although it might be expected that the insider would be better equipped to identify individual job success or failure, such is not always the case. It is quite common to find workers who themselves are unclear about the outcome of their work, their continuing progress, the scope of their jobs, professional growth and development, or the success or failure of an assignment or project. Such lack of certainty regarding success or failure is not restricted to managerial jobs. Commonly it afflicts clerical or production workers, whose performance, because of the nature of their duties, is difficult to assess. For example, there are machines whose speed and efficiency are out of the operator's control. In such jobs success is very likely to be defined as not being fired.

A key consideration in the evaluation of a person's previous performance is the tendency to look for total success or total failure; that is, to evaluate the total performance of an individual in terms of a single, isolated indicator of success or failure. In general, managerial jobs lend themselves least to this type of categorization.

Applicant Self-evaluation

One of the biggest problems in evaluating success or failure has to do with the method of measuring job performance. To the extent that a formal, accepted, clearly defined, regularly scheduled, and reliable appraisal system or method is lacking, the individual employee will substitute his own informal, unsure, and often biased evaluation of his performance. In so doing, he is as likely as not to use as measurements of performance invalid and unreliable bench marks. The less adequate the feedback he receives, the more obscure and irrelevant will be the criteria by which he measures his success and failure. When the feedback system is nonexistent or else so weak, untrustworthy, or generalized that it is viewed by the employee as not applicable to the job, or if the system is designed to reflect evidences of success or failure in terms with which the employee cannot identify, his evaluation of his performance may be characterized by uncertainty, confusion, and frustration; he may feel that he is unsuccessful or nonachieving (which is not the same thing). Such feelings of insecurity reflect this lack of feedback—communication between the employee and his superiors—more than it reflects the success or failure of his work.

Morale

The morale of the employee drops with his self-esteem and consequently his productivity after employment is unpredictable. He could run the gamut from initial optimism based on the confidence that if his work is faulty in any way someone is bound to tell him so, to abject disillusionment—a sense of failure and demoralization—as he comes to believe that he and the work he performs are so meaningless and unimportant that no one feels the need to communicate with him regarding the performance of the task. This belief could develop into a feeling that no one really cares; so not only the employee's work but also his mental well being could be threatened. These attitudes could clearly affect his achievement levels on a new job.

The harmful effects of this lack of interface are more likely to register in the employee's ability to set and achieve standards of performance than in the outcome of an immediate or current assignment, or in a production schedule, quality level, or work project. Without such standards, the employee has difficulty in evaluating his long-range progress and in keeping it in proper perspective with his short-run success and failure. Even if he is familiar with the job and has a good understanding of the relative importance of each task to the job's main purpose, he can be in the dark as to his performance, exaggerating or underestimating it.

Ill-defined performance standards also weaken the mechanisms of reward and punishment, which can be quite subtle in a business organization. The positive effect of a salary increase or promotion or words of praise (all mechanisms of recognition) is far greater when the employee has a clear picture of what he has achieved than when he has none at all. In fact, a reward that follows a long period of uncertainty about work performance may create confusion, frustration, or guilt—or even feelings of aggression. The worker will rarely turn down a salary increase or argue with a word of praise, but he may question either to himself or to others what he has done to deserve it. When the uncertainty is terminated by punishment (criticism or the withholding of an expected salary increase, bonus, or promotion), employees often react emotionally, sometimes aggressively.

Peers and Superiors

The criteria by which the employee may attempt to evaluate himself in the absence of properly defined, accessible performance parameters depend on the nature of his position, but basically are concerned with peer acceptance and recognition by superiors. The employee may seek indications in such subtle factors as the frequency with which he is asked his opinion, the rapidity with which his memos or recommendations are acknowledged, the attitude of his supervisor, and the frequency and quality of his contacts with upper management. Workers may compare their own daily or weekly production records with others doing comparable work or they may compare quality control levels. Employees have been known to judge their own success or failure in meeting immediate job demands on the basis of how much overtime they worked. The longer the uncertainty is protracted, the less valid the factors at which the employee will grasp for indicators. In extreme cases employees have construed the clothing a fellow worker wears, the model of car he drives, or the quality of his home as revelant for purposes of comparison in determining their own performance.

The way in which success or failure is evaluated on the job by management may determine to an appreciable extent how an applicant evaluates his own previous achievement, which in turn could influence the evaluation of the employment interviewer. It is not uncommon to hear sales people discussing the success or failure of a fellow salesman recall the time that he "pulled off a big one"—the one exception to an otherwise undistinguished record. Because of that solitary spectacular performance the salesman was for a considerable time thereafter considered a good performer. Even when he slipped back into his mediocre norm, he continued to receive the benefit of the doubt and remained, in the eyes of many, a man with topflight potential. The salesman's feat created a halo effect. Only after a considerable time period (this depending on the type of sales and the type of industry) with a below-average record will the salesman lose the halo.

Evaluating Managerial Performance

This halo effect is especially prominent in the evaluation of performance in managerial positions. At the management level the emphasis is on team effort. This is inevitable in view of the complexities of the management process and the many "special" occupations in the typical business organization today. It is, therefore, not uncommon to find management applicants who find it nearly impossible to evaluate their own total performance. When asked to describe their performance on the job, they may select words such as *satisfactory, steady, above average, average,* or *acceptable.* This is not simply a matter of humility. Basically their choice of such middle-ground words in preference to *exceptional* and *outstanding* is a reflection of their fragmented perception and also of their awareness of the management process; that is, they realize that in team effort individual successes and failures are absorbed unless they are spectacular and easily attributable to one person. It follows that managerial persons are rarely in total control of their achievement levels. It is not uncommon for an employment interviewer to hear such responses as, "My boss was extremely pleased with my work on the project, but the project was a total failure."

Understanding Success and Failure

An applicant's past successes or failures can be understood only by analyzing the system in which the successes or failures occurred as well as the scope of the job or jobs held. In many cases, the success or failure is selective; that is, confined to certain functions that *in that particular situation* were important enough to overweigh insufficiency in other functions. Obviously, such selectivity reduces the significance of success or failure. Some common examples of selective success: the manager who has the worst production or profile record in the company but who is an exceptionally fine trainer and developer of people; the secretary who is so bad at typing that she could not rely on it to hold a job but whose ability to deal with nuisance callers makes her valuable to her boss; the middle manager who never made an original suggestion or recommendation in his entire career but who can criticize the recommendations and suggestions of others so intelligently and to such good effect that he can be counted a success. Akin to selective success is the distinction that workers who have little control over their machines, work processes, or any of the tangibles likely to affect their production sometimes achieve success in ways unrelated to their specific job function. Such workers make themselves helpful to others, are punctual, and in general try to be liked and respected. Asked whether he considered himself a success or failure, an hourly rated worker replied, "I have always finished my work early and asked others if I could help."

In evaluating performance on the managerial level, the interviewer may be hampered by the fact that decisions do not always produce immediate results. Often the outcome of a decision may not be known for months or years; with major decisions an immediate outcome is the exception. Therefore the interviewer must concentrate on the manner in which the applicant went about making the decision, the methods he used to arrive at a conclusion, the extent and depth of the consultation, and the way in which he related and defended the decision to his superiors and answered questions regarding it. In the absence of a definitive result, a decision can only be evaluated on the basis of the style and the manner in which it was made.

Occasionally an employee is fired because he is too successful, or too efficient. In other words, he constantly makes waves. Such an employee may challenge supervision and unsettle the workforce. In the final analysis he may be said to be overqualified for the position. An example is the highly progressive manager who has achieved a remarkable record of success by rejecting statistical analyses and taking calculated risks, trusting to his gut responses. Probably this man has been applying his abilities to the wrong type of job and should be in a line of work in which his rapid-fire responses and instinctive approach are more appreciated and needed.

Aptitudes and Job Needs

The employment interviewer should not be interested in slapping a success or failure label on the applicant, but rather in evaluating his aptitudes and job needs. And yet employment interviewers are prone to seek out tangible indicators of previous success or failure, even when irrelevant. Certainly a typical employment interviewer would be loath to recommend for hire anyone who was fired from his last three jobs. Nevertheless, it is conceivable that the applicant is not a total failure. The relative significance and long-term career impact of these failures can be judged only in terms of the type of jobs the applicant held, his career goals, the type of company to which he is applying, his level of aspiration in relation to his abilities, and his ability to make the proper selection of an employer. It is the responsibility of the employment interviewer to be aware of the applicant's background and experience and of the circumstances that lead that applicant to express by actions or words his feelings of success or failure in order to form the most accurate picture possible of how the employee would function on the job. To accomplish such an analysis successfully, the employment interviewer must understand the dynamics of success and failure. The need for this understanding is increasing as corporations grow larger and the management and production processes become more complex.

Insulation of Corporate Life

If the employment interviewer is aware of no other influence on success or failure, he should appreciate the insulation that marks corporate life on any job level whether clerical, hourly rated, or managerial. The employee is insulated against risks and against clear-cut, obvious indications of success or failure. In the typical modern corporation, with its production technology and narrow profit margins, too much is at stake to rely on individual judgment. The old-style, single-minded, arbitrary, and unilateral decision making is giving way to conferences, discussions, committee activity, and buck sharing. With production and clerical jobs the individual role is being progressively curtailed by specialization, expedited by technology. In many jobs, the employee's responsibilities are limited to one small link in a chain of operations.

Typically, workers fail not so much because they are incapable of performing a specific job in a prescribed manner but rather for deficiencies in areas that are secondary or auxiliary to the specific job task. Many failures that result in involuntary terminations can be traced to inadequate or improper training methods, poor placement procedures, inadequate screening methods, unsatisfactory appraisal or feedback, or poor unit orientation—failure to explain to the worker that his work unit (small work section within a larger division) has a group responsibility (including its own production goals) that he must live up to. With some failures, part of the blame lies with a management group that is not fully sensitive to the needs of its employees. This is not to say that clear-cut instances of an employee's unwillingness to perform work satisfactorily are unheard of. Even then, however, there probably are other reasons for the failure besides the apparent unwillingness of the person to perform a specific job function. The fact of the matter is, the applicant may not have a deep enough understanding of the organizational structure and the interface with top management to be able to explain his own success or failure.

Job Hoppers

One type of applicant who merits more careful consideration than he usually receives is the so-called job hopper, the person who goes from job to job and seems never to build service time in any one company. At one time personnel managers regarded the job hopper as a bad risk. He was considered basically unstable, incapable of being satisfied, and emotionally immature, a potential rotten apple demoralizing to his co-workers. The assumption was that the job hopper does not take his work seriously because he has no stake in a job at which he does not intend to remain for long. This negative view has undergone a significant change in the past decade. To some extent this change has been forced on employers by economic and social developments. Business is growing in complexity, creating a need for trained and experienced people that has outstripped the supply and may continue to do so for years to come. Consequently it is now recognized that in some occupations and in some industries, the "child of the corporation" is less able to contribute to the profitability and success of the organization than the person with a more varied employment history. For example, managers with a background of experience with a number of major employers are quick to point out that, having enriched their job skills, broadened their abilities, and been exposed to a variety of management techniques and procedures, they are more valuable to a prospective employer than a counterpart who has spent the greater part of his career with one employer and is familiar only with the ways of that employer.

For their part workers worry less about job security than they once did. We have become a highly mobile people partly because of easier transportation, partly because of new patterns of industrial location, and partly because sectional barriers have weakened. There is a common bond between American workers that enables newcomers to a community to feel at home in a very short time.

The question of loyalty has diminished somewhat in importance in recent years because of the rise of professional managers, whose primary loyalty is to their profession or their technology rather than to the employer. This represents a shift in allegiance, but in the final analysis it may be that motivation has not suffered (in fact it may have improved because of the positive relationship between professionalism and self-actualization) and that the employer may be well satisfied. The new professionalism, however, raises some serious questions regarding the future of employee–employer relations especially in the clerical and management areas, where professionalism continues to grow under the impetus of technological developments. A manager, for example, may be chafed by the insulation that grows proportionately with service in one company and after two, three, or five years leaves a well-paying and seemingly challenging position to start anew in another organizational environment.

Yet the contribution of which he is capable makes the risk of hiring him worthwhile. No decision is possible until the employment interviewer can "explain" the applicant—understand his aspirations, motivations, and drives. A job hopper, for example, may be unable to conceive of himself as successful unless he continually seeks new frontiers to conquer. Experiments have demonstrated that the correlation of discernible, tangible, or objective evidence of achievement with the individual's own feelings of success or failure is not always possible.

Job Experiences That Affect Success

In understanding success or failure, the employment interviewer must be aware of the possibility that the individual will react differently to success or failure following a series of successes than he did previously. The employment interviewer must realize that each experience of success creates an appetite for another of slightly greater magnitude. Whenever a success is equal or inferior in magnitude to its predecessor (in a comparable endeavor), it is seen as a borderline failure; a true failure is seen as a near-catastrophe. For example, a production worker or a clerical person who produces 100 units a day feels successful at his task. He is recognized for his achievement, and the feeling of achievement and success are thus reinforced. On the second day, the worker may produce 150 units and again there is a feeling of achievement. On successive days the production of the individual may increase to a maximum of 500 units a day. Then he drops back to 300 units a day and undergoes feelings of disappointment and failure even though the 300 units are three times the number of units produced on the first day when the individual felt successful.

The same psychology is illustrated on the management level. A manager may recommend to his superior a certain change in method or procedure. The recommendation may be accepted easily and the manager feels successful. The next recommendation may be broader in scope and require more discussion, but subsequently it is approved. Again, the manager feels successful; he has achieved what he set out to do. As the manager's recommendations begin to embrace a broader scope of operations, there is more discussion prior to acceptance, with perhaps other persons called in. The possibility of failure (in this case, nonacceptance of the recommendation) increases. Let us suppose that the initial recommendation, limited in scope, is point A and that point D is a recommendation that is extremely broad in scope, is complex, and has considerable impact on end results. The remaining levels between these extremes, B and C, are points representing recommendations that gradually increase in their impact on the organization. A manager whose recommendations are accepted at points A, B, and C but are rejected at point D may have feelings of failure. There is clear-cut indication that an individual's evaluation of his success or failure is very closely linked to what he expects of himself. Therefore the interviewer should never accept the applicant's self-evaluation without careful consideration of that applicant's own standards and expectations.

Not uncommon is the manager who with a long history of non-failure broken by only the most modest successes scores an achievement that seems to dwarf all his near-misses. With this tucked under his arm he proceeds to leave the company and even change fields. He may have wanted to make a break for a long time, but felt he could not do so under the auspices of failure. Or he may have wanted to quit while he was ahead. Attitudes of this sort do not always result in abandonment of a chosen field or even resignation from a company. Instead they manifest themselves in the way in which a person approaches his job. An applicant coming to an organization after a series of job successes is more likely to respond differently to the organizational milieu than one coming to the organization after what he considers to be a series of failures. The person who considers that he has been successful has established for himself different (higher) aspiration levels than the person who considers that he has been failing. The successful person has learned to repeat those responses that lead to success. Therefore, he acts differently and approaches his superiors and subordinates in a different manner than the person who has experienced failure or only marginal success.

Motivation

How strongly the applicant is motivated toward success is a matter of importance and is not easily measured. The willingness to take chances may be a function of self-esteem or confidence based on past experiences of success; or his feelings of confidence and this willingness to take chances may be a consequence of his need for success and therefore of his motivations. On the other hand, a person who seeks not failing more than success may be hard working and loyal yet reluctant to contribute beyond the point at which he feels thoroughly secure or in general to act in a manner that may jeopardize his nonfailing (again, it is stressed, a situation different from failing or succeeding).

As the need for success increases, achievement levels increase; therefore, the person whose need for success is great is not the one who is making a concerted effort to avoid failure. The challenges he may or may not accept on his job—the opening of a new sales territory, organization and management of a new department, development of programs never before attempted, operation of a new machine for the first time, recommendation of a course believed to be right but known to be unpopular—all indicate the degree of need for achievement, a need that can affect an individual's conduct of his duties, determining his flexibility and adaptability and to a certain extent—and this may with continued research prove to be critical—the kind of company and the style of management that best suit him. The employment interviewer who does not fully understand the concepts involved in achievement needs cannot make the critical comparative analysis of the company's philosophy, mode of operation or expectations, and the needs of applicants, and employment interviewers who ask them about the future of their industry or occupation often receive a complete analytical treatment of the subject.

Self-concept and Achievement Potential

Employees with a high need (n) [1] for achievement are generally optimistic about their abilities. They are self-reliant (sometimes to the point of jauntiness) and willing to face challenges. At the same time they are realistic about the possibilities of success or failure. They tend to be somewhat impatient with low n achievers. It is not unusual to find high n achievers and low n achievers on the same salary level with comparable titles and rank in an organization. They may even be assigned to the same committee, with the high n achiever taking the leadership role. When high n achievers are required to work together, intensive competition may result, occasionally leading to friction.

To many high n achievers, money is the ultimate symbol of success. It is not unusual to hear one comment that the title is relatively unimportant, that it is financial reward that he is concerned about. The employment interviewer should recognize some of these characteristics and be prepared to reject a high n achiever if he realizes that his own company stresses low n achievement. The interviewer should ask himself the following questions. Is the company typically more generous in rewarding its employees by titles than by money? Is it low on internal status symbols? Is it highly conservative, conducting business strictly by the book? If any one of these questions can be answered affirmatively, the company is simply not the right fit for the applicant. There are many such companies today, and employment interviewers who place advertisements that in effect call for high n achievers may not be facing the reality of conditions within their own organizations. Too often managers, personnel administrators, and employment interviewers talk about the ideal applicant in such

[1] D. C. McClelland, *The Achieving Society*. Princeton, N.J.: D. Van Nostrand Company, Inc., 1961.

terms as "dynamic," "forward-looking," "goal-oriented," "creative," and "restless" when, for their particular company, the "successful" employee could be described in exactly the opposite terms.

The individual's concept of his success or failure at his previous job, and the manner in which he will approach his next job, is a function of both his experience and his expectations, but the expectations become perhaps the most critical aspect. The employment interviewer who in describing to the applicant the opportunities available in the company uses such phrases as "only your own inabilities will prevent you from rising" or "the sky's the limit" or conveys the impression that the company is sensitive to successful, aggressive people must remember that he is shaping the applicant's attitude toward the company and his future relationship to it. To the applicant who enters employment believing that he has a chance to be president of the company one day or a manager in the near future, these possibilities, however remote in reality, become idealized goals. From the time he begins employment he will be working toward the long-range goal of being company president and the shorter-range goal of being manager. With each success these goals will seem closer to fulfillment, thus more possible and more realistic. On the other hand, each failure seems to push the goal farther into the indefinite future.

The employment interviewer is wise to ask the applicant to describe whether a previous job was easy or difficult. The response will be important not so much because it objectively reflects actual work conditions, but because it provides insight regarding the attitudes of the applicant, his idea of his own ability and achievement needs, and opportunities and challenges that may or may not have been present on previous jobs. It is not uncommon in reviewing employment histories of self-evaluated nonachievers (clerical or managerial) to note a series of what might be termed junctions of achievement. In fact the employee has not failed, but his achievement level has not been satisfied; his aspirations have been satisfied quantitatively but not qualitatively. Simple, routine, easily accomplished tasks will not absorb the high n achiever's drive. On the other hand we find employment histories in which a series of failures are evidenced, but these may not be regarded as failures by the applicant. Here we come to a semantic fork in the road when an applicant views what the interviewer considers a failure as something other than failure; for example, as nonachievement. This is likely to happen particularly in occupations that are widely recognized as being extremely difficult, especially those in which circumstances beyond the control of the employee affect the outcome of work assignments.

The Applicant's Aspirations and Expectations

The employment interviewer must be sensitive to the fact that every applicant, regardless of whether he is applying for a clerical, technical, or managerial position, will make two separate, highly distinct anticipatory responses to a job situation. One concerns itself with what the applicant wants or is willing to *do*, the basis of aspiration; the second refers to what he hopes to *get* for doing it, the basis of expectation.

When an applicant declares that he is seeking a better opportunity the interviewer is furnished with a useful point of departure from which to explore the applicant. The opportunity sought may reveal the level of aspiration, which in turn influences the kind of work an employee wishes to do, the kinds of challenges and risks he will undertake, and his goals. It is important to remember, however, that the opportunity referred to may not be to achieve but rather merely not to fail; in other words, the employee is guided more by expectations—increases in salary, feelings of satisfaction, security, or some type of personal gain or reward. It is not uncommon to find cases in which the expectancy level of the applicant is high—he wants to get a lot from his work, the company, and even the industry—but the aspiration level is low—he is not prepared to do enough. This is most common with those applicants for whose services the demand is high but the supply is low (specialists, for example) or with those who are changing occupational fields. In general, the employee who has had a record of success on the job will be guided by aspirations, whereas for the employee with a record of failure the balance for or against the job vacancy will be tipped by expectations.

Effects of Anxiety on Motivation and Performance

Investigations into the relationship between expectations and longevity on the job have borne out the axiom of personnel people that, roughly stated, advises the employer to take the surprises out of the job before the employee is hired. In other words, the more the applicant knows about working conditions and advancement and salary potential the better equipped he is to make sound judgments.

Taking the surprise out of the job also reduces anxiety. Anxiety affects motivation and in extreme cases can produce physical or emotional breakdown. Anxiety is an emotional reaction to the possibility of an unpleasant or painful experience. It differs from frustration primarily in respect to the time element; frustration is associated with past and present circumstances; anxiety is anticipatory. Employment interviewers must not overlook expressions of anxiety by the applicant.

In a study of the employment histories of business executives an experimental psychologist was able to isolate some traits shared by successful managers.[2] He found, significantly, that these traits did not occur in those who on the basis of tests, biographical data, and performance histories could be judged as failing. The researcher was concerned primarily with categorizing the personality characteristics of successful persons. Objectively evidenced success outweighed self-esteem and self-concept as a criterion for grouping. He found that successful managers were all interested in promotional advancement and they felt able to accept and live with strong leaders to whom they might report. They all seemed to be realistic regarding achievement levels and aspirations.

The study also indicated that these successful individuals drew strength from organizational policies, rules, and regulations and felt uncertainty and even foreboding that they might not measure up to the demands of the organization. Therefore the employment interviewer should not interpret the applicant's feelings (regardless of how obvious) of anxiety as unmistakable indications of weakness, of a tendency to fold under pressure like a house of cards. Quite to the contrary; the individual may be chased by his anxieties to run as energetically as he can in the pursuit of success. Every hour and every day of hard work, every opportunity to throw himself into the fight, every indication of success helps him win the race against anxiety.

The signs of anxiety that an applicant reveals can provide the interviewer with important insights. The level of anxiety, for example, may be responsible for whether a person considers himself the key determinant of his success or failure or merely an instrument of forces beyond his control. It would appear that a typical work situation provides little means by which to deal with anxieties. Those who suffer from anxieties can often mitigate them by various defense mechanisms, but in some cases this only makes the consequences worse for the organization. Anxiety may have a stronger influence on an employee

---

[2] W. E. Henry, "The Business Executive: The Psycho-Dynamics of a Social Role," *American Journal of Sociology*, 1949, 54, pp. 286–291.

than desire for achievement. To defend himself against anxiety, an employee may be willing to reduce his aspiration levels and, even more critically, his job satisfaction, choosing nonachievement and nonfailure.

Typically he attempts to minimize decision-making responsibilities and pass problems upward rather than acting on them. For this reason he may prefer situations in which the work is routinized, even mechanical in nature, with little or no possibility of deviation from prescribed goals. Thus, when errors occur, the cause seems to lie in external circumstances beyond the control of the system or the individual operating within it. This kind of anxiety syndrome may be rooted in personal relationships, which the employee is seeking to minimize in his work. Into this class may fall the employee who tries to specialize his work, even attempting to orient a nontechnical job toward technological specialization. Symptomatic is the tendency of an applicant to refer to departments, functions, or broad divisions of the company in an impersonal way without mentioning people or to work units rather than to the persons responsible for or working in these units.

Employees with anxieties also tend to favor situations that offer on-the-job insulation; that is, where (at the price of increased operating costs) a system of built-in fail-safe procedures not only minimizes the possibility of mistakes by employees but also vastly reduces individual responsibility for, and vulnerability to, the consequences of error, failure to meet quotas, or miscalculation of any kind. Managers who in an effort to build some type of defense mechanism against anxiety in the work milieu organize their work into fragmented work units, thereby reducing the impact of each worker on the end result, may themselves be anxiety-ridden.

The employment interviewer should pay close attention to the applicant's questions about work situations and work style for evidences of anxieties. In addition, the interviewer can pose a series of well-thought-out hypothetical situations built around the type of work the applicant enjoys and his favored style of working. From the answers much can be learned about the employee's past failures and successes.

Aspiration Levels

Whether an employee succeeds or fails depends on his aspiration levels. Usually, these are the outcome of years of development and by maturity are an integral part of the personality. It is not uncommon for applicants to evidence high degrees of anxiety when they are told that a given project, assignment, or position is easily observed and that this will, in fact, be a significant factor in judging total job performance. Persons who express anxiety about such situations may be thought of as failure avoiders. Those who feel a strong need for success and achievement show little anxiety in a comparable situation.

In anticipating performance levels after employment and in attempting to predict success or failure, the interviewer has certain guidelines. We might expect the job performance of high-anxiety workers to be better than the performance of those with low anxiety or of the failure avoiders provided that the anxiety can be controlled to the extent that the individual does not feel personally threatened.

Anxiety will probably be a stimulus to the high-anxiety, high-achievement-oriented individual assigned to a job whose difficulty is well known and clearly overshadows the capabilities of any individual. The same may be true of jobs in which contingencies beyond normal control affect results. Conversely, feelings of being threatened seem to act as a stimulus to the low-anxiety worker. A high-anxiety employee who has once experienced failure might be expected to show a diminished work performance record. On the other hand, a low-anxiety person after having once failed might be expected to improve in performance in a threatening work environment. Anxiety has been characterized as emotions leading to uncertainty and a feeling of helplessness in response to apprehensions triggered by occurrences that threaten a valued and jealously guarded concept the individual feels is centrally important to him as an individual. It is not unusual and in fact is to be expected that, in the typical organizational structure, feelings of anxiety exist. In modern business settings, the absence of anxiety would be an indication of organizational abnormality.

It is impossible to understand feelings of anxiety as related to success or failure without considering the matter of frustration. Frustration is more likely to be externally caused than anxiety. It is largely a consequence of a situation or a series of events. The defenses against frustration are often devious. An applicant staunchly supports the former employer who fired him and makes excuses for his former boss, even to the extent of upholding company rules and regulations that helped retard his advancement. An applicant insists that the performance appraisal system used by his former employer was completely fair and honest although it evaluated him as borderline or failing. These defenses reveal much more than the applicant is aware.

Reaction Formation

The employment interviewer who is warmed by the apparent magnanimity of the applicant and interprets his attitude as a sign of maturity and generosity should take a closer look. In reality the applicant may be emotionally unable to accept the implications of what he has endured and, repressing these, goes to the opposite extreme in what Freud has called reaction formation. Instead of magnanimity, maturity, sympathy, and empathy, the applicant may be exhibiting an emotional reaction to frustration and disappointment. The former sales manager who tells the employment interviewer how, when his proposals for an entirely new sales approach and a new product line were rejected by top management, he returned to selling in order to get a better feel for his work hopes to impress the interviewer as a thorough, dedicated, results-oriented man of action—the type who channels injured feelings into constructive effort. But the fact of the matter may be that what the employment interviewer is seeing is regression. Frustrated and disappointed, the sales manager reverts to a lower level of achievement seeking. If this persists into the new job, the applicant may fail. The foregoing example illustrates the window dressing with which an applicant may disguise frustrations from himself and others. In some cases, the truth is often difficult to uncover.

Signs of Immaturity

In attempting to evaluate previous successes and failures and to anticipate the success or failure of an applicant, the employment interviewer must consider the depth of maturity, reactions to success and failure, and strivings. An inexperienced employment interviewer who confuses eagerness with effectiveness may get the impression that an applicant is a hot shot or an eager beaver. The fact is, eagerness may be a red flag signifying gross immaturity. Patience, and the accumulation, weighing, and evaluation of facts, may be far more desirable in an employee than the eager-beaver or action-now qualities.

Immaturity is a personality handicap that is often far from obvious. Immaturity may be associated with deep-seated conflicts that come to the surface under stress. For example, an employee relates, "My boss put me on the safety committee even though I didn't know anything about safety. He insisted that my managerial abilities would carry me through, and wouldn't hear of my resigning from the committee to do the work for which I was hired. I could see that there was a good deal wrong with the safety committee and our approach to it and I tried to point this out. Although the boss admitted that I was a good administrator, he criticized me for being a troublemaker. Finally, after a heated discussion with him, I quit."

The applicant presents a convincing picture of a confused situation in which there was the proverbial breakdown in communication leading to immature acts. About these he is candid because he can also point to his superior's (in this case, his boss) reverting to the same type of immature behavior. Thus he gains insulation. His comments about the fiasco are close enough to the facts to confuse the issue. Actually the applicant, unable to get relief from his duties on the safety committee, blocked the entire effort with his negative attitude. Similarly evidences of conflict and immaturity can be found in a statement like this: "No one really cared what I did; I was never encouraged or told things were going right, so I figured if they didn't care, I didn't care either." The employee withdrew from interface with the work milieu. Under the stress of conflict between achievement strivings and apathy, he became so personally and emotionally detached from the job and the incentives that went along with it and from the company that he sought other employment. If this behavior becomes a pattern the likelihood of his seeing a task through to completion regardless of obstacles may be questioned.

Origin of Conflict

Let us now look at some of the factors that may create conflict situations for a worker, factors of which he may be ignorant. The theory of cognitive dissonance has already been discussed. An employee has liked people all his life and has gotten along with them extremely well, being able to influence or persuade them because of his congenial personality. Yet he has been unsuccessful as a salesman. The applicant may give various reasons for his lack of success, none of which may point to a skills deficiency. By virtue of impressions gained from personal contact with the applicant and perhaps fortified by test results, the employment interviewer concurs that the applicant is, in fact, a natural "sales type." As a result the interviewer may be in something of a quandary about the applicant. (It is not unusual to encounter an applicant who scores well on a battery of tests, is alert, lucid, and communicative and yet has a work history of one failure after another.) A dissonance occurs because with his congenial personality, intelligence, liking for people, and ability to persuade or influence them, it should follow that the applicant is a success in sales.

Festinger, who originated the concept of cognitive dissonance, indicates that it can be a factor in motivation since the individual seeks to eliminate the dissonant nature of the relationships he observes.[3] For example, a person may continue to show respect, loyalty, and even admiration for a leader who repeatedly gives proof of his inability to lead. An applicant may boast to the employment interviewer that despite the many failures of his boss he continued to believe in the boss's ability.

The motivational aspect arises when the dissonance is so great that it must be resolved. When an attempt is made to resolve the dissonance, there may be confusion, conflict, and frustration, with the result that the applicant is unable to differentiate between previous success or failure. A well-educated worker, perhaps with a graduate degree, is placed in a job in which his work associates are noncollege people. He feels a strain on his status consciousness and becomes aggressive, perhaps resentful, and, unable to find a work environment more compatible with his status needs, may begin to question his success. The high school graduate working with college men in comparable job assignments, the bachelor-degree holder working with Ph.D.s, or the nonengineer working with engineers may feel inhibited and frustrated and gradually alienate himself psychologically from the job. In each instance the employee seeks to correct the situation as he sees it in the only way available to him.

Conflict, Anxiety, and Job Performance

Conflict, frustration, and anxiety in the applicant will not necessarily inhibit or aid future job performance. The employment interviewer cannot always rely exclusively on manifestations of psychological problems as a guide in his efforts to evaluate past successes and failures and to project prior experiences of success and failure to the job which the applicant is seeking. Certain basic principles will continue to be indispensable; for example, the concept that the higher the motivation and the stronger the need for job satisfaction, the more productive the employee will be. Regardless of an applicant's anxiety levels, achievement strivings, expectations, frustrations, and attempts at avoiding failure, there is no incentive known to man that can re-

[3] L. Festinger, "The Motivating Effect of Cognitive Dissonance," in *Assessment of Human Motives*, G. Lindzey, ed. (New York: Holt, Rinehart and Winston, Inc., 1958).

sult in higher productivity where there is a lack of ability, training, and experience.

The most immediate goal of an applicant, employed or unemployed, is a change from his present situation. There are basically two types of changes that an employee can make: *intra*organizational and *inter*organizational. The first usually involves a change in duties. The second may or may not involve such a change; if it does, it is in effect a compounded change. In either case, the employee must make an adjustment, and the capacity to adjust to a new job—that is, to reach satisfactory achievement levels in an acceptable period—varies widely between persons.

The upwardly mobile employee, who has changed jobs at perhaps two- to three-year intervals, always with additional salary and responsibilities, is psychologically (emotionally), physically, intellectually, and occupationally prepared for change. While there may be exceptions to any generalization, the employment interviewer is advised to accept this one as a virtual rule, at least at the outset. On the other hand, an employee whose record shows continual changes but limited upward mobility, or whose mobility is downward with acceptance or even active solicitation of changes and assignments that keep him relatively static in earnings and responsibility, presents quite a different picture.

Not only is attitude toward change an important clue to the motivations of the applicant but it may also be significant in the light of the opportunities offered by the interviewer's company.

Effects of Prior Discipline

If an applicant was ever discharged or otherwise disciplined, the incident deserves the closest scrutiny. Interestingly enough, employees are just as likely to be fired because of their reaction to the punishment for their misdeeds as for the misdeeds themselves. An employee whose daily production quota or quality of work is failing may not consider his lack of achievement as deviant or punishable behavior; an employee, tardy because of what he considers an act of God, is not likely to view his tardiness as a punishable act. It may have been that what the employee termed an act of God was part of a pattern of deviant behavior that management could no longer tolerate. The point is that a disciplinary measure does not have the same meaning for everyone. It becomes personalized, a part of the individual's cognitive existence.

In an effort to be fair to all and at the same time to comply with company policy and precedent, supervisors, foremen, and managers apply disciplinary action in a way that may be inappropriate for a particular person at a given time. An employee who is disciplined is rarely concerned with the consistency of the discipline where *others* are concerned; his single concern is the fairness of the punishment where *he* personally is concerned. This is because every person is ego-involved in the work situation to a different degree and has different needs, motivations, and achievement strivings from every other person.

For example, an applicant explains that he quit his former employer after he was chewed out for making an error. Under questioning the applicant acknowledges that he made the error and the supervisor would have been justified if he had "called it to my attention." Note the difference between "chewed out" and "called it to my attention." The employer reference may state that the employee resigned, that he was unable to take constructive criticism, and that according to his immediate supervisor the employee's actions after being taken to task for a serious error were immature. This is usually enough to rule out an applicant in many employment or personnel departments. The reasoning is that an immature employee who makes serious errors and who cannot take criticism is undesirable. This decision would be the only one possible if there were nothing more to know about the circumstances. In practice, however, there is always more to know.

The employee seeking high levels of achievement could view punishment or discipline for failing or deviant behavior (behavior inconsistent with rules, policies, general practices, or precedents) in one of two ways. He could take it as a crushing blow, a setback in his progress toward a goal, or he might view the punishment in relative terms, weighing it with his previous achievements and his aspirations. With the employee who seeks nonfailure, discipline could hopelessly shatter achievement-maintenance levels. An employee who functions at this level of aspiration is denied the opportunity to balance a failing situation with a strong comeback. But with the high achiever a comparatively minor disciplinary act could upset the delicate emotional balance, causing feelings of failure and disillusionment and ultimately resignation.

Punishment or the threat of punishment on the job can cause anxieties and neurotic behavior, when the employee is torn between the fear, humiliation, and ego-deflating character of punishment on one hand and the need either to continue the deviant behavior or to pay the price (of the effort) of controlling it.

Regression, hostility, anger, and even intense hatred may result, directed at management, the company, the job, or the circumstances of the employee's life in general, which put him in such a predicament. Psychosomatic illnesses following disciplinary action are not uncommon, and employment interviewers should be alert to this fact. A presumably failing employee disciplined for an act the supervisor felt was deviant begins to compile a record of tardiness or absence attributed to severe headaches, stomach disturbances, or dizziness. If the supervisor disbelieves the employee's pleas of illness, the employee is now in the position of having compounded the prior deviant behavior with unjustified absences. The outcome is that the employee is fired and is hampered in his efforts to find another job by a company reference that describes him as guilty of irresponsible, trouble-making, or refractory behavior.

The members of an employee's work group exert a strong influence on the effectiveness of discipline. The group forms a social structure within the work unit, and it may be expected to become especially cohesive when one of its members is disciplined in a way or for an act the group feels is too severe or unjustified. The group's concept of punishable behavior may be quite different from what management believes is punishable. When the group rallies to the support of the disciplined employee, it provides him with tangible evidence of his acceptance in it and in effect insulates him. Thus disciplinary actions by management can be weakened or negated.

When an employee is described in a reference as a "bad apple who infected the department and turned the employees there against management," there is the possibility that what caused the employee to be thus tagged was actually the behavior of the group, which reacted in his behalf. The employment interviewer who attempts to evaluate the previous successes or failures of an applicant on the basis of disciplinary action taken against the applicant by a former employer or the prior reactions of the applicant to discipline must understand the mechanisms of discipline and the behavior that may be expected in reaction to it.

Mechanisms Prompted by Anxiety

In the final analysis, success or failure, satisfaction and dissatisfaction on the job may be a matter of motivation. The subject of motivation, which is a vast and interesting topic, is discussed in another chapter. Here motivation is considered in terms of the relationship between the *sense* of success or failure and the *evidences* of success or failure. This relationship is an important factor in determining what might be called the frustration threshold. The emotional reaction that takes place when this threshold is passed varies with the individual. One way of exploring this threshold is by posing hypothetical problem situations.

A person who has been consistently thwarted and frustrated in his work or life in general may be expected to react in a highly predictable, even stereotyped, way. The highly motivated person may behave in a variable and unpredictable way. A rigid person who experienced frustration in a former job will probably respond to hypothetical problem situations in a static manner, approaching each in the same general way. In an interview and very likely on a job as well, he will not significantly alter his approach even in the face of correction, criticism, or punishment.

A person who shows strong indication of frustration at his job is likely to avoid admitting to acts or feelings of aggression even though these are for him the normal and predictable reaction. Corporations are not noted for providing the means by which to relieve or discharge aggressions. Their deficiency in this respect invites emotional problems, some of which even result in illnesses. A common reaction to frustration is psychological withdrawal from work and from the company, resulting in the isolation of emotions, drives, and, when possible, even the person of the employee. Frustration may result from too much of a good thing. For example, an operation that has been mastered, if performed continually with no prospect of escape through transfer or promotion, may eventually become a source of deep frustration and an obstacle to job success. Thus a manager who finds his work basically satisfying may become frustrated because the ladder of promotion is blocked. An employment interviewer who recognizes these circumstances as causes for the applicant's frustration should take into consideration the management philosophy and especially the promotional opportunities in the department in which the job vacancy exists as well as in the company to ascertain whether the same circumstances will again haunt the applicant. The highly ambitious applicant who enjoys overcoming challenges is the most ready to become frustrated when unable to realize his goals. There is a difference between passive frustration, or a simple blockage of goal attainment, and active frustration, in which passive frustration is combined with a feeling of being threatened.

By way of illustration, there is the familiar situation of the newly transferred or newly hired executive who becomes the boss of an employee with some 20 years of service and threatens not only to block the older man's progress but even to eliminate him from the department. In such a situation some form of aggression can be expected. The degree of the aggression will probably be in direct proportion to the severity of the frustration.

When direct retaliation against the cause of the anxiety is impossible or unsafe—as, for example, when the cause is the boss—an employee may attempt to displace his frustrations by venting his anxieties on his subordinates. A managerial applicant who describes himself as a hard-driving man, respected although not liked by his employees, but "loved" by his superiors may be exhibiting displacement of frustration. An applicant who insists that his fellow employees were against him because he knew the score and because his superconfidence and unwillingness to be duped or shoved about made him a threat may be covering up his frustrations by projecting. An employee who professes to hate gossip on the job and continually denounces those guilty of this offense is in effect gossiping about the gossipers and thus gratifying and justifying his own need to gossip. Sometimes dangerous and unwholesome characteristics are attributed to others to enable the person to avoid recognizing these same characteristics in himself. By convincing himself that his reactions are strictly defensive or no different from normal, he escapes feelings of guilt or self-condemnation. Feelings of aggression and hostility resulting from frustration can be masked from the interviewer, whose understanding of the reasons for failure on a previous job may consequently be incomplete.

The employment interviewer who detects evidence of frustration and anxiety should not assume that these necessarily work against the applicant. These pressures may be sublimated; their objects or causes may be disguised or hidden while the behavior of the applicant may be unaffected and his efficiency unimpaired. Sublimation involves substitution of an acceptable attitude for an unacceptable one, so that the drive originally associated with the unacceptable attitude is redirected into safe and constructive pursuits. One familiar personality type that exhibits the mechanism of sublimation is that of the mild-mannered employee who has rarely created a ripple in his department, but who on the job is a perfectionist, controlling every aspect that comes within his scope and demonstrating an attitude toward productivity commonly believed to have prevailed in the era before unionization, and who in his off-duty hours is the High Exalted Supreme Ethereal Potentate of his lodge, ruling with an autocratic hand. This example underscores the importance of interpreting sublimated conflicts in the context of the applicant's aspirations and performance record.

Obviously, these psychological mechanisms have endless implications. The employment interviewer is cautioned against the unlicensed practice of psychiatry. Some understanding of behavioral mechanisms is necessary to the employment interviewer in his dealings with applicants. But nothing in this discussion is intended to suggest that the employment interviewer should attempt some form of therapy through job placement. While it is true that certain forms of work are therapeutic, therapy is not the employment interviewer's function or responsibility, moral or professional.

Success or Failure Versus Satisfaction

The sense of success or failure is intrinsic to self-esteem. It is a function of what we think we *are* as opposed to what we think we *have done*. According to certain theories of motivation, man wants and needs to be challenged. The advocates of this theory postulate a hierarchy of interrelated and occasionally overlapping needs, ranging from the biological and physiological to those concerned with self-image and ego fulfillment. Therefore we might view an employee fired for incompetence as one who is not to be stoned but only to be placed on a job in which he may recover his confidence. The machine operator who is consistently absent might not be basically worthless or fundamentally dishonest; in fact he may not even be unhealthy. He may simply be venting his frustrations in the only way available to him.

Every person has his own special way of satisfying his needs. When he cannot do so, he may consider himself a failure; when he does, he may consider himself successful. In the absence of opportunities for personal and occupational fulfillment, a person's on-the-job performance may deteriorate, and he may become a statistic on a turnover chart or a nonpromotable nonentity whose name seems forever to haunt salary review committees. This by no means suggests that the applicant who was fired from a previous work situation should automatically be excused for his behavior deviations: People must be held accountable for their acts, and employees are no exception. However, the extent to which the employee is to blame, as well as the implications of the unsatisfactory performance for his employability, can be adjudged only when all the factors are considered.

Job Satisfiers

The relationship between success or failure and satisfaction varies between persons. Two persons who achieve the same level of success do not necessarily achieve the same levels of satisfaction because their needs may be different. But in evaluating the success or failure of an applicant the level of satisfaction he has attained is as important as his achievement of his objectives.

To a very great extent it is the nature of the reward that determines how an achievement is evaluated. For example, an employee who has acquitted himself creditably in an assignment may consider himself more successful if his contacts with upper management permanently increase than if he merely receives a salary raise. This is a subjective matter, and the employment interviewer's own predispositions may conflict with the applicant's values, such as in the foregoing example the belief that broadened contacts with superiors are more important than money. An interviewer who reviewed an applicant's résumé and commented on how well he had done over the past few years was shaken by the offhand reply, "Not very well at all." The interviewer may have been led to believe that the applicant was unduly modest, when in fact he was merely being honest. By *his own* criteria, the employee was not a success. Despite an objectively good performance, he was frustrated because the goals he had set for himself had not been achieved.

Job Challenge Versus Success or Failure

The interviewer should not make the mistake of attempting to reduce the challenge of the job. This approach almost always backfires. The temptation is strongest with applicants who have had failures. The interviewer who tells such an applicant that he will have no trouble succeeding in the proffered job is almost certain to lose him. The well-meaning invitation to succeed could easily antagonize the applicant, who might not only reject the job but also tell off the interviewer, leaving him to wonder what in the world applicants do want.

Another point to remember about success and failure is that where the possibility of failure is slight or nonexistent the sense of success is also slight or nonexistent, and the statement is of course equally valid if success is substituted for failure and failure for success. If every coin put into a gaming machine were a winner, very few people would find the game even remotely intriguing, and the same applies, of course, if every coin were a loser. The exuberant production line foreman who sets an impossible goal for his crew and then is shocked because the crew not only fails to reach the goal but to a man refuses to acknowledge failure does not understand this essential truth about success and failure.

The employment interviewer who asks an applicant what he hopes to accomplish, either in the near future or over the long range, is really inquiring into the relationship between the applicant's level of performance and his aspiration level. If the interviewer wished to indicate this relationship diagrammatically, he could draw two lines one above the other on a blank sheet of paper, labeling one line P for performance and the other A for aspiration. If it becomes obvious that the individual's aspiration level is below his performance level, the upper line is the A and the lower line the P. In this case, the applicant feels successful. If, on the other hand, aspiration level is above performance level the labeling is reversed. Here the applicant probably has feelings of failure or, at best, frustration. It might be useful to construct a series of these P-A lines representing various phases of the applicant's life history and career strivings. One possibility to explore is the use of the distance between the two lines to represent the extent of the gap.

Private Life

The social context of a person's private life can shed light on his motives and aspirations. It is natural to be influenced by the achievement level of the group with which we identify. The applicant whose personal associates are high achievers, whose personal references are from people with status in the community, the applicant who is in general in fast company will probably make every effort to keep up with his associates and to reflect their achievement levels in his own. To some extent, this identification is a reflection of a person's self-concept or self-esteem; in other words, how he feels about himself. Of course personal achievements outweigh social and professional relationships in reckoning self-esteem.

An applicant's feelings of success or failure (as well as indications of probable success or failure in the job applied for) are a function, in part, of his needs, values, self-esteem, aspiration levels, expectation levels, job skills and aptitudes, past disappointments and achievements, and social environment and, in part, of the working environment of the job and the management policies and practices that govern it.

Tangible evidence of success or failure, beyond what the applicant is aware of, may be as elusive as any fact that the employment interviewer may try to isolate. This elusiveness, in large part, is the result of the fragmentation of work, the insulation against feelings of failure made possible by management by consensus, and the almost fail-safe character of some management styles.

6

Motivation: Implications for Screening and Placement

THE EMPLOYMENT INTERVIEWER sat across the desk from the executive and, while thumbing through voluminous notes and preemployment documents, said of the applicant, "No question about it; he's motivated." There was a sense of pride in the interviewer's voice and in the manner in which he made this proclamation, suggesting that he had managed to uncover something important and could now "explain" the applicant. However, the executive did not respond to the employment interviewer's note of pride and simply asked, "Motivated to do what? Jump off a bridge!" The employment interviewer countered, "No, motivated to accomplish something." "But," said the executive persevering, "jumping off a bridge *is* accomplishing something."

Motivation is a highly complex matter. But through an understanding of what motivation is—its mechanics and function in the employee-work relationship—the employment interviewer will be better equipped to deal with certain matters of critical importance relating to the applicant's work history. As a result, the interviewer will be in a better position to evaluate the feasibility of employment in terms of the work environment and management philosophy of the company to which the individual is applying, and to some extent in terms of the applicant's job needs and career goals as well.

Motivation and Turnover

The reasons the applicant left his former employer are of great importance. There will always be reasons beyond the control of the applicant; for example, changes in personal life, layoff, spouse transferred, transportation difficulties, and other comparable circumstances, which probably signify nothing particularly important except that the interviewer should ask certain questions regarding the possibility of the recurrence of involuntary transfer. Typical questions would concern job situation of spouse, plans with regard to children, and transportation. With women applicants, availability of babysitters and conflicts between school and work hours are relevant considerations. These purely circumstantial factors are comparatively easy to evaluate. But resignations or involuntary terminations usually result from intangible pressures, and the understanding of these presents a critical area of concern to the personnel manager.

There are no statistics on resignations or involuntary terminations. Such statistics, though they might be accurate (as far as they go), would be misleading because personnel departments typically have not broken down causative factors sufficiently and in fact do not always maintain statistical records detailed enough to make this possible. Generally, employment departments and personnel files will list such motives as job dissatisfaction, desire for more money, inability to do the work, and other such shotgun, broad-gauged categories of little use in personnel research. There are basic disparities between what personnel people think they know about employment attitudes regarding work and turnover and the typical categories into which personnel departments dump statistics regarding the movement of employees into and out of a company. Regrettably, far too little has been done in the way of research to uncover basic truths about people and the work process.

While the degree of satisfaction may be difficult to measure and is perhaps exaggerated, there is ample evidence to support the contention that the majority of American workers are reasonably or moderately satisfied with their work. And yet people continue to express unhappiness (or, more accurately, to reflect levels and degrees of satisfaction and dissatisfaction) and to resign positions and to be terminated involuntarily. Thus we are inexorably drawn to the conclusion that it is not so much the broad fact of work satisfaction that is important but rather the quality of the work satisfaction and the ability of the factors that conduce to it to mediate long-range goals. If, through deeper understanding and more enlightened methods of analysis, employment interviewers can affect job placements that do not perpetuate old dissatisfactions and frustrations or breed new ones (not in a counseling sense but in a highly professional, personnel-placement approach), they will have made a Herculean contribution that will fortify their own professionalism and strengthen their value to the business community. But in order to do this, they must be aware of the mechanisms of motivation, job satisfaction, and dissatisfaction and of the relationship between human needs, present-day organizational structures, and modern work styles and obligations on one hand and the resulting behavior on the other. The employment interviewer must determine in what circumstances and conditions the applicant would be motivated to leave. This requires not only tact and insight but also, in certain circumstances, innovation, imagination, and even courage.

In a study of some 600 women employed by the Michigan Bell Telephone Company during a three-year period, the researcher attempted to predict the probability of turnover by the use of biographical information and preemployment test scores.[1] The initial finding was that there seemed to be little predictability in either of these approaches. What seemed to determine whether employees stayed or left the company was the amount of ego-involvement and sense of commitment to the job and subsequently to the company. It was found, interestingly enough, that those employees who left the company were no more critical of company policies, procedures, or methods than those who remained, and their comments regarding salary were not terribly significant. They differed, however, in the amount, degree, or intensity of their personal involvement with the work, their need to feel that their work was important, that they could make decisions, that they were needed as people, and that they were contributing to their own best interests and those of the company. The circumstances responsible for the lack of fulfillment may be extremely difficult to demonstrate. Objectively the employee may have had a highly responsible job with considerable decision-making power. But as long as the applicant *feels* a lack of fulfillment or satisfaction, then for him there is none. Therefore an applicant who admits he disliked a particular type of work on a previous job yet for all intents and purposes seems to be applying for exactly the same type of work is

[1] F. R. Wickert, "Turnover and Employees' Feelings of Ego Involvement in the Day-to-Day Operation of a Company," *Personnel Psychology*, 1951, 4, pp. 185–197.

not necessarily being contradictory. He may have nothing against the work itself, but may have found that certain features of the work environment, the management philosophy, and the general circumstances of the work milieu deprived him of ego-fulfillment.

Thus we see that job satisfaction and the consequent desire to remain with a company are more a matter of personal needs than of the external circumstances of employment; that is those circumstances outside the worker himself, such as salary, working conditions, fringe benefits, policies, rules, and work specifications. To learn whether there is, in fact, a relationship between certain psychological needs in a typical work situation and turnover, was shown in a study that attempted to measure the effects of affiliation, achievement, autonomy, recognition, and fair evaluation.[2] The researchers found that, when personal needs in these five areas were not satisfied and when the job seemed to the employee to be interfering with or inhibiting his off-the-job activities, there was a great likelihood of turnover.

Motivational Theory

At this point it will be useful to consider some fundamental theories of motivation. According to the needs-hierarchy concept, the more basic or animal a need, the higher the priority accorded it; that is, human needs are arranged in hierarchies of prepotency. The appearance of one need usually rests on the prior satisfaction of another and more prepotent need. Thus, man is a perpetually wanting animal. An attempt to apply the needs-hierarchy concept to practical and tangible considerations has distinguished five basic needs: physiological, safety, social, ego, and self-fulfillment. The physiological needs of food, rest, activity, and protection must in general be satisfied before the next highest order of need, which is safety. (Once satisfied, a need rarely remains a motivational factor.)

After the physiological and safety needs have been satisfied, attention may be given to the social needs, which have been defined as needs for belonging or association, for acceptance by fellows, for giving and receiving friendship and love. (The act of isolating employees, controlling and restricting their activity and social interaction, thwarts this need.) When the social needs are satisfied, the ego needs—self-

---

[2] I. Ross and A. Zandor, "Need Satisfactions and Employee Turnover," *Personnel Psychology,* 1957, 10, pp. 327–338.

confidence and self-esteem—become motivational. Status, the appreciation and respect of one's fellows, is an ego need. It is thought that
ego needs are less easily satisfied, and it must be admitted that
in modern industry the emphasis on dehumanizing working methods
makes satisfaction of this class of needs increasingly difficult. In fact,
the systems, procedures, methods, practices, philosophy, and commit-
ments of the modern industrial scheme seem diabolically to be designed to make it impossible. The highest order of ego need is for
self-fulfillment. Self-fulfillment comes from the awareness of being a
creating animal, of realizing a subjective potential. In modern jargon,
the quest for self-fulfillment might be characterized as striving to do
your thing. It is rarely achieved.

A somewhat more sophisticated motivational concept was advanced
by Herzberg:

> Factors involved in producing job satisfaction (and motivation)
> are separate and distinct from the factors that lead to job dissatis-
> faction. Since separate factors need to be considered, depending
> upon whether job satisfaction or job dissatisfaction is being exam-
> ined, it follows that these two feelings are not opposite of each
> other. The opposite of job satisfaction is not job dissatisfaction but,
> rather, no job satisfaction; and, similarly, the opposite of job dis-
> satisfaction is not job satisfaction but no job dissatisfaction.[3]

He goes on to say that the satisfiers or motivating factors include
achievement, recognition for achievement, the work itself, responsibility, and growth or advancement. The dissatisfiers, or hygiene factors,
are company policy and administration, interpersonal relations, salary,
status, security, and supervision. As Herzberg points out, in a work
situation two separate sets of needs must be considered: the pain-
avoidance and the biological needs on the one hand and the personal
growth and achievement needs on the other. Thus it would follow
that we grow, develop, and achieve in work situations in terms of
job content or the scope and latitude our jobs allow.

Emotional Need for Job Security

Now let us consider an employee who resigned to seek other work
because one of her friends was fired, "for no good reason at all." On
further questioning, it turns out that the person to whom the applicant
referred is not a close friend. In fact, they have not maintained any

[3] F. Herzberg, "One More Time: How Do You Motivate Employees?" *Harvard Business Review*, January–February, 1968, pp. 53–62.

friendship ties subsequent to the time they worked together. On the strength of this the interviewer might consider the applicant headstrong and immature and reject her. But it may well be that what was really bothering the applicant was not the firing of her friend but rather insecurity and especially fear of management practices that, in the applicant's opinion, were unfair and biased. Because she felt threatened, the applicant's motivation level fell and she finally fled to seek employment elsewhere. Thus she responded to an unfulfilled basic need for safety.

One consequence of modern industrial turnover is that workers with specialized skills cannot always find a ready market for them. Sometimes the specialization is so narrow that a worker who loses his job can only regain his former salary level at a new job by retraining. Applicants in this position are often near desperation and declare themselves willing to consider any type of work. They must be handled with sensitivity and understanding. With such an applicant it may do little good to dwell on such ego-level incentives as opportunities for creativity, development of potential, and close association with high achievers. If the applicant appears only lukewarm, it is probably because he is feigning interest. This response is entirely normal in the circumstances. When a worker is unable to find employment, he becomes concerned with survival; that is, the basic physiological and safety needs are paramount, and the higher-order needs are temporarily shelved. The employment interviewer who understands this will be in a much better position to evaluate the applicant in the proper frame of reference.

Job Enrichment Versus Job Enlargement

Consider the applicant who gives as his reason for leaving his last employment lack of opportunity and advancement possibilities. The employment interviewer doubts that the applicant has been completely candid because during the course of his last employment the applicant was assigned to no less than four different jobs, and furthermore in his last job was given a semiprivate work area, a concession strongly suggestive of status and prestige. How then, the interviewer asks himself, is it possible for the applicant to maintain that he has not been given opportunities? If he is quick to form judgments, the employment interviewer may conclude that the applicant really does not know what he wants and cannot be satisfied. As a result, an exceptionally fine worker may be rejected.

The motivational problems in this example are complex, but we can explore the fundamental implications. To begin with, the employment interviewer would be well advised to investigate each of the four jobs at which the applicant served. It is quite probable that these involved little more than lateral transfers; they may have involved nothing more. What the interviewer must look for are signs of either job enrichment or job enlargement. The distinction between these two terms is significant. *Job enrichment* seeks to improve both task efficiency and human satisfaction by means of building into jobs, quite deliberately, greater scope for personal achievement and its recognition, more challenging and responsible work, and more opportunity for individual advancement and growth.

Job enlargement, on the other hand, is simply a series of job changes in which the employee masters new tools, methods, or practices, yet continues in effect to do the same work. In job enlargement, the succession of tasks does not provide the capacity for personal or occupational growth. The employee who punched holes at job A now punches squares at job B, or instead of filing purchase orders he files purchase receipts or completes ten case histories a day instead of six. Sometimes certain aspects of the job are eliminated, usually on the suggestion of an industrial engineer, so that the new job has less content than before but is more error-proof, more quickly learned, and easily automated. Returning to the example, if the job changes that the employee underwent amounted to job enrichment, then the interviewer may feel justified in an unfavorable verdict. But if they were in fact no more than job enlargement—alternate expansion and contraction of duties productive of no real satisfaction—the interviewer may feel that incentives were lacking.

It is also possible that the applicant suffered from the effects of isolation. It has been demonstrated that when workers are isolated in a social sense from other workers job dissatisfaction can result. Researchers have found that rates of turnover as well as absenteeism were higher for employees isolated from their fellow workers than for those who worked closely with co-workers. Other studies demonstrate conclusively that there are motivational benefits with job satisfaction, lowered turnover, lowered absentee rates, and higher quality levels when employees are allowed to talk with one another and are not inhibited in developing and maintaining social relationships. In his fourth position with his last employer, the applicant was denied this social interaction and his motivation suffered. With social needs unsatisfied the higher-order needs were stifled. These are matters the employment interviewer must discover and isolate in order to satisfactorily judge the applicant's motivations.

Social Interaction

Any suggestion of problematic social behavior in an employee's record evokes an immediate red-flag reaction in most employment interviewers. Personnel managers have a tendency to fear the consequences of this type of problem even more than absenteeism and poor work performance. Partly this is because of the uncertain quality of human interaction and partly because of the traditional (but not always valid) desire that employees function as a happy family, a concept that has for a corollary the belief that an employee who is not adaptive to the group or who causes friction will damage morale and perhaps impede production.

Employment interviewers usually disbelieve or heavily discount the explanations offered by applicants for such characterizations as "unable to get along with others." The interviewers tend to assume that they are hearing only one side of the problem. This attitude, while it is often tempered with caution, is nevertheless a bias and may affect the final evaluation of the feasibility of employment. Here, too, relations with others in the work group are highly relevant. In certain circumstances an employee may feel little obligation to contribute to the work or to the employer. This lack of personal commitment results in a motivational nose dive. Such circumstances can occur at any level in an organizational hierarchy from that of unskilled, hourly rated personnel to top management.

Social interaction is an integral part of the work milieu. To understand its effect on motivation, it is mandatory for the employment interviewer to investigate the social relations in previous jobs. But the interviewer must avoid stereotyping certain patterns of social behavior as indicative of motivation or the lack of it.

Peer Attitudes and Roles

A theory of "social certitudes," concerned with the relationship of an individual to the group, helps explain how individual productivity is linked to employee interrelations. The workings of this theory can be illustrated in the two examples, one involving a woman production worker and the other an administrative or executive secretary. The theory begins with the premise that groups, like individuals, have attitudes regarding the behavior, background, personal habits, and general life style of members and that these attitudes form the basis for the collective judgment of the group. The individual's conformity to that judgment in turn determines that person's status within the group. When the production worker enters the work group she will, in all likelihood, encounter others of roughly the same social and economic background, and their standards and ideals probably are compatible with her own. What differences there are will not be so great that they cannot be tolerated. Thus the woman is accorded the acceptance of the group and will take her place in its status ranking. A typical reference comment for such an employee might note that by the time of the morning coffee break on her first day at work she had already managed to make friends, a circumstance judged to be indicative of her ability to get along with people. Although the observation may be correct, the explanation is less a matter of social adeptness than of the social certitude that results when the newcomer and the group meet each other's standards.

In a certain respect, this interaction is a form of role playing in a highly structured organization where shared standards protect the participants from jarring surprises. Such surprises as do occur are not the kind that will threaten the social fabric of the group. Even work productivity becomes, to a significant extent, a function of the social relations within the group; shared production goals become personalized.

Let us now consider the second example, a woman hired as an administrative or executive secretary in a medium-size corporation. She is married, has three children, and is not a college graduate. Her husband is a salesman. Although in the same age bracket as the other secretaries, she has worked up through the ranks and has a history of having worked in semiskilled clerical positions. As a result, she finds herself in effect an unknown quantity or an ambiguous social entity.

This fact may not be readily apparent without some understanding of the attributes of the typical executive secretary. An unpublished research study conducted in a moderate-size insurance firm showed a high degree of uniformity in the backgrounds of the executive secretaries. Typically they were college graduates, either single or divorced (with no more than one child). The women studied were comparable in working habits, personal relationships on the job, leisure-time interests, and type and location of residence. There was evidence of a common socioeconomic base; many of the women knew one another before joining the firm, saw one another outside the office, and had mutual friends in the community. In such circumstances, employees can be expected to relate to one another in a reasonably patterned manner.

By virtue of her position in the organization, the executive level of the man for whom she works, and her professional capabilities the newly hired secretary in the second example may earn status points and gain a kind of acceptance. But this is purely formal. She is not a member of the group in the full sense. Because of differences in her background and private life, she cannot share the interests of her co-workers. For example, she does not have the same amount of leisure time as the others and if she did she would not put it to the same use. The conversation at coffee time or lunch holds little interest for her. The fact that she earns more than many group members does not lessen these differences.

There is confusion in the minds of the other women about what they can expect of her—and in her mind about what she can expect of them. As a result there may be some conflict. The others may not confide in her, the ins and outs of office politics may be kept from her, and she could be denied many of the intangibles that may be important to executive secretaries. The predictable response is a rise in the employee's anxiety level, with detrimental effects on her performance. In a reference for this woman an employer might comment to the effect that, although an extremely capable secretary, she was not quite right for the job or not yet ready for executive-level responsibilities.

When work relationships are marked by shared understanding and when group expectations are confirmed by an individual's values and life style—in short, when there is what one industrial psychologist refers to as high group status congruence—we might expect to find labor turnover and absence rates low, which is another demonstration of the important fact that interpersonal relations within a group have marked effects on individual motivation. For this reason and from the point of view of placement, the applicant's personal relations in his former job should not be passed over.

The Work Itself—the Prime Motivator

As important as the effects of the work environment are on motivation, the study of motivation must center on the work itself. It has been shown that job satisfaction, and thus motivation, leading to productive and achievement-oriented behavior is most likely to be found where the job is satisfying to perform and there is scope for advancement, a sense of responsibility, and some justification for pride. The individual who has experienced growth on a former job and who indicates growth as one of his aims may really be seeking a sense of independence in the work and the work environment. Specifically he may have in mind fewer external controls such as job constraints, limitations on the use of knowledge, restrictive production schedules, or quality quotas—the freedom from which he believes necessary to job competence and increased skills. Such a person wants to exert an influence on the environment rather than merely react to it. For him growth is an incentive to further growth.

But there is a cutoff point in this growth cycle. Unfortunately no job offers unlimited opportunity. Once the limits are reached, frustration and discontent set in. This may happen just when the employee is beginning to became a profit center for the company, clearly able with his skills and efficiency to pay his way. But now his threshold of boredom is lowered, the challenge is gone, and his motivation is no longer directed toward the job itself but toward upward mobility. Thus the very motivating factors that make for outstanding success on the job can lead to loss of interest and a possible drop in productivity.

At this point the employee may seek promotion of the job-enrichment (but not job enlargement) kind. He may also seek more money. But monetary reward without job enrichment is unsatisfying, and so it is not uncommon for an employee to resign immediately after a salary increase. The reasons given, such as a desire for greater advancement opportunity, can be highly misleading to anyone not aware of the limitations on the power of money. Constantly increasing the salary can deter an employee from leaving an organization for a time, but it may not hold him indefinitely. The employee may feel the need for the recognition and status that come with promotion as well as for money. If the employer cannot oblige, the employee may change jobs.

This emphasis on promotional opportunities is increasingly evident in middle management and executive applicants, and is even becoming noticeable in clerical workers, who are acquiring new technical skills in connection with their duties. Employment interviewers may be disconcerted by the applicant's willingness to change jobs for a very small salary increase or no increase at all. However, there may be nothing wrong with the applicant's motivation. He may simply be willing to take a temporary salary setback in order to get a job with a higher salary ceiling than the one he left.

Some applicants are not interested in promotions. They are perfectly content with the same title and responsibilities as long as their salary advances. An employment interviewer might judge this to be a lack of initiative. Motivating elements that contribute to this attitude are found in persons whose job advancement has been slow and difficult. These are persons who have invested many years in minimal career gains. They appear to be satisfied with what they have and do not feel secure enough to try for anything better. Such an employee's ego needs are confined to reassurance that he is not slipping. For this purpose salary increases serve perfectly. If significant increases are not forthcoming, however, the employee may change jobs.

Motivators Versus Satisfiers

Let us consider fundamental differences between what we have been calling motivators and what we refer to as satisfiers. A motivator is not necessarily extinguished by satisfaction; in fact, satisfaction tends to keep it alive. If satisfaction is withheld long enough, the motivator may recede only to return again in a totally different form. As the motivator diminishes, its place is taken by other motivators directed toward more attainable satisfactions. Thus the salary increase can substitute for other, less tangible forms of recognition and growth.

Every person strives to fulfill his unconscious image of himself. This self-image becomes a kind of motivator. Since it is not the same for any two persons, it follows that everyone has his own reasons for working, be it money, security, prestige, or passing the time. Regardless of how a person develops, what satisfiers he attempts to substitute for those he cannot obtain, and regardless of how he masks his needs, there will generally be a consistent thread, a general pattern of motivation, however subtle. Each person creates certain fictions about himself and may strive unyieldingly to realize them. The man who decides that he is destined to reach managerial or executive heights would find it extremely difficult to work for a totally production-oriented supervisor operating on, say, theory X. In this position he would be unable to salvage any fragment of his self-concept and would be unable to continue pursuing the ambitions related to it. Predictably he would be unable to tolerate the supervisor who in effect has destroyed the very motivational aspects around which the employee's entire life is built. In the resultant antagonism and friction, the employee might make every effort to thwart the supervisor and consequently could earn an involuntary termination and a poor reference. The same person working under a theory Y supervisor may flourish because he is allowed to pursue the satisfaction of his needs. If the theory Y supervisor is the kind who believes in allowing his employees to set goals for themselves and that employees who are positively motivated will *seek* responsibility not attempt to avoid it, he should respond favorably to the managerial aspirant.

When an employee is positively motivated, minimal controls are necessary. His goals are the foundation on which his life is based and are intimately tied in with his self-concept. Every element in the work environment associated with the attainment of those goals is potentially gratifying. If a person is able to visualize the advantages to himself in terms of his need, he will be motivated. Certainly with self-disciplining needs, such as for achievement, recognition, responsibility, and advancement, this condition is fulfilled.

For a possible clue to motivation the applicant could be asked his opinion of his former supervisors and also of the type of supervision he visualizes as best for him. In pursuing this line of investigation the interviewer is cautioned against snap judgments based on the applicant's hostility to a former supervisor. It is a common belief that applicants who denounce a former supervisor or employer cannot be trusted or are troublemakers. It would seem that there is a sacred unwritten code that requires the applicant to bear courageously and silently the burden of any type of supervisory malpractice.

Management Styles and Motivation

Supervisors can be grouped into three broad categories. The first could be described as the laissez-faire or the hands-off category. Supervisors in this category do not lead or follow, nor do they challenge or interfere with the workers. The workers, in fact, determine their own goals and perhaps even their own methods of working. As a result this sort of supervisor is sometimes labeled "accommodative" and even "abdicative."

The second category is made up of production-oriented supervisors. These are almost completely dominated by the production schedules, quotas, and work methods and procedures established for the department. To them a good employee is one who does what he is told. They tend to be autocratic in their approach, keeping the actions of the workers under careful control. Thus they are the complete opposite of the accommodative supervisor.

The third category comprises the employee-oriented supervisors. Their primary interest is in the training, development, self-improvement, and motivation of the employee. They value such qualities as initiative, confidence, ability to set reasonable goals, sense of humor, and relaxation. The employee-oriented supervisor establishes goals jointly with the employee. In effect, he and the employee mutually agree to achieve, whereas the accommodative supervisor and the employees mutually agree that the employees will dominate and will seek their own levels of achievement unfettered by supervisory influence. The production-oriented supervisor is the most inhibitory to motivation. By discouraging innovation, he blocks employees from influencing or affecting their work and their work environment. Work satisfaction is lowered and on-the-job relations suffer.

Thus it is obvious that supervisory style can affect the motivation of an employee and color his relations with his employer. Therefore, when these relations appear to have been unsatisfactory, the interviewer should be receptive to the possibility that the supervision was in some measure at fault.

Technological processes also influence motivation. To a significant extent they determine the type of work the applicant is seeking and the self-imposed limits of his productivity. Technology can be an underlying source of employee discontent. Typically the reasons given for dissatisfaction are vague and undefined. The employee cannot point to low wages and, in fact, makes his rate each day. The employer is generally considered to be advanced in terms of technological and mechanical devices, and working conditions are considered good or above average. On questioning it is found that the employee is suffering from frustrated self-esteem. The work may be over "technolized"; systems and procedures or automated processes make it impossible for him to contribute to the job, to innovate, or to affect his work environment. The efficiency of the operation is practically predetermined and virtually invulnerable to human error. The employee has established his membership in the group, and his status in terms of social relations is secure, but this remains the highest order of need that is satisfied.

One research study showed that coal miners, who have some control over technology and in fact may contribute to it, see technology as the means to an end, the accomplishment of a goal. Automobile workers, on the other hand, although a part of the technological process rarely have an opportunity to affect it in any significant way. Thus they derive little incentive from it.

Work Rules and Job Constraints

Job satisfaction and motivation can be correlated with the degree of personal control an employee can exercise in his work environment. (A poll of industrial workers produced a consensus that the degree of supervision has a direct bearing not only on job satisfaction but also on productivity.) In general this applies regardless of the nature of the job, whether it is running a train, digging in a mine, or putting bolts in car frames. It has been found that when work is highly repetitious, when workers cannot free themselves even for short periods from the work at hand or pace themselves, storing units of production (sand bagging) to cover periods of lesser productivity, then absenteeism, accident rates, and turnover increase. Workers feel the effects of these constraints in their social relations and even in activities supposedly not regulated. This is the situation on a typical production line.

On the other hand, workers in occupations in which there is minimal contact with supervisory personnel, such as truck driving and certain railroading jobs, enjoy high degrees of job satisfaction and self-esteem. The same appears to be true of coal miners (to judge from a study of questionnaires), although a sense of team spirit, or working together, seems to be a contributing factor. Team spirit can serve to mitigate the dissatisfactions that arise in automated or closely supervised operations. It is a factor in the steel industry but is lacking on the auto assembly line.

It can be seen from these limited examples that when the needs of the individual are either thwarted or denied job satisfaction, motivation and subsequently productivity both suffer. Typically, job satisfaction surveys and other research indicate that automobile assembly line workers are probably the most dissatisfied with their lot in life. Most prefer to get off the "line" and onto a job in which they can exert some influence on the pace of the work. Despite the fact that the entire mass-production field is dominated by machines and technological methods, a worker can generally find some operation where there is greater latitude in respect to pace setting and social conversation.

In discussing motivation there are certain basic principles that must be kept in mind. For example, every person has certain ideas about the kind of person he is. Sometimes these ideas are quite vivid and can be related in detail. At other times, they are vague, hazy fictions. Taken together these ideas constitute a person's self-concept. The self-concept guides behavior; in other words, people make every effort to behave, think, and achieve like the person they believe themselves to be.

When anyone is unable to act as he feels he should, he experiences frustration. The environment in which we live, our surroundings, the world itself thus become a highly personalized place. We interpret the world as we see it, and it is a rare occasion when two people understand and explain their environment in exactly the same way. Impressions about the environment come early, in infancy and long before a person has had an opportunity to experiment with his environment. Inevitably he is locked into certain ideas, fears, anxieties, and hopes, some of which do not change through adulthood. Thus the self-concept is modified by the limitations and inhibitions the person sees in his environment. It is this modified self-image, a product of a kind of real-world compromise, that the person strives to fulfill. But the extent to which he succeeds depends on how closely his self-image and his view of the environment conform to reality.

Productivity and Risk Taking

In keeping with this concept, behavioral scientists suggest that to maintain high levels of productivity, which means motivating employees, it is necessary for management to make sure that the psychological needs of workers are not blocked or totally thwarted. And yet, as a practical matter, it would be totally impossible for every department in every business organization to be run on the basis of this kind of "ego-consensus." Therefore a kind of natural selectivity has been evolved to accommodate needs to the extent possible. This policy, however, is difficult to apply because of the apathy of employment interviewers, managers, workers, and applicants.

While most business organizations still prevent a person from being himself, by means of prescribed policies, procedures, rules, regulations, and technologies, there are ways of countering the inhibiting effect on motivational drives. Some of these have been discussed in this chapter. With burgeoning business organizations straining under the weight of complex technologies, advancing automated techniques, and pressure for change from employees with advancing levels of education and increasingly divergent socioeconomic backgrounds, management techniques will grow more varied. Traditional management will recognize the need for different management approaches to the problems of leadership and control in accordance with the amount and quality of innovation needed on a job, the nature of the job (mechanical or automated, repetitive or varied), the level of skills required, the motivational drives that characterize the worker, and finally the demands of the environment.

Anyone who makes decisions about hiring someone must eventually realize that people do not fit into neat categories. Each person reflects his own pattern of experiences, motives, and frustrations, as well as his individualized self-concept. On the other hand, a certain amount of classification, if only tentative, is necessary to the decision-making process. Thus the interviewer begins his evaluation of the applicant by deciding which of two fundamental motivational types he is: achievement-oriented or maintenance-achievement-oriented.

The difference in these types lies in the motivational stimuli to which the employee responds. Employment recruiters are instinctively drawn to the achievement-oriented applicant. But both types contribute to a business organization in the proper circumstances and in a specific way. Certainly every person has a blend of achievement and maintenance-achievement within his motivational structure, and it is the degree to which one or the other predominates that determines his type.

Achievement and Achievers

One of the first things the employment interviewer should try to determine is the applicant's attitude toward risk taking. A common trait of the achievement-oriented type is the disinclination to take either long-shot gambles or ultraconservative, minimal-gain risks. The tendency is to seek some middle ground where the risk is sufficient to satisfy his need for a challenge. Such people generally prefer situations in which they have some chance of affecting the outcome over situations in which they would be wholly the captive of luck. Achievement-oriented persons usually exhibit a strong sense of responsibility for their own destiny. They want to take credit for their accomplishments and they are willing to be held accountable for their failures. The maintenance-achievement-oriented employee refuses to involve himself that personally and he protects himself from involvement by one of two courses. Either he takes extreme risks, knowing that his role ends with his decision to take the risk, or he minimizes risks by playing the game so closely that his gains are miniscule.

High achievers, as we have suggested earlier, want to know how they are doing. They need to have rapid and accurate feedback, and this means precise answers to their questions about their performance. The maintenance achiever is perfectly satisfied to know that he is getting along well, that people like him, and that people say he has a pleasant attitude. This is never enough for the achiever, who is easily frustrated in an atmosphere in which everyone is a good guy and nobody loses. Thus he will probably respond better (and, in effect, be more highly motivated) when he is told that his applied efforts are successful than he will to the information that his attitude is good.

Achievement-oriented people tend to be very realistic. Because it is important to them that they succeed, they can be expected to seek goals that, if not easy, are nonetheless attainable. In the pursuit of these goals they can be remarkably impersonal, acting with a coolness and deliberation suggestive of a classical type of ruthless businessman. But this does not mean that they are ruthless or obnoxious. On the contrary, they are most often likable because they have learned to channel their abilities along lines that will help them succeed in a typical business environment.

Biographical Data

It is important, in addition, to obtain some idea of the applicant's family background and social class. Personal contacts, friendships, and acquaintances formed through the years especially within the same socioeconomic group or class tend to reinforce attitudes, concepts, and thinking about many subjects, including the environment, career goals, and achievement levels. The influence of acquaintances, who constitute the peer group, is reflected in a person's tendency to conform to their attitudes and opinions. Typically, people do not want to risk group criticism.

A word of caution: Simply because a social class, peer group, or background is clear-cut does not mean that an applicant's motivations, needs, and personality differences are necessarily easy to isolate and define. Certainly, these influences tend to shape the person and guide his activities, but motivations and subsequent behavior may serve more than one purpose and one need.

The family is the primary social unit; the basic formative tie. Likes and dislikes, prejudices, and strivings originate at the family level. The family also serves as the medium of social continuity. Religious beliefs and life styles are perpetuated through it.

A social class is a subgroup of society with which a person may identify or be identified by others. The subgroup may be defined or conceived of in terms of economic status, education, religion, geography, ethnic origin, and even race. Self-concept, attitude toward environment (and toward authority, including of course management), and particularly toward aspirations are all influenced by socioeconomic identification. In American culture there is a definite reluctance to admit that there are social classes here as in many other countries. But for the behavioral and social scientists, social class structure is a real and meaningful consideration.

Social class is the result of stratification or ranking of people and the groups they constitute in accordance with some scale, value measurement or observable characteristic, and life style or pattern of behavior. The most recent trend in American sociological thought is against the idea of social class as a collectivity of easily segregated, clearly defined, discrete categories. Instead, social class is seen as a continuum of status, power, and privilege running through society, with a pattern of broad distinctions clearly observable in life styles, values, and motivations.

It should not be assumed that the following brief review is by any means a complete treatment of the relationship between social class and occupational as motivational factors. Inasmuch as social class may not be easily recognized, the interviewer may find it difficult to apply specific social class criteria to career goals and biographical information. The application of specific criteria may be dispensed with, however, if the interviewer is prepared to take into account some degree of social class influence when attempting to interpret the results of the interview.

Social Class

Social class differences begin to make themselves felt during the preschool and school years. Typically, lower-class children have a wider range of real-life experiences than do middle-class children. They care for brothers and sisters and learn the value of collecting refundable bottles. They get accustomed to contacts with strangers and learn the ways of the street. The quality of their childhood experiences, however, does not lend itself as readily to institutional expectations as does that of middle- or upper-class children. A child in school who is not familiar with middle-class vocabulary, who finds out early that his teacher does not talk like his parents, inevitably has an adjustment problem. He may be unwilling or unable to identify with the classroom situation, where everything is transacted by a verbal communication that is unfamiliar to him and unrelated to those whom he knows, understands, and trusts. Years later, when he encounters supervisors, foremen, and managers who embody middle-class values in their standards of performance and conduct, he may respond unconsciously as he did in school. While the language may no longer be foreign, the system under which the employee operates remains so.

Middle-class children are encouraged to excel, to be neat and clean, and to respect authority, which is explained to them in positive terms. In most middle-class homes, fighting among boys, for example, is not viewed as a sign of manhood or as a part of growing up but rather as a delinquent practice that serves to lower the status of the boy and his parents. The middle-class child is told to use his head not his fists. These attitudes do not change markedly through life. Although they may be modified through education, changes in economic status, and strong motivation reinforced by realistic, attainable goals, it is quite another thing to shed them entirely.

The wider a person's exposure to other classes and cultures, the more receptive he is likely to be to ideas and opportunities. Employment interviewers dealing with high school graduates or even applicants with some college or trade school experience with cultural, social, or ethnic groups other than their own often find the applicants unresponsive to certain incentives or benefits, such as a tuition refund or development and training program.

Sociologists are concerned primarily about the mobility of persons within the social continuum: upward (achievement-oriented), downward, and lateral (achievement-maintenance) mobility. Most studies concerned with social class use occupation as the basic criterion by which to measure upward or downward mobility since this seems to be, at least at this stage in a relatively new field of study, the most productive approach.

We may begin by citing the results of a research study that indicate that significant changes in career status take place *within* work categories or occupations and not *between* them.[4] The applicant, though upwardly mobile, is likely to remain in his blue collar or white collar occupational category because to do otherwise may require training, retraining, and educational experiences as well as employer acceptance of his new status, all of which may be difficult to obtain.

The study also found that upward mobility throughout the career life was most typical of persons identified as members of the upper and middle classes. Members of those classes have a wider selection and can exhibit more freedom of choice regarding occupations or employers because of economic, cultural, and educational advantages. Lower classes more typically may be expected to seek job placement by default. Upper-class members typically marry at a later age than members of other social classes, so that with certain white collar positions involving heavy travel or other inconveniences discouraging to married men with families, a high proportion of applicants come from this class.

We might expect that the middle class, with its heavy representation among professionals, entrepreneurs, managers, specialists, and

---

[4] R. Bendix and S. Lipset, eds., *Class, Status and Power* (New York: The Free Press, 1953).

educated people in general, will produce the achievement-oriented or achievement-motivated applicants. These people who value educational experience as "something no one can take away." Middle-class virtues have been satirized over the years, but they are not dispensed with so easily. Management tends inexorably toward middle-class standards in evaluating employee performance. These standards are often betrayed in the language used to describe the successful employee. Broadly speaking, the achievement motive is less pronounced and less well defined in lower- and upper-socioeconomic groups.

Middle-class applicants may, typically, show concern about security, educational assistance, and benefit programs. During the interview they may stress educational, intellectual, or academic abilities and accomplishments as well as their personal responsibility and integrity, and they may indicate friendship with well-known individuals in the community. They are often willing to trade salary for security on a job or in a company that also offers some status. Unlike lower- or lower-middle-class applicants (who are perhaps conditioned by long-time union membership to feel secure), they seldom express distrust of management.

Middle-class people are generally quite sensitive about living within their means. For example, much as they value status, they will scorn a status car if they feel they are not economically ready for one. Members of the lower classes may be less cautious because of the desire to break out of the confines of their status. In fact, however, the affluence of the American laborer today makes the classic identification of him as lower or middle lower class obsolete, at least by many of the criteria used to measure social class.

Mode of dress may be significant with upper- and middle-class applicants as reflective of self-image. An emphasis on style may indicate identification with (or aspiration toward) the upper strata; an emphasis on quality and durability, the middle strata. Ethnic identification should not be overlooked. Certain ethnic groups tend to coincide, in fact or in the public mind, with certain socioeconomic levels. This identification and the resultant value adoption may be significant and may supply the interviewer with important clues.

Unquestionably social origin or background may function like a kind of caste system, weighing heavily on a person and overriding his preferences or abilities in the determination of his career path. Similarly, identification with a social class can shape definite inclinations toward types of employment situations, such as protective, paternalistic, autocratic, theory Y, and so forth. Thus it is a factor in the total makeup of the applicant.

Job Skills Demand and Motivation

One of the most fundamental changes brought about as a consequence of the dehumanization, fragmentation, fail-safe sterilization, and labor-saving "technolization" of most jobs, both management and clerical, in an economically advancing society is the growth of what might be termed transient skills. A transient skill is a proficiency at a technical operation used exclusively or almost exclusively by one company, and for which accordingly there is virtually no demand elsewhere. The worker is trained by the company and his value to it depends on the company's need for the special skill. As the technological need increases so does the employee's value and vice versa. It is possible for a marginally educated employee to reach impressive salary and hierarchical levels solely through his adeptness at a transient skill. It is also possible for the employee to topple unceremoniously when the transient skill on which his entire career is based diminishes in value or even disappears. Retraining may be offered, of course, and the company may make an effort to utilize the background gained from the use of previously learned transient skills, but the employee still finds himself in the situation of having to fight the battle all over again.

Thus clerical, production, and managerial employees can become locked into a job, department, company, or industry because of transient skills. Education is no protection. The broad background that college provides equips a man for learning advanced skills. A highly educated employee may find that the skills that he is required to master as he rises in the executive hierarchy and that become the basis of his value to the organization (and therefore of his earning capacity) are all of the transient type.

A worker with a transient skill has a limited marketability, or chance of getting other employment at the same salary level or of advancing. The degree of his marketability depends on the portability or transferability of his skill. Where the skill is transferable, the employee may represent that he has a general background in or exposure to the subject. But portability is generally highly restricted. Therefore the employee with the transient skill is generally described as having potential, signifying that he can supplement the narrowness of his experience with his own personal adaptability.

As a product of technological change, the transient skill is sometimes difficult to describe in conventional occupational terms. A worker may be unable to find an appropriate title for his function. When answering a query, he may either put down the title he held (which may be meaningless outside his former company) or else use some all-inclusive term such as "manufacturing," "accounting," or "management," hoping to avoid the problem by resorting to an encompassing abstraction.

The knowledge that his skill is transient can have profound effects on the behavior and motivation of an employee. Limitations on the ability of others to understand and appreciate the value of his skill rob the worker of certain recognition. The worker may tire of using special terminology to explain how he earns a living. Moreover, he is not always sure of job advancement or enrichment. He may not understand the technological theory that gave birth to the need for his transient skill. Someone, somewhere, perhaps a scientist, an engineer, or a mathematical theoretician, developed the operation or recognized the need for it. And, although it may have portability, the skill is of value primarily to the company for which it is performed. Knowing that a change in technology can affect job security; feeling that he is at the mercy of management and locked into a situation over which he has limited if any control; suspecting that his own imagination, abilities, and needs (if they can be expressed) may be of only small value in demonstrating his ability to pull himself up by his bootstraps, the worker whether management, production, or clerical may have difficulty in mediating his job function with his self-concept and responding to internal and external motivational stimuli in quite the same manner as the village smithy.

Whether or not a worker is repelled by the hygiene factors in the work environment, regardless of what level of needs he is seeking to satisfy, or of whether he is an accomplishment, responsibility, or security seeker, his capacity to control or adjust to his environment is affected by the pressure and impact of industrial need. Industrial need preshapes the work environment. The implications where motivation is concerned are profound.

Motivation and the Work Environment

It is within the context of this preshaped industrial environment that motivational stimuli are defined or, put another way, reinterpreted in terms of rewards available to the worker and the needs of the organization. With a highly achievement-oriented applicant, the interviewer should be concerned with the extent to which the existing work milieu can fulfill the applicant's needs. The carrot–rabbit technique is still much relied on in industry. A study of managers, which showed that, qualitatively and quantitatively, performance kept pace with reward, suggests that the technique is sound.[5] In management, efforts exerted in low-responsibility functions produce far lower rewards for the employee than the same efforts in critical functions. Thus the nature of the job assignment should be related to the psychological needs of the employee. Additional dimensions must also be considered in terms of motivational effect; for example, the reward versus punishment system in relation to the work or, to put it simply, process versus result. Rewards may be forthcoming for effort, efforts and results, or simply for results alone. To be effective, the employee must have confidence in the appraisal method. If the employment interviewer recognizes these implications, he can understand the sensitivities that may be touched off when the matter of performance appraisal, rewards, recognition, and the entire matter of motivation are topical during the interview. A system for identifying employee performance could be interpreted as a reward system, a need-fulfiller and satisfier by one employee while another employee could perceive the same reward system as a sinister mechanism devoted to stalking him and "finding him out."

[5] L. W. Porter and E. E. Lawler, *Managerial Attitudes and Performance* (Homewood, Ill.: Richard D. Irwin, Inc., 1968).

7

Interviewing Techniques

Among the more fascinating aspects of employment interviewing are the various techniques available to the employment interviewer. No one technique is successful for all applicants all of the time. What elicits highly useful responses from one applicant can fail miserably with another. A technique that works well with clerks may fail with managers. An approach that was effective in drawing out a withdrawn applicant proved totally wrong for a gregarious, highly achievement-oriented type who must be controlled and directed. The method that triggered a chain reaction of self-analysis by the failure avoider drove a highly motivated applicant into a doldrum of boredom. The gambit that put the disingenuous applicant off guard so that he could be maneuvered into subtle contradictions about his past was useless with the applicant whose candid response to questions was designed to disarm the interviewer. The conversational approach may have appealed to the management generalist, but it disconcerted the detail-oriented specialist. The humor that delighted and charmed one applicant evoked rigid, reflex behavior from another. One applicant when challenged, doubted, and verbally attacked collapses in an effusion of guilt and recrimination, while another is stimulated and battles back forcefully.

All this points up the fact that a technique is designed to accomplish a specific purpose with a specific candidate for employment at a given time. It is not the fault of the technique if it is misused by the interviewer. In selecting a technique, the interviewer must thoroughly understand the job that is vacant. He must know what skills are required, the ways in which these skills are learned, and the experience and education necessary. He should know something about those employees who were successful and unsuccessful on the job in the past, and he must have a realistic understanding of job progression and organizational ascendance probabilities. Finally, he must be thoroughly familiar with the functional relationship between the job to be filled and the objectives of the organization.

The interviewer's generalized knowledge about applicants will direct him to the selection of an appropriate technique. Although there is no certain formula, the experienced interviewer knows that he can make certain basic assumptions about educational and occupational backgrounds, career objectives, life styles, geographic labor market, and patterned behavioral characteristics of applicants seeking specific types of employment such as secretaries, clerk–typists, junior accountants, skilled and unskilled trades, management trainees, and some sales and management personnel. He is, of course, always prepared for exceptions. And the more the interviewer understands about human behavioral patterns, achievement needs, and the relationship between socioeconomic identities and motivation, the fewer the surprises he will experience and the more the confidence he can place in his choice of techniques or in any plan that he might devise for the interview. Usually more than one technique is called for with any given applicant. This results in an interplay of techniques that do not, however, differ radically from one another. Changing of techniques in the middle of an interview requires some experience, but the ability to sense when a technique is failing and to shift to another is as important to the successful conduct of the interview as making a reasonable selection of techniques (or plan) before the interview begins. An employment interviewer who must grope for the appropriate technique during the interview fails not only himself but the applicant as well.

Gaming

Business theorists have used gaming principles to analyze business transactions and organizational relationships. The classic work of Neumann and Morgenstern attempted to define rational human behavior through mathematical principles applied to socioeconomic circumstances.[1] They showed that strategies could be charted when the probabilities of anticipated and unanticipated occurrences are known, and when the outcome is not wholly the consequence of human decision making.

In terms of the game theory as laid down by Neumann and Morgenstern, it should be possible to predict the outcome of an interview with certainty if the variables can be specified. In an interview this can be done only in a gross sense; gross because the variables are infinite and many are subtle and related to unanswered questions about human behavior and motivation. Yet such broad categories as the ability, experience, and education of the applicant, his interest in the job and in the company, job specifications, salary ranges, working conditions, opportunity for personal and professional development, and a host of others are all capable of specification.

There is considerable speculation that game theory is still too abstract for practical application. But the gaming approach has unalterable advantages. In any situation in which there are opposing interests, it provides a system for analyzing responses and planning moves.

Game theory assumes that each of the players understands the other and that each reacts in a logical way. They will then engage in a series of transactions that may be variously termed moves, ploys, maneuvers, and the like. Each transaction builds on the one that precedes it and usually has a positive or negative effect on the outcome. A game is a repetitious activity since the same or highly similar transactions continue to occur. Each transaction seems reasonable, contextual, logical, or plausible because each transaction is germane to the game. The strategic purpose of a transaction, however, is always concealed by the participants. Therefore deception is inherent in gaming, a fact that is of course void of ethical significance.

Zero-Sum Games

In certain games the purpose is to win or lose. But business rivalries seldom lend themselves to a win-or-lose outcome; the parties are concerned only with achieving some gain over their original position. Games in which the alternatives are win or lose are classified as zero-sum. In a two-party, zero-sum game no degree of cooperation is possible between the players. What one wins the other loses. Card games are typical. Games in which neither party wins or loses are non-zero-

---

[1] J. von Neumann and O. Morgenstern, *Theory of Games and Economic Behavior* (Princeton, N.J.: Princeton University Press, 1947).

sum. In such games a strategy (or a range of strategies) exists by which both parties can gain; in other words, an element of cooperation is present. In general, bargaining situations and employment interviewing fall into this category.

Role Playing in Gaming

Before examining the various ways in which game theory may be applied to an interview, a contributory concept must be introduced—that of roles. A role, in the psychological sense, is a pattern or blueprint of behavior. It is learned and therefore is not capricious or based on a whim of chance. Everyone acts out a specific role in accordance with his perceived social position, purpose, or status. It can be said that in rational circumstances an unspoken bargain is struck between the role players, to the effect that they recognize each other's roles and the expected patterns of behavior and attitude consistent with that role. This interawareness is known as a role set. Role theory requires that roles do not exist of and by themselves, but only in relation to or in interaction with other roles. The theory of roles is extremely useful in explaining the behavior of interviewer and applicant.

If the applicant's behavior is not as the interviewer expected, the interviewer changes his strategy. Obviously, the interviewer had some criterion of the appropriate social role of the applicant in mind or he could not have had expectations. The role of the applicant was defined in the mind of the interviewer on the basis of the social situation we call employment interviewing.

As a rule the applicant who is seeking to persuade the employment interviewer in his behalf and to impress him favorably by communicating the responses and attitudes he perceives as being desirable or advantageous assumes the focal role, that of role sender. The role receiver is the interviewer, who has the power to affect and to mold the cognitive behavior and attitudes of the applicant. Sometimes, in what is generally an undesirable situation (as in an extremely tight employment market with respect to a specific skill), the interviewer may assume the focal role (role sender), seeking to persuade the applicant to join the company. This type of role adaptation does not always imply dishonesty or a devious motive. Nevertheless, this adaptability can be turned unscrupulously to advantage by the role player to convey false impressions of his attitudes or opinions.

Essential to the application of game theory is the determination of what the parties are striving for. There are a number of possible formulations for interviewing, but the following two are perhaps the most generally applicable.

Who You Are—What You Can Do

In this game the stake is information. Specifically, each party wishes to learn as much as he can about the other and at the same time prevent him from learning anything unfavorable about himself. Commonly the interviewer checks off everything favorable to the applicant, much as he would the items on a skills checklist. Mentally the applicant may do the same. Both parties may also keep negative listings. This strategy entails a certain amount of trading, which supplies the necessary element of cooperation characteristic of a non-zero-sum bargaining game.

Give and Take

This game is characteristic of negotiation. It can most readily be played when the applicants are at the managerial level, highly skilled technically, or have skills that happen to be in short supply. The negotiations may be concerned with salary, deferred income, benefits, profit sharing, relocation reimbursements, commissions and bonuses, job titles, reporting relationships, and other considerations. In this game both parties normally have predetermined limits within their stated demands. But neither player knows the extent of this flexibility in the other.

The interviewer begins by stating his conditions as if they were irreducible, and the applicant counters with his. The greater the gap, of course, the longer the process of negotiation. The give-and-take game can be played very close to zero-sum, with neither party making any concession to the other. This is undesirable and may result in the withdrawal of one of the parties (or what is worse, an unsatisfied employee). In practice, it is to the advantage of both parties to find an equilibrium, or cooperative strategy in which the gains of both (considered jointly) are optimized.

Besides the basic game formulations, there is an almost infinite variety of techniques or stratagems from which the interviewer can select. In theory, only lack of experience and imagination can limit him in deciding how to arrange his repertoire. In practical terms, however, such factors as the experience, background, personality, motivation, and career objectives of the applicant, coupled with the nature of the job vacancy to be filled and the special characteristics of the job, the organizational milieu in which the job exists and other perimeters defining the job, the organization, and the industry, narrow the selection. The following stratagems are among the most useful.

You the jury. The purpose of this subtle stratagem is to put the applicant in an honesty-versus-conformity dilemma in order to test his integrity. For example, one seasoned interviewer tells the applicant (in a conversational way and in a pseudoconfidential tone) about an unnamed individual who, although in management, always locked his desk at five sharp. The story ends with a smile of ridicule and the words, "Can you imagine such a thing?" With that rhetorical question the applicant–player is now placed in the role of juryman. The interviewer–player has presented his case. The expectation is not only that the applicant will get the message but also that he will respond. The applicant–player understands that he is expected to indicate that he cannot imagine such a thing, although both players realize that, in fact, he perfectly well *can.* If the applicant–player, however, refuses tacit compliance, he is in effect challenging the principle expressed in the example. Whether or not this response will benefit the applicant depends on the value attached to the policy or principle that he challenges.

Go–no-go. This stratagem is an excellent way of opening a give-and-take game. The interviewer outlines the company's expectations and standards and demonstrates the advantages of affiliation to the applicant. If the applicant accepts these points, the interviewer has an excellent starting position. If the applicant attempts to bargain on these points (indicating perhaps that he has parallel expectations and offers parallel advantages), the interviewer, pretending to yield reluctantly, leads the applicant into a give-and-take game at a disadvantage. One result is that the interviewer may have to negotiate on fewer items.

Persuasion. Sometimes in the standard give-and-take bargaining game, the interviewer is convinced of an applicant's desirability, but the applicant holds back. In this situation direct persuasion can be effective. In essence the applicant is made to feel that he has won a zero-sum game and need only assent to being hired. This usually works with college graduates, but with more experienced applicants it is often less successful. The latter tend to hold their ground, knowing that the interviewer can go only so far and still stay within the bounds of truth and reason.

Persuasion is a tricky ploy because the interviewer puts himself at a disadvantage. The tactic should be used in conjunction with others to which the interviewer should be ready to switch when the applicant shows signs of a favorable response.

How we *do it.* This is an instructional tactic. The purpose is to help prepare the applicant for employment by giving him helpful information and insights about the job, the company, or his prospective superior; telling him what technical skills he should build even though his present skill level is adequate for employment; suggesting personal development needs and even indicating social demands that may be made of him. It is more than an orientation, for it is intended specifically to direct the applicant's personal activities.

The applicant's response is usually cautious. On the one hand, he must continually reinforce his present level of skills and development to uphold his acceptability. On the other hand, he must (as a result of role expectations) indicate that he is willing to seek out developmental opportunities that will make him a better employee and to adapt to the new job circumstances, new skill demands, new procedures, and new people. He cannot emphasize the second point at the expense of the first. The interviewer must be careful not to downgrade the applicant's skills or make it appear that his experience and knowledge are obsolete.

Rapport. This tactic is perhaps one of the most commonly used of all. It is an outgrowth of the superior–inferior relationship between applicant and interviewer. Anxiety is normal for applicants. In some cases getting the job is of crucial importance. Even if he passes the test of acceptability, he may have to face many and significant changes in his work style or in his family circumstances (relocation, for example). This anxiety underlies his conduct and affects his relationship with the interviewer. The applicant is guarded in his responses, for he knows that every move may be judged and analyzed; every manifestation verbal or nonverbal is potential input. The interviewer, therefore, must strive to create a supportive environment during the interview. Some authorities actually advocate responses calculated to put the applicant at his ease. Others merely stress an ambience of benevolence.

From a psychological standpoint, rapport is simply the fluid exchange of thoughts and ideas. This fluidity is of advantage to the interviewer, whose objective is to learn all he can about the applicant. The interviewer makes the first move and observes the reaction. If the response seems neutral, the interviewer applies more of the same rapport-producing small talk and humor with appropriate facial animation. Only when it is clear that the anxiety level is rising alarmingly does the interviewer assume that his chosen method or technique is not working. If it does work, the applicant recognizes the interviewer's desire to establish rapport and makes efforts to respond to it. The pretext is played out until the interviewer feels that fluidity will continue. Once rapport has been established, it should be maintained. There should be no shift in approach to a harder-hitting technique. One danger that the interviewer must guard against in the rapport approach is that the consequences of faulty technique may not be obvious. The applicant counters with as relaxed and affable an exterior as possible, producing an artificial fluidity that may deceive the interviewer.

Sometimes the applicant is aware of the purely tactical nature of the interviewer's moves to establish rapport and resists them. This defense can sometimes be overcome by catching the applicant off guard, as, for example, by telling a joke and waiting for a response, or by a friendly and constructive personal comment. Clothing often furnishes a pretext: "My, that is *quite* a tie (or blouse). Certainly nothing shy about it." This ploy has overtones of the how-we-do-it stratagem. A more delicate maneuver is the trap-play, wherein the interviewer makes a comment or statement that he really does not believe in order to elicit a response. An applicant's counterplay may be to pretend not to see the ploy or to respond neutrally to the probe, without commitment or emotion. This interchange can momentarily produce a zero-sum confrontation and antagonize the applicant, but this effect can be dispelled if the interviewer relinquishes his winning position quickly by making light of his statement or acknowledging that the joke was a poor one.

There are several techniques that can be applied to almost any interview game and in the proper combination can be most effective. There is no formula that specifies which technique is best suited for each game or that can take into account variances in the role played by either the applicant or interviewer. Again, much depends on the situation at hand, the type of job to be filled, the background and objectives of the applicant, and the interviewer's understanding of basic behavioral patterns.

Applicant-centered Interview

One of the most useful techniques in any type of employment interviewing is the applicant-centered interview. This technique does not require much creativity on the part of the interviewer; usually it consists of following an application blank or résumé, confirming facts, obtaining and clarifying detail. It is generally used early in the interview before more elaborate techniques are called for, but for most unskilled, semiskilled, and general clerical jobs or for applicants about whom too little is known to serve as a basis for evaluation, it may be exclusively relied on.

The applicant-centered interview uses the more obvious facts about the applicant, usually those that have been committed to writing. This makes it somewhat restrictive for the interviewer but not necessarily superficial. Typically the technique concerns itself with three broad categories of inquiry: personal, educational, and occupational. The line of inquiry is factual and chronological, so that the responses are usually patterned. Little introspection is required of applicant or interviewer, but there is a heavy stress on open questions, those that cannot be answered yes or no. For example, "How did you happen to work for Profit Makers, Inc.?"

Quite early in the interview the applicant realizes that inquiry is based on what he has already made known about himself, and his anxiety is quickly reduced. This relaxed frame of mind may be fruitful of insights for the interviewer. In his elaborations, asides, anecdotes, and reiterated references to himself, the applicant may supply important paths of inquiry.

Another advantage in this approach is that the interviewer's responses are immediately perceived and serve as a kind of feedback that tends to reinforce the applicant. The interviewer usually nods in affirmation of his understanding, makes a notation on the application or résumé, or makes brief comments indicating his understanding.

The applicant-centered interview and indeed most interviewing techniques play down the superior–inferior relationship as a way of reducing the applicant's anxiety. At the same time, it can be desirable to take the opposite approach—that is, to heighten anxiety as a means of analyzing how the applicant reacts under pressure and how well he maintains his poise, coherency, sense of direction and role—because the nature of the position is such that the applicant will need those attributes. The methods used may involve manner—flat voice tone and stock closed questions that do not invite elaboration, challenging the applicant's qualifications—and props—a squat, armless chair set back from the desk of the interviewer forcing the applicant to speak a little louder than he might otherwise.

Interviewer-oriented Technique

Foremost among the techniques that rely on the deliberate height-ening of anxiety is the so-called interviewer-oriented technique. This is one of the most difficult of all techniques for both parties, although of the two, the applicant probably has the more trying time. The interviewer's posture is challenging and accusatory in the extreme. Typically he is stern, cool, and distant, uttering perhaps a crisp "How do you do" and not even inviting an answer. He has the application or résumé on his desk but appears to regard them with contempt. In fact, he gives the impression of being annoyed at the applicant's pres-ence. Almost at the outset, he attempts to deflate the applicant, taking the offensive with an observation to the effect that, after having re-viewed the résumé or application, he is having difficulty determining exactly what the applicant is qualified for and would appreciate clari-fication on this point. The applicant can become angry and lash out at the interviewer; he can retreat; or he can quietly stand on his merits, using sound logic to defend his qualifications.

Unlike the applicant-oriented technique, the interviewer-oriented technique is not usually phased into another approach. The inter-viewer keeps the pressure high; he wants to learn the basic job-related facts about the applicant, but he also wants to know how well the applicant will stand the heat in the kitchen—and for how long. Anxiety builds in the applicant, then frustration and perhaps psychological fatigue. Those pressures may find outlet in aggression displayed in the form of hyperdefensiveness. All these manifestations contradict tradi-tional role expectations.

In an interviewer-oriented interview, the interviewer ignores the mood of the applicant and relentlessly superimposes his own mood; he does not react to or show any sensitivity toward the feelings or attitudes of the applicant. For all practical purposes, he throws rap-port to the winds. But he does not relinquish flexibility. The highly skilled interviewer can move from a sterile, impersonal, accusatory gambit to a congenial, warm, even humorous approach, then revert to the sterile approach to test for the applicant's adaptability and maturity. The success of this technique depends on the proper choice of applicant and on timing. Its misuse, particularly with nonmanage-ment applicants or applicants in most lower-level and many middle-level management jobs, is needless and can prove disastrous.

Conversational Approach

A third technique quite different from the preceding ones is the conversational approach. This is one of the most deceptive of all techniques. Typically, the interviewer's desk is cleared of all papers at the time of the interview except for a pad and pencil for notes. The interviewer is seemingly conversational and nothing more. Thus a relaxed atmosphere is engendered and maintained throughout the interview. Everything is done to make the applicant feel that he is not being subjected to a fine scrutiny. Gradually he lowers his guard, revealing much about himself.

The conversational approach affords the interviewer the logical prerogative of "hopscotching"; that is, not following a single line of questioning through to completion, but moving from one subject to another. This facility gives the interviewer an exceptional opportunity to judge the mental alertness and adaptability of the applicant. For example, in a nondirective situation of this sort a good deal of the responsibility for structuring the applicant's presentation falls on the applicant. Whether he keeps to the point or rambles, indulging, as many do, in speculation and self-analysis, is of course a useful insight.

Note taking can be performed without disturbing the desired effect if excessive body movement (for example, hunching over the pad) is avoided. Also the action of writing should be artfully disassociated from the applicant's responses. There should be no simultaneous writing and commenting, and if possible, new questions should be asked while notes are being written.

Naturally the interviewer must do his homework carefully if he is to dispense with the presence of the key data sources—application, résumé, and test results—during the interview.

For eliciting multiple responses from the applicant, the so-called pregnant pause is devastatingly effective. Its execution is rather simple, which may account for its huge success. Following an applicant's response to a question, the interviewer withholds comment, does not nod or affirm understanding, or even indicate that basic communication has taken place. There is no facial expression or note taking. It is as if the applicant had not spoken at all. A situation very much like gaming occurs. The interviewer's move is intended to make the applicant feel that he gave an insufficient, incomplete, questionable, irrelevant, or otherwise unsatisfying answer. The interviewer appears to be waiting for more or better, and the applicant, assuming this response is negative and not knowing whether the fault is in the quality or the quantity of his response, begins to elaborate and expand on his reply.

The interviewer now has an advantage; by withholding positive responses, he can draw out the applicant. The technique has the drawback of making the applicant feel insecure, and if carried too far may cause him to lose his composure. The undesirability of this is obvious. Another drawback is the possibility of eliciting irrelevant responses.

The pregnant pause works well because applicants, playing a non-aggressive role, do not usually counter the challenge that it represents. When a counterchallenge takes place, as, for example, in a statement like "I think that answers the question, unless there is something else you wish to know about that point," the interviewer becomes the respondent. He cannot maintain silence for, if he does, the applicant may remain silent. By asking another question on a different subject or pursuing the previously asked question, the interviewer can break the pause and reestablish the feedback.

The pregnant pause should be used sparingly. It is generally most effective when it interrupts a long chain of affirmative feedback from the interviewer. It is also more effective when the applicant happens to be reciting complicated or significant facts.

Forced Choice

Another technique used by interviewers is the forced choice. The interviewer asks a question the applicant cannot answer without affirming or denying the assumption on which the question is presumably based. Thus the applicant is set against the interviewer and is out of his expected role. Examples of such forced questions are: "Every major executive in this company enjoys the excitement of statistical detail. You *do* enjoy statistical detail?" or: "What type of leadership experience have you had?"

The first question assumes enjoyment of statistical detail; the second, leadership experience. To deny these assumptions is tantamount to concluding the interview. If the applicant attempts to resist these questions he is forced to abandon the role that he and the interviewer expect of him. Therefore the interviewer should not lean too heavily on this technique unless he wishes to induce the applicant to terminate the interview.

Group Interviewing

A broad technique that has been given attention in the past few years is group interviewing. This practice is based on the theory that consensus is the best way to make certain that an applicant (usually for a management position) is, in fact, qualified. A group of management people are singled out for the educational, occupational, and personal attributes that appear to make them seem logical choices to interview particular candidates for specific job vacancies. Each interviewer is furnished with an outline of the applicant's background and aspirations and sometimes with a list of topics he is to cover. The list of topics, no two of which are alike, represents an effort to prevent the interview from straying into unproductive channels.

In theory, this approach may seem sound, but in practice it breaks down rapidly because of the human factor. In the final analysis, while the members of the executive team may be highly qualified in their fields of endeavor, there is no guarantee that they can sustain a productive interview. The assumption that a representative group of management talent can bring to the interview enough practical and theoretical knowledge to formulate questions and to interpret the replies has not been borne out by practical experience.

Interviewing Members of Minority Groups

The problem of racial minority applicants is one of the most difficult the interviewer has to face. Members of the more seriously discriminated against races (for most purposes this would exclude such groups as Jews and Orientals) tend to approach the subject of employment with defeatism, and their attitude toward the interviewer is tinged with hostility. When the interviewer is working under prejudices and misconceptions, the combination of negative attitudes can reduce the interview to a shambles.

Minority applicants, particularly blacks, do not yet fully believe the words "Equal Opportunity Employer." They know that the door may be open, but they have no assurance that their chances for employment are any better, in the main, than they have been. This is to be expected. Blacks are aware that they have long been served poorly by the majority, and the attitudes built up over a lifetime cannot be corrected overnight.

The interviewer also has attitudes to cope with. Total objectivity is unattainable but, when the applicant is a member of a minority group, the barriers to objectivity are especially formidable. For one thing, there are psychological and semantic gaps that magnify misunderstandings. For another, there are subjective weaknesses, such as the tendency to level blame, or the opposite tendency—to lean over backward and ignore certain background factors that would never be overlooked in a white applicant. Conscientious interviewers aware of these pressures may subject themselves to self-scrutiny, constantly questioning their motives, wondering whether they are being too paternalistic, too permissive, and too big-brotherish on one hand, or too stern and unyielding on the other. This uncertainty has the effect of undermining their authority in the interview. Furthermore, in attempting systematically to neutralize their subjective tendencies, interviewers may emphasize objectivity to the point where the interview lacks warmth and becomes a disagreeable exercise.

In general, the interviewer and the minority applicant have very little in common. Their life styles, experiences, expectations, and in certain respects even their basic psychology are quite different. It is difficult, for example, for a white interviewer to understand why highly qualified blacks often apply for jobs far beneath their levels of occupational skill, or why they sometimes conceal job skills and take lower-paying positions. The interviewer may not realize that in the first instance the black employees hope to increase their chances of getting work, and in the second they are avoiding not responsibility or demanding duties but merely competition with whites, whom they deem better qualified than themselves. Thus employment interviewers assume that the aspiration levels of the black applicant are low, when in fact the black may be facing the realities of the situation in the only way he knows. Some black applicants go so far as to devaluate their earning power by quoting a desired salary far below the going rate. Again, this is an effort to avoid head-on competition; by pricing themselves well within the market available to them, they believe that they are making it difficult to rule them out of consideration. These applicants do not realize that they are weakening their case and providing a prejudiced interviewer with ammunition.

Minority Group Employment Patterns

The history of the typical minority applicant shows patterns unlike those of the rest of the community. The reasons for these differences can be understood only in the light of the conditions that shaped them. It is recommended that the interviewer read as much as he can on the condition of minorities in this country. It is also a good policy to consult with social welfare specialists and with the educated members of the various groups who can supply additional insights.

The following discussion outlines and explains some of the employment handicaps common among minority applicants.

The employment history of minority applicants is quite likely to be spotty. Many are trapped in unskilled or semiskilled jobs that offer little or no training and practically no upward mobility. Not only are such jobs vulnerable to economic downturn, but also employers, aware of the replaceability of this type of worker, are prone to a certain complacency when it comes to working conditions—prompt dismissals for minor infractions are an example.

The insecurity of employment is reflected in the life styles of minority workers. Many are without a.permanent address. Because they cannot afford to live far from their place of work, which changes constantly, these workers move frequently. Thus they do not form ties with their neighbors as do lower-middle-class people. Their lack of possessions makes this frequent change of place somewhat easier.

There is also the matter of police records. Here hypothetical constructs of the ideal employee and the ideal background must give way to social realities. Yet on closer examination the facts often do not bear out the damaging implications of an arrest. When a minority applicant, particularly a black, points out that an arrest is not a conviction, he isn't just playing with words. In many parts of the country it is routine police practice in ghetto areas to make arrests in connection with minor infractions or for information on friends, acquaintances, or relatives. Extensive investigation shows that many arrests simply reflect community attitudes about minorities. A favorite catchall is criminal conspiracy, which could mean anything from the numbers game to consorting with known criminals.

Communicating with Black Applicants

Probably the very best technique the employment interviewer can use with a black or minority applicant is no technique at all. And that in itself is a technique of sorts. The point is to meet the applicant on his own ground, not the interviewer's, and to begin talking and listening with only a general interview program in mind. The interviewer may be able to anticipate certain milestones in the white applicant's recitation of his past. Where the minority applicant is concerned, there is no certain way of knowing the twists and turns his life may have taken. Under a general plan it is not the practice to anticipate responses. The interviewer, in effect, reduces his susceptibility to shock. This is terribly important because the minority applicant has learned to read even slight changes in facial expressions.

The minority applicant may use words and phrases that the interviewer has never heard before. These are colloquialisms and slang

that are a part of the vocabulary of his social milieu. They do not signify disrespect, ridicule, or arrogance. By the time the more popular
phrases work their way into the middle-class vernacular, they are
passé in the ghetto. The employment interviewer should not try to
speak this idiom unless he knows it well and unless his entire de-
meanor is consistent with it. When badly done it backfires.

It is best to steer clear of first names. Some interviewers believe
that use of first name on both sides builds rapport. But to minority
applicants it is likely to appear as a palpable affectation and may only
contribute to his uneasiness. Of course, use of first names by the interviewer without extending a similar license to the applicant is insult-
ingly paternalistic. Also taboo are such gaucheries as approving references to well-known minority personalities or folkways (for example,
soul food), boasts of liberal hiring policies, and use of such expressions as "you people."

The Facts Do Not Always Speak for Themselves

It is advisable to allow the minority applicant to complete his
employment application after the interview rather than compel completion before it. While this may make it somewhat more difficult to
structure the interview, it relieves some of the applicant's anxiety. Bald
facts can create a misleading impression, and the applicant is naturally
apprehensive that by the time he can present the mitigating circumstances the damage may be done. Therefore he is often reluctant to
answer any questions until after he has had the opportunity of explaining himself to the interviewer.

Minority applicants tend to be highly sensitive toward certain
interview questions touching on personal life. The fact is that traditional justifications for many of the presumably routine questions have
been weakened by valid challenges both from within and outside the
personnel field. Minorities want to know what ownership of a house
or a car—standard application form questions—has to do with a
worker's ability. Credit standing is a particularly sore point with many
minority applicants. The relevance (if any) of such questions is not
always easy to explain and the prejudicial quality is often keenly felt.
Thus a young mother who is asked about her use of "Miss" on her
application is not easily convinced that the company is concerned
with how the child is looked after, indebtedness, or other related matters, not in subjecting her to moral judgments.

When questions of this nature must be asked it is up to the interviewer to educate the applicant to understand the need for them.

This requires more than lucidity and reason; it requires rapport.

Employment interviewers must also analyze most carefully school records of grades. Employers are finding that school grades are not reliable predictors of job success or failure where whites are concerned. They are equally bad predictors where minorities are concerned. Similarly, preemployment testing of minorities often fails to produce results comparable to test results of white applicants. This is due in part to poor educational experiences and to the hostile or defeatist attitude with which the applicant regards the test. But an important extenuating circumstance is the fact that test standardization has seldom been done with a significant sample from the minority population. (See Chapter 9.)

Every interview is an occasion for the interviewer to give the applicant information about the company, its products, services, and benefits to help him in judging the company as a place in which to work. But such information is helpful only if the applicant can relate it to himself. If he cannot, the information is meaningless. Where the minority applicant is concerned, the interviewer must explain why he wants the applicant to know these things and of what use such information will be to him. Unless this is done, such information is just another way of telling the black applicant how nice things are in the white world.

8

Campus Recruitment

Nowhere have traditional interviewing techniques undergone more dramatic change than on the college campus. The changing intellectual climate has forced college recruiters to modify the well-established structured approach. Their success has created a mild revolution in the field of employment interviewing. Long-standing theories and methods are being critically reevaluated and a number of sacred cows have been banished or at least are regarded with growing suspicion.

Changing Trends on Campus

Recruiters can no longer afford to create the impression that they take their presence on campus for granted or that they consider themselves a boon to the college or to the student. A recruiter for a well-known tobacco company can no longer concern himself with whether a student smokes his company's product or doesn't smoke at all. Informality is the rule. The best atmosphere is one that is comfortable and familiar to the student. A shirt-sleeve chat on a campus bench or an old-fashioned bull session at a fraternity house may soften student antibusiness attitudes far more effectively than the more formal and stilted approach traditionally associated with campus recruiting.

Most university and college placement directors attempt to exert some influence on the student applicant's attire. Some even rigidly enforce dress codes. However, the campus recruiter who scurries to the director in rage and indignation at the sight of long hair, love beads, sandals, and even beards is out of touch with reality. Such "in" appearance may not get a student past the recruiter and into the company's employment office, but it should not deny him an interview. If this signifies a startling departure from traditional recruitment standards, it is nonetheless a fact of life. Actually the recruiter should bring up the subject of dress when he feels that the applicant holds some promise, but this must wait until a fairly advanced stage in the interview. Initially a certain degree of bizarreness should be accepted.

Most students are alienated by elaborate wining and dining, by the use of representatives who are also alumni (part of the company's unofficial campus recruitment mothball fleet, dredged up when pressure is needed in the form of the old college spirit), and by any maneuver the student considers false or insincere.

Today, the well-equipped campus recruiter goes into the field with a superhoned but well-concealed team of specialists behind him. He is provided with printed information of a high order, which neither smacks of Madison Avenue nor glosses over areas of sensitivity to students. Besides being knowledgeable about every aspect of his company's products, markets, and policies, he is fully prepared to discuss special issues if he must. He knows what to say about his company's involvement in community-oriented affairs, and he can speak with clarity on any subject from Mao to McLuhan. He is prepared to face the student who has no interest in a business career but who makes appointments with recruiters for no other reason than to express his feelings about the American business community.

The modern campus recruiter has learned not to attempt to speak in the student vernacular but to understand it and respond to it with aplomb. He knows every interviewing technique in the book and quite probably has developed a few of his own. He is highly discriminating in his use of techniques, knowing that formulas are not always successful with the up-tight generation unless applied with considerable skill. He knows when and how to approach such matters as grades, extracurricular activities, career objectives, and preemployment test profiles, which many students consider little more than establishment hang-ups, and still maintain rapport. His interviewing, therefore, is guided as much by industrial psychology as it is by standard corporate recruitment methodology. Indeed, if business ever produced a man for all seasons, it is the successful college recruiter of the 1970s.

Problems in Meeting Recruitment Objectives

Today's graduates are the product of a generation that—as many have observed—is the most communicated with in history. This may account for their overall superiority to their predecessors in aptitude for certain types of problem solving, especially their demonstrated ability to handle complex or "categorically ambiguous" problems. It is not surprising that top-level management considers them the smartest, best-prepared, and most intellectually sophisticated body of young people ever to confront American business.

The college graduate is well prepared and business has a critical need for him. Yet all is not well. College men in sales work showed a 50 percent turnover within three and one-half years of employment.[1] In other occupations the turnover norm for college graduates seems to be about 50 percent after only a few years of employment.[2] In the words of a behavioral scientist, "The turnover of these young people is probably the prime managerial personnel problem."[3]

Not all studies bear out this assessment of the turnover factor. But in the matter of recruitment there seems to be little disagreement. A survey of 180 manufacturing company executives by the National Industrial Conference Board revealed that two out of five companies were unable to fill the job vacancies slated for college recruits.[4] Some firms experienced such difficulty in attracting college recruits that they stopped campus recruiting completely, preferring instead to catch the graduates they needed on the rebound from other employers. Forty percent of the companies surveyed failed to achieve their recruitment goals and the remaining 60 percent had considerable difficulty in doing so. Among the reasons given by the companies were the inability to meet salary demands, the high number of students either planning to attend graduate school immediately or seeking employers located near graduate schools, the draft, dissatisfaction on

[1] A. E. Pearson, "Sales Power Through Planned Careers," *Harvard Business Review*, Vol. 44, No. 1, January–February 1966, p. 105.
[2] E. E. Schien, "How to Break in the College Graduate," *Harvard Business Review*, Vol. 42, No. 6, November–December 1964, p. 68. Also A. L. Kyte, "Personnel Administration Revisited—In One Company," *Management Record*, Vol. 23, No. 10, October 1961, p. 7.
[3] T. H. Patten, Jr., "The College Graduate Trainee: Behavioral Science Perspectives on Management's Prime Personnel Problem," *Personnel Journal*, August 1969, p. 581.
[4] S. Habbe and J. K. Brown, "College Graduates and Business," *The Conference Board Record*, The National Industrial Conference Board Record, February 1968, p. 51.

the score of size (usually the company was too small), and lack of interest in the company, its products and services.[5]

A certain amount of discontent is inevitable in the transition from the university to the business world. Despite all his training and his high level of intellectual discipline, the college graduate learns quickly that most entry-level positions mean a prolonged period of super apprenticeship. In the words of an industrial psychologist, "There still exists a considerable measure of mutual suspicion between the graduate and management. After having spent four years at a university, studying a particular discipline—developing his power of analysis and his eye for the evidence—the modern graduate is unattracted by industry which appears to make no little immediate use of his expertise." [6] Many companies spend considerable amounts for recruitment, relocation, and various incidentals to hiring and then place the college graduate in a routine office or factory job where the emphasis is on form rather than on content. This, even though well-organized education can supplant experience to a considerable degree.

Student Unrest, Protest, and Social Conscience

The traditional problems of absorbing graduates into business are complicated by the current revolution in the thinking and mores of college students. In recent years an intense social consciousness has emerged and has found expression in protest against many of the institutions of modern society. Hand in hand with this idealism has gone a rejection of certain key norms of appearance and behavior.

As a mainstay of the American way of life, business has naturally been a prime target of student protest. Once the ideal of aspiring youth, business awoke to its horror to find itself the object of antipathy. Well-known firms, long respected on campus, have been boycotted by students, and their representatives demonstrated against. What has been called the "business-is-for-the-birds syndrome" is the main challenge American industry must face in recruiting college graduates today.

The recruiter can no longer rely on the traditional formula devices for identifying the potentially strong recruit. The old guideposts have disappeared. The red carpet treatment accorded college recruiters by students in years past is mostly a memory. Students want to talk with college recruiters but not in the same context they once did. They

[5] Ibid., p. 48.
[6] J. Kelly, *Organizational Behavior* (Homewood, Ill.: Richard D. Irwin, Inc., and The Dorsey Press, 1969).

challenge where once they acquiesced: "Where does your company stand on EEO?"; "What are you doing about pollution?"; "How many government contracts does your company have for making war materials and how many do you plan to keep?"; "What does your company do to help train impoverished or hard-core unemployed?" Students show as much concern with these questions as they do with their own development and career goals. And these are the questions that recruiters must be prepared to answer, factually and simply.

Behavioral Approach to Campus Recruiting

From this brief review of the apparently conflicting worlds of business and the college recruit, it can be seen, even without analyzing all the causative factors, that the behavioral approach to the problem of college recruitment is probably the best. Without it, recruiting is a hit-or-miss affair with no possibility of qualitative measurement—even the grossest and most imprecise—of success or failure. Until businessmen make an effort to understand the attitudes and basic behavioral patterns of businessmen *and* college graduates and until they become more aware of the psychological needs these attitudes serve, they cannot hope to gauge the effect of the methods they use. Only then will it be possible to "refreeze" the college recruit; that is, integrate attitude changes into the total personality—in effect, meaningful internalized change as opposed to the more superficial cognitive adjustments.

Now that we have outlined the perimeters of the problem, let us examine some of the more critical behavioral mechanisms involved.

Identity Needs of College Students

There is a widespread belief that all college students are members of an invisible universal cult with all-embracing monolithic ideals. College recruiters are not immune to this false idea although consciously they think in rationalistic rather than in superstitious terms. Obviously, campus youth is a highly diversified collection of people. If they have, indeed, a common need, it is for some degree of self-identification that will enable them to valuate their environment in a more personalized (involved) way. This need, of course, has been in the process of manifesting itself since early adolescence.

At least a nodding acquaintance with the theory of the value-expressive function of attitudes is indispensable to the understanding of the attitudinal forces that propel so many college students into seemingly irreversible and unalterable behavioral paths. According to the theory we gain gratification from making known those attitudes that we cherish or those that are central to our self-concepts. We may have no other purpose than that of standing up and being counted, of identifying ourselves by our association with a concept or idea. The establishment of this identity reinforces the self-image and lays down a blueprint or pattern against which we can further develop. The young adult who rejects subordination to his elders and expresses this rejection in a kind of ostentatious declaration of independence in regard to dress, speech, and life style is demonstrating the mechanism of value expression. This behavior is typical of certain stages in the process of maturation, characterized by the search for self-definition (self-image).

In childhood, authority figures, such as parents, teachers, or preachers, seem to categorize all human beings as either good or bad. TV and the movies support this dichotomy. Consequently the maturing child becomes character-conscious. Yet, though he is continually striving for acceptance by authority groups, he must also build a satisfactory self-image. One of the measures of his success is how well he manages to reconcile these two pressures. The process of compromise requires that, when the authority figures are in dissonance with the self-image, that image (and with it, certain values) be altered. When he is more mature, however, the person may reject this accommodation and express attitudes more in keeping with his own preferences.

Career Orientation and Expectations

The very fact that an interview takes place indicates that the student has done some thinking about his future. His objectives are likely to be short range and specific and (unless he is one of a small minority who enter college with a generalized idea of their career preference) were probably not formulated until his junior or even senior year. Generally, specific job objectives emerge as the student begins to think about postgraduate employment. The longer-range career objectives, when they exist at all, are usually of the haziest sort.

It has been pointed out that college postpones the requirement to make a decision. If students take full advantage of this period of grace before deciding to enter business, it is partly because of the difficulty of forming a picture of career life styles and of the business world in general. The student brings with him to college a certain set: ideas, concepts, attitudes, or expectations, all formed from second-hand observation. He may have relatives and friends who held jobs at various levels in the business hierarchy. He has probably read fictionalized versions of business life and has seen motion pictures and television dramas depicting the world of industry and big business. He is familiar with all the stereotypes: the ruthlessly ambitious climber; the bungling, well-meaning secretary; the benevolent despot. But rarely as a student does he have a chance for direct, meaningful observation.

As the student clarifies his ideas of the kind of job he wants, he becomes more specific about what he expects from an employer, focusing on training and developmental opportunities that can potentiate his education as well as on salary. Very likely he hopes to be assigned to a specific functional area in the early stages of his training, in the conviction that such experiences will eventually lead to the kind of management positions he is seeking. For him, however, the word "eventually" is internalized to mean "quickly."

A student who is committed, who has specific job and career objectives tends to be less patient with long-range trainee and internship programs than a student whose career path remains undefined. The latter has few expectations about employers and employment; he is more likely to be impressed by the way in which the recruiter presents the facts than by the facts themselves. For example, he may fail to appreciate an exceptionally well developed internship program or liberal promotion policies, not because he is insufficiently bright to recognize their merits (he does so in a generalized way), but because he cannot relate to them.

Student Alienation

A recruiter who approaches every college student in the same way, without first determining his attitudes and career objectives, runs the risk of boring or alienating him. There is little advantage in holding out the promise of training and development and tuition refund programs, liberal promotional opportunities, salary advancement, stock options, and the like to a student who finds such incentives repugnant.

Unfortunately, the expectations of many students regarding business hierarchies, personal relationships, and the role they will play reflect their experiences in the intellectually freer academic environment. They anticipate "meaningful" personal relationships with all levels of the organizational hierarchy and see their role as being anything but limited. They expect an organization that resembles an open community instead of a rigid bureaucracy. They anticipate the freedom to challenge the ideas of their superiors as well as what they are taught in formal training, orientation, and development programs. Many companies are not ready to regard this kind of behavior as anything other than deviance or inability or unwillingness to assume the proper role in the organization. They counter with an unflinching, "That's the way we do things around here; you can't argue with success," expressive of an attitude for which the graduate is almost always unprepared.

The graduating college senior who has a clearly defined job or career objective, who feels he knows where he wants to go and is impatient to get there presents a very special kind of problem for the recruiter. When expectation levels are this high, alienation occurs readily. The student whose goals orientation is not reinforced by the recruiter, or who encounters unacceptable alternatives with no room for modification or mediation, may simply turn off. The risk is very great when the recruiter is unaware of this or is unable to read the overt signs so that he can backtrack, modify his approach, or present the facts in a different perspective before the turnoff point is reached. The turnoff, of course, is a frustration response to the recruiter or to what he seems to represent—a dead end insofar as the student's aspirations and expectations are concerned. Once an applicant is alienated, the process of winning him back can be arduous.

The interesting fact is that the alienation syndrome typically does not occur during an initial meeting. These initial meetings tend to be brief and almost wholly social. However, during subsequent meetings, when the conversation begins to penetrate beneath the surface, frustration can develop as the recruiter reveals more and more that is distasteful to the student or clashes with his goals. The alienated student tends to become inflexible. He does not respond at all to either reward ("Come with us and your future is assured") or challenge ("We want bright, innovative people but we have no room for deadwood"). As a consequence, the student's responses do not—and this is a key clue—build up toward making a favorable impression. Instead, each response, verbal or manneristic, is complete in itself. The cumulative effect of such responses leads nowhere beyond the student's expression of frustration. The student responds at will rather than with deliberation. He may show signs of aggression (although rarely does this reach the overt stage) or he may attempt to rationalize, defending his goals in terms of the values of his age group. Appeals to the peer group are common in such situations. To emphasize the identification, the student may use the first person plural instead of the singular whenever he expresses such supposedly shared values.

Other reactions of thwarted students include—

Reaction formation. The student seems to capitulate entirely, supporting the recruiter's position and disavowing his stated goals as vigorously as he maintained them earlier.

Withdrawal. The student seeks a job, generally far beneath his potential, on his own.

Nonadjustive reaction—fixity. The student persists in irrelevant and unproductive dogmas and refuses to be shown any alternatives. The recruiter should not exclude the possibility that his own presentation is at least partially to blame.

Adjustive reactions. Apathy and resignation: Responses are routine and uninspired, verging sometimes on the mechanical. This behavior is most often found in students whose work experience or social contacts with persons in business are limited or nonexistent. Compensation: The student intensifies his efforts to find a position on his terms, without modifying the attitude or the approach that has been responsible for his repeated failure to do so. Compensation is similar to fixity except that in compensation some factor of intensification is always present.

Conversion. Various pretexts are found for discontinuing the interviews. Physical symptoms are much in favor. The ailment may seem real enough, but actually it is a psychosomatic product of the desire to escape the appointment.

New Approaches to Loyalty

The indifference of students to the idea of loyalty is of growing concern to many interviewers. Usually the interviewer responds at first with bewilderment and then exercises his own form of adjustive behavior by rationalizing that nonloyalty is after all not disloyalty and that such behavior is part of the game. Loyalty is, in fact, a matter of attitude. Typically, college recruits do not express anything akin to what traditionally has been meant by loyalty. Students think of a trainee position as contributing to their careers. They reason that experience will probably make them more valuable, but that they will undoubtedly not receive the salary commensurate with this increased worth until they change employers. In other words many recruits will value their trainee experiences more from the standpoint of future jobs than of their present job. The recruiter should make it his responsibility to counter this attitude. As realistically as possible he should outline what an entry-level position with the company can mean to the trainee and to the company now and in the immediate future.

The acceptance or rejection by students of company offers can hinge on these matters of loyalty, longevity, and subsequent utilization by the employer. A student attracted to a company by the possibilities for growth that it offers is more likely to identify with those possibilities than with the company itself.

Graduates feel mistrustful when a recruiter is unwilling or unable to outline specifically what will be required of them as trainees. They want early opportunities for development, and this means challenging work assignments. And they want to be able to put their education to use. An employee who has applicable educational experience that his employer is not taking advantage of feels wasted. He may consider that he made a mistake in selecting either his major or his employer. This attitude is not conducive to high morale or feelings of loyalty. The value that a business organization places on educational qualifications can significantly affect the value that the recruit attaches to them. When job placement and promotion are tied to education the effect is to induce many recruits to continue their studies while working.

Selection Criteria

There are two other vital considerations in college recruiting: recruitment selection and the adjustment problem of the newly hired graduate. In evaluating management applicants with previous significant work experiences, it is normal procedure to rely heavily on work history and to project the evaluation to the job vacancy in question. Although this approach is at times invalid, a methodology has nonetheless been formalized with procedures developed to accumulate data. The danger lies in applying it to college recruits, who are sometimes subjected to the same standard tests, interviews, and reference checking (usually directed to former teachers and professors) as experienced applicants.

Evaluating an applicant with a proven work history and evaluating an unproven college recruit are totally different exercises. In the case of the experienced manager, selection is based on history and on the projection of conclusions about that history into the future. In the case of college recruits, selection is based on academic records, which do not wholly support any such projection.

The recruit may fail because he is either educationally, occupationally, or emotionally unprepared for a management role or because the company is not better prepared to properly evaluate his potential and create appropriate (personalized) developmental opportunities to help insure success. Yet there is at present no infallible way to identify management potential in advance. Recruiters and employment specialists are compelled to base their estimates of potential on the extent to which the applicant seems to possess the elements or characteristics required by the particular management position. Recruiters attempting to fill lower-level management positions usually stress the need for technical or specialized, easily evaluated job skills that can produce immediate short-term results (return on recruitment and orientation investment). Recruiters attempting to fill higher-level management positions stress skills that are more difficult to measure, emphasizing background experiences and exposure to training and development activities. This conflict is resolved only by establishing objectives for management recruitment and deciding on the kind of applicant, college recruit, or experienced manager the company needs and can accommodate.

Certainly, many predictors of success or failure are illusive; college students have long been critical of business because of its love affair with the freakish grade curve. Yet business is learning that grades alone are not predictive of success or failure on the job in terms of either adjustment to peers and supervisors or of operational productivity. Business is also learning that the best recruits are not always tall and handsome. In a study of the recruiting practices affecting 211 business school seniors it was found that handsomeness was the one criterion of selection always present and was the strongest, most consistent attribute of the recruits. But analysis revealed that extracurricular activities, although not held significant by recruiters, seemed along with grades to be more predictive of success than handsomeness.

The recruiter who stresses security, for example, by outlining career path development as though there were few if any contingencies or by suggesting that the student need only hitch his wagon to the corporate star and hang on, is sowing the seeds of discontent from the very beginning. Worse still, this type of emphasis tends to attract the failure avoider, who is willing to be carried along on the waves of fate, and to discourage the achievement seeker, who is prepared to take a certain amount of risk and to face challenges.

Adjusting to the Role of Worker

The disillusionment that is evident in college recruits before hiring is sometimes very slow to dissipate after it. There are sharp discontinuities between the academic and work environments, which can make the transition between the two extremely trying. The graduate must learn new rules and modify or drastically revise certain ideas and expectations. For example, there is the matter of feedback. From the time he entered kindergarten until the time he graduated from college the graduate trainee was able to measure his progress according to carefully planned calendar periods: quarters, semesters, and terms. He began an educational experience on a given date and finished it on a given date, at which time he received the all-important performance feedback, in the form of a report card. The feedback was always on time, was related exactly to task completion, was part of a known and understood system of performance and tests, and carried with it the clear understanding that a passing grade or grades meant advancement to the next grade.

One need hardly attempt a comparison with appraisal methods used in business. The systems of measurement are often obscure and not easy to relate to specific performance factors. If there is any feedback at all, it is irregular. Rewards commonly have only the barest relation to a formal appraisal system; undue selectivity may be exercised in granting them, with certain aspects of performance unaccountably neglected. In addition, business displays a marked preference for nonspecific rewards usually taking the form of broader recognition by supervisory management. Inclusion on special mailing lists, participation in meetings and conferences, and increased on-the-job social contacts with persons of higher rank are examples.

A particularly jolting dicontinuity is felt in the area of training and development. In the academic world, teachers, instructors, professors, and administrators concentrate all their energies in this direction. In business, the focus is not exclusively on training and development. The trainee has a job to perform *in addition* to his learning responsibilities. He does and he learns as often as he learns and does. In fact he is not expected to confine his learning experience to the classroom or formal training session, because these cannot substitute for firsthand observation and practical experience.

Though in some ways the counterpart of a professor, the supervisor is somewhat more aloof because he is concerned with a broader spectrum of activities and his leadership role is more pronounced. Typically, he avoids intellectual equality with an employee. The college recruit cannot opt for a supervisor with whom he feels he will be compatible as he formerly selected professors and courses of study. And he most certainly cannot select a training experience because he decides it will be less rigorous than others or more to his liking. In the business environment he lacks many of the prerogatives that he enjoyed in the spacious halls of academe.

Commitment Versus Adjustment

The graduate trainee's job is usually narrow in scope and insufficient to support his former self-concept. From a highly sought after, analytical, culturally aware, and clearly identifiable person he may diminish in his own estimation to a supertechnical, lower-level specialist. Some graduates in trainee jobs resign. Others remain, achieving perhaps what has been termed situational adjustment, the internalization of relevant norms and the acquisition of new, more acceptable roles through a succession of on-the-job or job-related learning experiences. For a few intensely committed individuals, situational adjustment is unnecessary. This type of employee refuses to change his career goals and will persevere in any job that furthers these goals, even though another job might better satisfy his needs. Obviously, this loyalty to a long-range commitment requires a high degree of stability and fixity of purpose.

Neither the committed nor the situationally adjustive individual is necessarily neurotic or otherwise disoriented. In fact, the organization that accommodates both benefits in the long run. Keep in mind that, while we have discussed commitment and situational adjustment as if each represented wholly opposing psychological configurations, degrees of both can be present in any person at different times, although one or the other is dominant.

Black Students on Campus

Where black graduates are concerned recruiters face special problems. There was a time when black students could be ignored. They were few in number and effective civil rights legislation was nonexistent. Most blacks knew not to sign up for interviews and most companies did not encourage them to do so. In fact, most recruiters did not bother to visit black colleges. How and why these conditions changed is the history of the 1960s and beyond the scope of this writing. We are concerned with the fact of the change. Today, the black graduating college senior has become a precious commodity to many corporations, a fact of which many black students are aware. Nonetheless, despite more effective social legislation, the power of government contracts, mass demonstrations, consumer boycotts, and progressively more enlightened public opinion, all the walls of discrimination have not come tumbling down. The American black has won official legislative equality; he now demands equality *in fact.*

The quality of recruitment where black students are concerned remains weak in terms of long-range effectiveness and relevance to the needs of blacks. For the college recruiter, the problem is twofold. First, there is the need to understand the psychological mechanism of black student reaction to white-dominated industry. Second, there is the need to face up to the realities of employment in general and corporate life in particular where blacks are concerned.

The black student has come a long way from the childlike state of social development that stereotyped him for so many years. One sign of this is the virtual disappearance of all evidences of identification reaction from his overt behavior. Identification reaction is the feeling that one can strengthen his social worth and elevate his status by sharing or adopting the values and styles of another person or group. This mechanism may be highly internalized or may only be a facade, contributing to shallow, cognitive behavior, which helps disguise personal differences. Although few verbalize it, many campus recruiters still expect to encounter identification reaction in the black student and, when they fail to do so, their entire recruitment pitch collapses.

Analysis of Conflict

Many college recruiters have been stunned by the rebuffs they received from black college students. They reeled in wonderment that their overworked black-and-white-forgive-and-forget approach was rebuked. They discovered the hard facts of aggressive projection. If whites had blocked black progress for so long, blacks could thwart white efforts at recruitment. This was not intended as a vindictive little game. It was and is the outcome of black selectivity, a refusal ever again to be sold short. Blacks in effect are fighting for an equal opportunity *to fail.* They reject paternalistic employment offers. And they reject ultra-liberal permissiveness, blind acceptance of all things black, and oversolicitousness. To the black these are new prejudices more injurious to his cause today than naked hatred. "What do they want now?" is the oft-heard lament of college recruiters whose "you've got it made" approach fell flat. The only answer possible is an equal chance to succeed and to fail.

College recruiters must understand what may after sufficient research emerge as the most useful explanation of the psychological relationship between the recruiter and the black student—Schelling's basic theory, which demonstrates the conflict and mutual interest between game opponents.[7] Let us assume that the role of recruiter is played by the white and the role of college recruit by a black. If recruitment were performed in a discriminatory or prejudicial way, a zero-sum game evolves; that is, whatever one player wins, his opponent loses. Recruitment in a nondiscriminatory setting results in a game that is non-zero-sum. It is carried on as a bargaining process in which neither party can afford to annihilate the other.

For an illustration, consider an airplane trying to bomb a truck. As the plane gets closer to the weaving vehicle it suddenly becomes impossible for it to drop the bomb without endangering itself. The bomb is not dropped. The contest of nations to see which can build the more destructive superbomb is another example. A superbomb becomes useless if the radiation fallout endangers the user as well as the foe.

To conform to the pure bargaining game the interview should be conducted with a very minimum of negotiation. Communication regarding social status or the social condition of work should also be kept to a minimum. Except for the basics of salary, benefits, and the other hygiene factors, developmental advantages may be introduced, but not in a negotiative manner (because negotiations on this point would be zero-sum). There is no need for tolerant attitudes. These might be appropriate in a zero-sum game, where the recruiter might wish to soften the harshness of the operating principle. But in a non-zero-sum game such attitudes may confuse the issue and give the applicant the wrong impression.

In the white–black interview the moves of the participants are often strongly influenced by other forces such as the Congress, stockholders, masses of black people, and public opinion. The fluidity of the situation mediates. What the student does in relation to accepting a job offer, how he reacts to a recruiter, how he views a company,

[7] T. C. Schelling, *Strategy of Conflict* (Cambridge, Mass., Harvard University Press, 1966).

and his subsequent behavior either as a consumer, a recruit, or an employee are all subject to the moves the recruiter may make. In the view of the black student whether or not he reaches his objectives depends on the moves of the recruiter, the policies of the company he represents, or even on the image of the company or industry as the black student perceives these. In the view of the recruiter the moves of the black have a small but definite bearing on whether he achieves his recruitment objectives and his company maintains a government contract, avoids a black consumer boycott and bad publicity, and keeps the goodwill of all its markets. The same premise governs both parties with each facing different but equally compelling consequences and alternatives.

Campus Recruiters and the Credibility Gap

The recruiter should not deliberately raise questions of race relations or politics. To do so is likely to be considered intrusive. If the recruiter thinks he is demonstrating his concern for the feelings of the applicant, he is deceiving himself. And, if he is only feigning interest, most black students will see through the sham.

At the same time, the interviewer should not attempt to hide or soften the realities of corporate life where blacks are concerned. In any organizational milieu, some degree of interpersonal conflict is inevitable. It is obvious that the mere presence of blacks and whites competing in a corporate milieu could, conceivably, foster a certain amount of conflict. Insecurity, unclear social relationships, ill-defined hierarchical authority, defensive personalities, frustration, negative attitudes, and inner conflict all potentiate and aggravate prejudice. Blacks instinctively understand this situation and, if the recruiter is less than candid about it, he risks losing the student's confidence. At the same time the recruiter must not in any circumstances suggest that the black employee will receive any favoritism. The black student must understand that the company would demand of him the very best he can do. Any other policy is discrimination in a highly injurious form.

Fundamentally the black student is looking for credibility. He is fully aware of the bitter job-hunting experiences of his family and friends. He knows that the statement of equal employment opportunity in the help wanted ads is no guarantee against the polite brush-off, the extended delay, or the humiliating round of indecisive interviews.

A black student may feel pangs of guilt about his interest in the job. He may question whether entry into corporate life is justified from the point of view of social responsibility and self-fulfillment. Social consciousness is not the sole property of black students, and the college student's uncertainties about business are shared by black and white alike. But these feelings are generally more pronounced among black than among white students.

Another factor is that corporate life is not a part of the black experience in America. There are few black capitalists with whom a black student can identify. One study of black capitalism suggests that what is needed is a contingent of knowledgeable men able to explain the principles of capitalism to the uninitiated and to assist them to become practitioners.[8] There is no reason why this process cannot begin during the interview.

Today's college graduates are not wholly confident about the future. Many are interested of course in salary potential and the chance to get ahead. But the importance of these goals should not be over-emphasized. Graduates accord equal rank to such factors as stimulating work, compatible work associates, opportunity to be creative, and leisure time. It is symptomatic of the prevailing attitudes of college people toward business that the vast majority of graduates are not interested in a chance to become the chief executive of a company. Graduates seem to be concerned about the risks, pressures, competition, and uncertainty of executive life.

[8] L. L. Allen, "Making Capitalism Work in the Ghetto," *Harvard Business Review*, May–June 1969, pp. 83–92.

9

Testing and Conjunctive Interviewing

O<small>NE OF THE MOST</small> controversial subjects in the field of personnel is testing. Business executives and personnel people seem either to embrace testing with wild-eyed enthusiasm or to have little or nothing to do with it. If testing is vulnerable to criticism it is not because the principle is unsound but because the practice is subject to certain abuses. Among these are unqualified application, particularly making test results the sole determinant of decision; administration and score analysis by inexperienced or ill-trained persons; and use of tests as screening tools in connection with jobs or companies for which they are not valid. Unquestionably tests must be selected with considerable discrimination and with a clear advance conception of what they should accomplish. Otherwise serious problems arise.

A test is simply a way of measuring behavior. It tells us something about a person. That something may be past or present and may be susceptible to projection into the future. The major caution is that, no matter how accurate the measurements, test results are worthwhile only in relation to a standard. Another caution is that a test result is no more a person's *ability* than the temperature reading of a sick person is itself the *disease*.

There are certain practical considerations that every employment interviewer must recognize if he is to properly integrate the interview with the testing procedure. Testing can never be justified as a substitute for interview analysis or the subsequent "torment of decision" that ensues. Second, testing and the combination of testing and interviewing, which we call conjunctive interviewing, are not a substitute for on-the-job motivation, job enrichment opportunities, effective and enlightened management leadership, and training. But testing can help introduce into the organization personnel who will be responsive to these elements in the work milieu.

Testing is only justified if the personnel department is willing to reject unqualified applicants in a tight labor market. When scarcities in the labor market compel the hiring of almost anyone who applies, there is no point whatever in testing. Testing is, after all, a screening method.

While it is possible to administer a test that measures many factors, the most effective tests are those that do not attempt too much at one time. For example, it is better to use a test that concentrates on one aspect of the personality than to administer a general personality test. Separate tests for typing, shorthand, and numerical aptitude, when their results are combined, give a clearer indication of ability than a general clerical test.

Selection Tests

Personality, aptitude, achievement, and performance tests are grouped under the heading of selection tests. These tests not only help in placement; they also are valuable in formulating prerequisites for employment and subsequent success on the job. Selection tests are savers of time and money.

Most tests should be administered after an in-depth interview. Common practice makes an exception for general knowledge, aptitude, and job interest tests, in an effort to screen out the obviously undesirable applicant. Heavier testing, however, should be postponed until the interviewer has determined specific testing needs. Standard test procedures are terribly limiting to the interviewer and may not be responsive to individual applicant needs. Once an in-depth interview has been completed, a specifically designed testing format can help redirect the interviewer or clarify areas about which he was uncertain.

The first responsibility of the interviewer is to make certain that the proper tests have been administered. A personality test does not give results about performance in a job specialty; achievement tests do not help very much in determining aptitudes. General educational achievement tests enable personnel people to confirm that the educational attainment level indicated on the application was in fact achieved. Proficiency tests do the same for the skills indicated on the application.

Once the interviewer is satisfied that the appropriate tests have been selected, he must then make sure that each test used has validity; that is, that it measures what it is supposed to measure. Content validity refers to the fact that the items that constitute the test logically support the purpose for which the test is used. Predictive validity refers to the ability of the test to predict future performance. The number of variables on a job is such that the validity, in order to be realistic, must be spoken of in terms of possible or acceptable limits or even ranges. The interviewer who looks for pinpoint predictability is deceiving himself and making claims to knowledge that cannot exist, at least at our present level of psychological theory.

Even though the most appropriate and valid tests have been selected, the interviewer must still be certain that the tests are both reliable—that is, consistent or accurate in their measurements and objectives—and constructed in such a way that more than one person can score them and get the same results independently. An interviewer who uses tests that are not reliable or objective is no better off than a carpenter who depends on an elastic yardstick. From the standardization information furnished by the test publishers it is possible to learn whether the test has been administered to enough people, in controlled or uniform circumstances, to establish norms or standards.

Adaptive Testing

The interviewer must make a decision regarding whether, in his best judgment, adaptive or consecutive testing will produce the best results. With adaptive testing the tests are selected in keeping with the specific information requirements of the interviewer, the applicant's educational and occupational background, and his emotional state. The administration of adaptive tests and even the sequence—difficult-to-easy or easy-to-difficult—is suited specifically to the applicant's personality, his work methods and habits, and his special capacities, to the extent that these are known to the interviewer. This is one of the reasons that, except for superficial, gross, preinterview testing, major test administration should be deferred until after an in-depth interview.

The term "adaptive testing" is also applied to the technique of varying the test so as to require adaptation to new and uncertain circumstances in the midst of stress. Marked changes in behavior that occur in response to an adaptation requirement could be an indication of psychological illness. While the interviewer is not expected to be an expert on the subject, he should at least recognize certain warning signs. Such basic instructions as "Omit questions 1 to 10," "Answer only the questions on the last page," or, "Complete only those questions in this test booklet that seem to you to have pertinence on the job for which you are applying" are examples of adaptation. Alternating the sequence of test questions and changing the timing are other ways of challenging a person's capacity for adaptation as well as the strength of his drives, his maturity, and his intelligence.

Adaptive testing is controversial. Its proponents argue that, because people are different, tests must be adapted to the differences. Its opponents cannot accept the changes in the difficulty and general conditions of the test, although it has been pointed out that with a given test battery the interviewer will more likely than not adapt the test in about the same way.

In all testing caution is essential. The interviewer cannot assume that the applicant with the highest test scores is necessarily the right man for the job. And by the same token a low test score does not necessarily mean that an applicant is unhirable. Hiring must be based on other supportive analysis, primarily the interview, which is itself a kind of a test. Therefore to hire in the face of low test scores does not necessarily contradict the testing principle.

Intelligence Testing

The difficulties that surround the measurement of intelligence are worth investigating if only to bring out the dangers of uncritical application of testing. There is considerable lack of agreement as to what "intelligence" means. Intelligence has been defined as the ability to adapt to the environment and to environmental change. Quite different from this biologically oriented definition is the concept that intelligence is the capacity for abstract thought or analysis. According to another major concept intelligence is a function of testing and therefore it is what tests measure. Another, more recent theory holds that intelligence is a developmental process that includes perception, emotional development, and the usable and appropriate assimilation of stimuli from the environment.

In reviewing the scores of an intelligence test, the interviewer should not as a rule accept a score as significant unless he knows the test specifications; that is, the distribution of scores used to validate the test by the test publisher. In any sample of the population, the middle range of intelligence contains the most people, with the high range coming next, and the low intelligence range last. Yet tests can be designed with any standard deviation, which means that depending on what test is used IQ can be significantly different for the same person.

Standard Methods and Uses

It is vitally important, not only with intelligence tests, but also with all other tests of behavior that clearly defined uses, standards, and objectives be established and that the methodology of test administration not vary. There must be consistency of test application, scoring, and interpretation. Furthermore a test cannot be valid unless it is consistent with the actual work situation. And, since work environments, the scope and duties of jobs, and management objectives and leadership styles all change, validation cannot be performed once and then forgotten. In updating validation the critical point is to isolate the on-the-job criteria for success—as defined by the organization in which the work is performed.

It is impossible to even approach an absolute degree of validation and measurability since, for example, production output can vary at different times of the day or at any time during a production period. In addition, the operators against whom validity studies were made might be experienced or still in the learning process. Such factors might significantly affect test score analysis and mislead the interviewer.

It happens quite often that the applicant's results on a vocational proficiency test are low but his references from a former supervisor or foreman are quite good. In the face of this contradiction the interviewer may question either the validity of his tests or the truthfulness of the applicant's former supervisor. Actually the probable explanation is that two different criteria of success have been used. The test represents an objective criterion. Other examples of objective criteria would be productivity in terms of actual units produced, quality control, salary history, promotions, and developmental training for which the applicant qualified. The reference, however, was subjective and judgmental. Thus a comment by a former supervisor, "Bill did not always meet his quotas (or deadlines) but, overall, he tried hard and was a good worker," supplies two subjective criteria conflicting in tendency. Since both are equally valid, the interviewer must determine which he wants for input data.

The tests, if properly validated, will reflect the productive effectiveness of the present workforce. But, if the purpose of interviewing and testing is to help upgrade the manpower resources of the organization, it is not always sufficient merely to meet the norms of performance. They must be surpassed, or standards do not improve. This means that when tests are administered and scored the minimum performance that qualifies for consideration should exceed the norm. This criterion should be carried over into the interview.

From a practical standpoint it is not always possible to reject persons who satisfy the norm of performance or surpass it by a slight margin. Obviously, if numerical test scores were a true measure of the qualities tested it would be comparatively easy to justify rejection for applicants who fell below any arbitrary limit. But true differences between the low and high scorers may be slight and validation techniques, when practiced, are uncertain. Normative test performance can be acceptable, however, if the interview methods are decisive, applicable, and practiced by trained personnel and if testing is validated as accurately as possible.

Intellectual abilities usually rank high among the characteristics desired in managers. A number of important research studies have demonstrated a direct correlation between intellectual factors and managerial success. While it is generally accepted that above-average intelligence potentiates managerial success, there is considerable doubt that the level of effectiveness advances simultaneously with the degree of intellectual superiority. The evidence indicates that, although a certain degree of superiority in a leader is advantageous, when the leader's intellectual level is very much higher than his subordinates', effectiveness suffers.

Judgment

One of the most vital aspects of intelligence is judgment. Judgment is not a simple concept either to define or to isolate by means of testing. Judgment can be measured by certain problems involving discrimination of facts, verbal aptitude, and selection of the most favorable alternative. These testing methods are well adapted to conjunctive use with in-depth interview techniques.

The interviewer calls on the applicant to analyze and comment on circumstances in his personal or occupational background that may have contributed, for example, to success or failure. The interviewer has a threefold purpose. First, he wishes to test an opinion or assumption he has formed about the applicant or, in the absence of his own opinion, wants the applicant to elaborate before arriving at one. So the first order of business is the quest for pertinent insights leading to the definition of the facts. Second, the interviewer is interested in observing the analytical or judgmental processes of the applicant. The applicant will be asked a clear and pertinent question. In his response not only his words but also his facial expression and body movements, such as shuffling of feet or wringing of hands, are carefully noted. How does the applicant express himself? Does he stammer, make false starts, wander, or is he clear, concise, and penetrating? Finally, the interviewer attempts to relate the qualitative aspects of the applicant's judgmental responses with the analysis of the test results. This should include verbal confirmation of test scores and probing with interview techniques that produce problem-solving and alternate-choice requirements similar to those on the test.

Management applicants fall into two broad categories: those with experience, interested in all levels of management, and those without experience, applying for entry-level jobs. The problem with the former is to determine the amount and quality of experience and the likelihood of the effective transfer and reapplication of this experience to a new work situation. While tests for both categories may need to be both evaluative of current skills and predictive, it is not a valid assumption that one test can necessarily be used for both. It may be, but this must be ascertained by careful analysis of the test.

Management-oriented Tests

Tests aimed at the management levels have gained less acceptance than specific job skills tests. Management-oriented psychological tests are woefully lacking in validation. Test schedules for management effectiveness are usually designed to reflect executive management's attitudes about those attributes that are valued in the organization. If, for example, top executive management places value on human relations efforts, people-oriented leadership, or sensitivity to the feelings of others, the tests will be oriented toward such qualities. Yet the interviewer may find that efforts to measure empathy and relate this attribute to managerial effectiveness have not been highly successful. To evaluate empathy with any degree of certainty, the test results must be correlated with those of the interview. Here the technique calls for pursuit paths that elicit responses the interviewer feels will provide the necessary indications. It must be understood that without factual investigation of past job performance this procedure cannot be considered conclusive. It is also necessary for the interviewer to have a conception of the desired empathic qualities. This will most likely be derived from observation of successful managerial employees in the interviewer's company.

Verbal ability is considered important to managerial effectiveness. But although verbal ability tests are available a measurable correlation between the two has yet to be developed. Vocabulary measurement is not enough. The size of a vocabulary has nothing to do with the ability to use it, especially the judgment to adapt it to the understanding of those to whom it is directed. Consider the college graduate working as a shop foreman, who sends a memo to his staff reading: "Consistent with regulatory measures instituted by our management group, and, in the interest of maintaining proper decorum, expectoration in unauthorized areas is frowned upon." What he could have said was: "Don't spit on the floor."

Verbal Ability

The matter of verbal ability cannot be isolated from semantics, personality, and leadership styles. Surely, certain verbal styles and skills may be directly related to effectiveness on the job, particularly where the job is of a technical nature (requiring some form of professional preparation, as opposed to mere practice or assistance of co-workers). But this relationship between verbal ability and technical job know-how is a narrow one, and no reliable correlates have been uncovered. The best that can be assumed is that the ability to write clearly and convincingly and to understand what is read, together with a vocabulary at least comparable to those of subordinates and most superiors, is an important contribution to job effectiveness. This is not to say that the absence or underdevelopment of communication skills will necessarily inhibit effectiveness.

In evaluating verbal skills the employment interviewer has the problem of determining the level in relation to which the applicant must be judged. In the example, the college graduate foreman's verbal skills might be deemed satisfactory for management levels but unsatisfactory for lower levels, beginning with his immediate supervisor.

Job Interest Levels

Regardless of the job category, whether clerical, management, or labor, most organizations require that the applicant be interested in what he does on the job. If this concern is necessary, it is because of management practices that reduce jobs to their lowest common denominator, oversimplify the work, and reduce it to a mechanical procedure void of personal and occupational developmental opportunities. Except for persons with low mental capacity, immaturity, or limited career objectives, interest in such work is difficult to maintain. In measuring an applicant's interests the purpose is to determine what he *will* do rather than, in aptitude tests, what he *can* do. *Will do* is a function of motivation, values, and attitudes. Interest can be a compensating element that strengthens technical know-how or fills the gaps in it, but it can never compensate for lack of a motivating or enriching job content. Of course, this is a personality matter, but it would not be accurate to indicate simply that a personality test is sufficient. For the achieving employee, interest is consistent only with jobs that uphold goal orientation. Testing for interests that will not be reinforced on the job is a meaningless exercise.

Considerable research has demonstrated interest patterns that relate to managerial effectiveness. For example, research shows a similarity between managers in general and successful sales managers, purchasing agents, and top executives in manufacturing. Other evidence indicates that successful managers are interested in politics and economics but not in things esthetic. And other research findings show that successful managers in government appear to have a low level of economic values but quite a high level of theoretical interests and social values.

The interviewer is strongly cautioned against applying these conclusions as stereotypes. Certainly, interests, attitudes, and values are significant among other personality configurations in helping to identify managerial effectiveness. However, it is important to guard against formularized patterns or quick and ready indicators. The interviewer must be aware of changing values and of intrinsic value differences between industries and even geographical areas. It is far more important and relevant to judge interests on the basis of what is known about a company, an industry, and regional influences than to be inflexibly chained to test norms and theoretical patterns.

Measuring Managerial Potential and Attributes

Effective managers are believed to be characterized by confidence, poise, and maturity. As yet the correlation between these attributes and managerial effectiveness is not highly valid. The relationship is simply not capable of reliable measurement; and, although this reflects the unsatisfactory status of technology in human behavior research, it does not negate empirical belief that there is indeed such a relationship. In any case since there are situations in which managers may be deficient in any one of the three attributes, the uncovering of such situations should be the object of tests and of supporting interviews aimed at these attributes.

One of the major problems, if not *the* major problem, in determining the measurable relationship between the many, many personality attributes and skills believed to be linked to successful or effective managers (and workers in general) is the absence of any testing method to determine the influence of the work milieu. It is one thing to develop a list of the significant managerial attributes (somewhat on the order of a Boy Scout credo), but it is quite another to develop a milieu supportive of these attributes and to be able to measure that milieu qualitatively.

In fact it would be possible (but hardly productive) to list every attribute believed to contribute to managerial effectiveness and the test most commonly used to measure it, together with paragraph after paragraph of research studies demonstrating the weak validity or unreliability of the test and strongly cautioning against taking some test results at face value. This by no means argues against testing, nor does it imply that the attributes believed to be significant to managerial effectiveness are as much myth as fact. It does, however, argue against the practice of administering numerous tests, requiring long hours of testing and even longer hours of test scoring and analysis, solely on the assumption that more testing is better testing, and against indiscriminate decision making based primarily on test scores. And it strongly supports the case against employment interview techniques that are wholly influenced by tests and not simply guided by them. The impracticability of testing for significant managerial attributes underscores the need for prudent use of psychological testing and the delicate, cautious handling of test results.

The Applicant as Test Taker

Any test, good or bad, is built on the premise that the applicant knows little about tests, testing theory, and even less about how to take a test. Those who administer tests, particularly personality or subjective types of tests, may know as little. Neither realizes that the ideal type toward which most personality tests are oriented would be either an organism somewhat akin to a walking vegetable or the invention of a liar. The astute test taker can, by analyzing multiple-choice questions, quickly determine what the test is trying to discover and will be able to see through seemingly innocent questions designed to reveal prejudicial traits.

The trouble with this kind of deception, of course, is that it is caused by some test makers who believe that personality can be divided into neat little categories, all psychotic or neurotic in nature. Commonly, in the minds of such designers, a score in the upper 25 percent of the sample qualifies the neurotic as acceptable; a lower score as unacceptable. What is being tested, however, is the applicant's ability to *deal* with test questions rather than his actual personality. The applicant who assumes the mental set of Mr. Mainstreet, USA; who responds to personality test questions in an unimaginative, basically contrived, prosaic, red-white-and-blue apple-pie way, emerges as an employable more times than not. The applicant who indicates on a personality test that he still identifies with his parents is suspect. Applicants who respond pessimistically to sentence-completion tests are in trouble with the test maker's norms. The one who unfurls a potpourri of meaningless but generally revered executive mumbo jumbo—"maximize my potential," "gear for growth," "synergize with co-workers"—delights the test makers.

The applicant who admits to fearing black cats or to constant diarrhea, who considers himself an earthbound extension of a deity, who admits being thrilled by inflicting pain, who loves mom more than his wife may have his own special problems. But for the interviewer the problem is to find out what is *really* wrong with the applicant (the interviewer assumes that he has enough educational background and the right to determine this) and then to decide if in fact the applicant is unemployable.

There are, of course, moral and ethical questions surrounding such probing. Even if judged by the company to be pertinent, is it an invasion of personal privacy and, if so, what confidences must be kept? Some testers consider information highly confidential and share only the final scores with decision makers. Some tell all and others are selective, sharing only the information they feel is pertinent. When one considers the impact test results can have on the career life of a human being, indiscriminate testing and the faulty decision making that can result become almost criminal.

The Value of Tests

The fundamental value of a test depends on many factors. Besides the theoretical, structural, and contextual properties there are many variables—the test administrator, for one. Another area of concern is the relevance of the form of the measurement to the decision being made. In the case of preemployment testing, mathematical symbols are substituted for human action and are representative of human behavior—past, present, and future. These symbols are, of course, theoretical. Their purpose is to fill the gap between hypothesis and practice. Too often, however, decision theory has been concerned with mathematical constructs at the expense of relevant application. An authority on decision theory warns that it places great burdens on the decision maker because every possible state in nature must be numerically evaluated but no human being possesses the ability to evaluate the utility of the various actions in all possible states.

A great many decisions the employment interviewer must make are of the institutional kind. An institutional decision is made up of many smaller decisions that are comparable in terms of impact, determinative criteria, and level of difficulty. These decisions reflect an attitude, and a set of values, that can be applied in a uniform way only by translating them into some standard of measurement.

Attitude and values cannot be varied from one applicant to another. But, in order to differentiate between applicants or between segments of an applicant's occupational experience, some system of classification is necessary. The basic distinction between acceptable or unacceptable in the mind of the interviewer represents a simple classification.

Analyzing Test Results

In mathematical figuration this distinction would be represented by plus or minus. Or the classification may be based on quality. In this case it must take into account other factors, such as circumstances, events, achievements and failures, or behavioral patterns, which offset the defined classification. For example, the ability of an organization to develop potential in an applicant would lessen the overall significance of an "unacceptable" classification.

When tests are used to determine acceptability or unacceptability, they must be administered individually; for example, two aptitude tests, one very specific and one general. Next a general personality test may be given with tests intended to measure specific personality traits. In any case, the results of these series of tests are multivariate, in that they consist of a series of dissimilar components. The employment interviewer, however, cannot formulate a decision on the basis of multivariate data, so he seeks a composite or univariate score. With this approach, a constraint is placed on the decision maker's flexibility. In the employment or selection process there is a maximum number of vacancies and a minimum quality for acceptance. If a univariate score is used to make a decision, the decision must be better than chance or, put another way, there must be an improvement over chance as a result of using tests (multivariate and then univariate test results), or the exercise fails. It has been suggested, however, that chance is not necessarily the alternative to testing. The point is that, while tests support decision making, they do not always produce better decisions. An improved automobile makes driving more comfortable, faster, perhaps safer, but it does not produce better drivers. Thus, it has been contended, when other means in addition to testing are used to make decisions about applicants for employment, the value of tests cannot be judged by comparison with chance selection. Instead the comparison must be with the value of nontest methods. Tests are best judged, therefore, on the basis of what they contribute above and beyond the best available selection methods that make use of knowledge of current employees and the applicant.

As an example, consider typing speed. A typing test becomes a work sample. Such tests usually have high validity because the work itself is actually reproduced. But the typing test could be eliminated if highly accurate past performance ratings were available and could be compared with actual and expected typing production rates of the current staff. On the other hand, tests that deal with leadership, creativity, emotional adjustment, ability to analyze and solve problems, human relations sensitivity, and the like usually have very low validity. However, such tests are useful, the usefulness lying primarily in the way in which their results are applied by the employment interviewer. Psychological tests of this kind can provide greater insight into the applicant than achievement tests because they can identify or warn of the existence of *qualities*. Qualities cannot be measured with pinpoint accuracy, but this is not necessary because the results of qualitative tests are not meant to stand alone. They are to be used in conjunction with other methods and their value lies in the fact that no other method can duplicate them.

The Dangers in Generalizing

The employment interviewer can review past employment history in detail and listen to the applicant's recitation of his achievements and still not isolate how or why these achievements were possible. It may have been that organizational instability, manpower shortages, the inability of the former employer to develop younger managers or to recruit qualified managers from the outside were factors that significantly affected the applicant's upward progression and even made it possible. When the applicant is tested he may reveal few if any of the characteristics associated with such upward mobility. In this case, achievement tests by themselves would not tell the story.

It is important for the employment interviewer to remember that, merely because a particular method enabled him to arrive at a correct decision in one instance, it does not mean that it will produce a correct decision in any other. The interviewer must avoid quantifying or generalizing his decision-making process. Payoff is not the same for all persons; that is, the company does not gain the same benefit from the employment of each applicant. Some will be immediately productive but will have limited future development. Some applicants have little promise from the point of view of the organization's current needs but show prospects of satisfying staffing needs in the future. If the tests and the interview do not corroborate the short- and long-run payoffs reasonably possible in terms of the applicant and desired by the company, a poor job of selection is certain.

The next point is a matter of methodology. The employment interviewer may make a decision about an applicant solely on the basis of his estimate of the applicant's worth, or his decision may be based on a comparison with other applicants. The test theory and the interview technique must be adjusted to satisfy these decision-making methods. For example, if applicants are compared and the best of several is selected, then what one applicant gains must result in a loss for another. A score of 120 on a test by Applicant A must result in the elimination of Applicant B, whose score was 115. And yet there may exist strong indication of acceptable qualities in Applicant B. These may be such that at the score level of 105, he would be worth hiring. More than one test may be used, in which case either applicant may cancel the other endlessly.

On the other hand, if the methodology of the interviewer is sufficiently defined, it may be that in a multivariate situation an applicant may fail to approach an acceptable normative level on a given test and thus be disqualified, provided of course that the interviewer considers the result significant. In many clerical and most technical, accounting, engineering, and skilled job categories, this may be a valid approach if the achievement test is a direct reflection of the work criterion. However, in management positions or in job categories where it is virtually impossible (and at best invalid) to attempt a strict point value for an intangible attribute, the univariate approach is best. An applicant either qualifies or he does not, or he qualifies but is equally qualified when compared with other applicants. The latter situation produces a dilemma for the interviewer. The selection process becomes a contest, but the contest proves inconclusive. The effects on the interviewer, however, are not so easily canceled; he is likely to find himself interviewing Applicant A in terms of Applicant B and vice versa. Applicants are weighed against one another and the result may be not the best applicant for the job but rather the best selection among available applicants. The interviewer has overtested without obtaining sufficient clarity to make a meaningful selection, and in his frustration he selects the applicant without regard for statistical or interviewing method.

Testing Minority Group Applicants

The testing of minority applicants places special responsibilities on test administrators and employment interviewers. Such testing has been a hotly contested issue. Those who oppose it argue that many methods are invalid and uncertain when applied to minority applicants, particularly when test norms typically exclude samples from the minority population, and that tests intentionally or otherwise create additional barriers to minority employment.

Title VII of the Civil Rights Act of 1964 authorizes aptitude testing, the tests to be administered for the purpose of helping determine qualifications for hiring and promotions. This law further stipulates that applicants may be required to take such tests and that employers may act on the results. But certain conditions were imposed. The tests, the method of administration, and the subsequent decision based on the results must not be discriminatory. In an effort to guard against invalidity and unreliability, the law limits the tests that can be used to professionally developed ability tests.

To assist employers in developing a testing program that will comply with these antidiscrimination provisions the Equal Employment Opportunity Commission developed a set of guidelines. These guidelines are oriented toward a total personnel assessment system. Basically they require that, before a testing program is launched, job descriptions be developed that are exact and accurate in terms of the duties actually performed on the job and that the skills and standards expected for qualification and on-the-job performance be defined. EEOC further requires that interviewing and other screening methods, including testing, be specifically related to the requirements of the job. This, of course, is a much simpler matter with nonmanagerial than with managerial jobs. This provision reflects the commission's awareness that tests specifically adapted for one screening situation may be useless in another, one of the basic problems involved with the selection of tests by employers.

Rather than specify what tests should or should not be used, EEOC adopted the *Standards for Educational and Psychological Tests and Manuals,* prepared by a joint committee of the American Psychological Association, American Educational Research Association, and National Council on Measurement in Education.

The guidelines also require that actual job performance shall be made the basis of test validation. The commission supports retesting opportunities for applicants who failed preemployment screening tests once but who after additional work experience or training feel ready to attempt such tests again.

The commission has also been concerned about methods of test administration, realizing that not only the structural qualities of the test itself but also the way in which the test is administered can have a significant influence on the outcome. The commission advocates test administration that does not heighten or create anxiety or tension (reactions that can be allayed by carefully explaining the purpose of a particular test), reviewing instructions, and using conversational tones that reassure the applicant. It argues for conditions that are conducive to testing—the absence of noise, distractions, and other inhibitors.

The Problem of Validity

In the final analysis, the commission subscribes to the theory that a test, by its nature, must assure that those who pass it will be better qualified for the job for which the test was given than those who failed. This is of course a basic requirement for validation; yet the courts are not in full agreement on it. In *Griggs* v. *Duke Power Co.,* 292 F. Supp. 243 (MD NC, 1968), a North Carolina court ruled that the Civil Rights Act of 1964 does not actually require the use of tests that accurately measure the skills and abilities in relation to a job or group of jobs. This court further judged that it is reasonable to measure the level of general intelligence, even if such specific testing is in itself unrelated to a particular job.

The *Griggs* case further clarified, at least for the North Carolina court, the matter of a company's right to require a high school diploma and passing grades on preemployment ability tests. The federal district court found no violation of the Civil Rights Act in either instance and disagreed with the EEOC guidelines. The act does not, of course, restrain an employer from establishing educational standards provided that such standards are not instituted for the sole purpose of discriminating. Disagreement with the EEOC guidelines centers primarily around the issue of the employer's right to set standards and test for a *specific* job. It has been argued that tests for "qualities" that the applicant would logically be expected to possess are sufficient to satisfy legal requirements. The matter of guidelines for testing has by no means been settled either by the courts, EEOC, or employers. However, some basic, practical considerations should be understood by the employment interviewer so that he can more effectively deal with minority testing problems.

Nearly all applicants feel some degree of nervousness during interviewing and testing, but it is believed that such feelings are magnified in many black applicants. This nervousness may be translated into hostility and distrust. The applicant probably has had little experience with written testing. He may have a problem expressing himself and may feel that the entire screening process is designed to exclude him from employment. Efforts by the employment interviewer to explain the technical statistical validity of testing, theory of standardization, normal distribution curves, and other testing factors are usually ineffective in dispelling anxiety or building trust and confidence in either the test, the system or the employer. The interviewer must explain in nontechnical language why a particular test is given and why it is important and valuable to both the applicant and the organization. If he is unable to get this point across, he is not doing an effective job. (It is not impossible, however, that the fault may lie with the test, which may be deficient in validity and relevance.)

The Equal Employment Opportunity Commission has found that the cultural differences that exist between white and black, and that complicate employment interviewing and testing, also exist between many ethnic groups. Thus certain tests may predict job performance more accurately for one ethnic group than for another. The same disparity may occur in testing the inhabitants of different geographical areas. Tests that are not properly correlated to take these differences into account may screen out valuable employees. This is illustrated quite frequently when home-office tests are applied to a field operation in widely different areas without validating the tests to adjust to geographical or cultural differences.

Cultural and Social Impact on Test Results

Certainly, cultural and social backgrounds along with educational and occupational experiences can have a marked effect on test results and subsequent employment interview pursuit paths. For example, an applicant who has experienced little if any reinforcement for tasks performed quickly or well might reasonably be expected to achieve a lower score, particularly on a standardized test, than an applicant who has received constant encouragement. Thus some tests accord an advantage to certain types of backgrounds. The U.S. Commission on Civil Rights, in its booklet "Employment Testing: Guide Signs, Not Stop Signs," emphasizes this point by reproducing several test questions included in widely used selection tests.[1] Two examples are—

Does R.S.V.P. mean "Reply not necessary"?

A man who spends his money lavishly for nonessentials is considered to be (1) fortunate, (2) thrifty, (3) extravagant, (4) generous, (5) economical.

Certainly, the cultural background of an applicant would help determine his response to such test questions. (There is also the point of how relevant to the job such questions really are.) For example, in the second question illustrated, the applicant's background might lead him to check choice number one. The same report shows that cultural bias in testing is a real and not a fictional issue by reproducing tongue-in-cheek test questions that could discriminate against whites. An example—

Cheap chitlings (not the kind you purchase at a frozen food counter) taste rubbery unless they are cooked long enough. How soon can you quit cooking them to eat and enjoy them?

  1. 15 minutes   4. 1 week (on a low flame)
  2. 2 hours   5. 1 hour
  3. 24 hours

    (The correct answer is 24 hours.)

Another question asked the opposite of square. The correct answer was hip. Thus cultural background can have a direct effect on test results. Obviously, the questions would have little direct relevance

[1] U.S. Commission on Civil Rights, U.S. Government Printing Office, Washington, D.C. 20402, Publication No. 10, 1968.

to the vast majority of jobs. Multiple-choice tests are usually highly discriminative against most culturally disadvantaged people because the multiple alternatives are so confusing to them.

In the final analysis, the same cautions that should be exercised in testing and interviewing in general should be exercised with black or other minority group applicants. These applicants may dress differently from those whom the interviewer has been accustomed to; their cultural background may be different, and thus their verbal forms of reference may be foreign to the interviewer. But essentially it is the interviewer's responsibility to understand and alleviate any resulting strain, and to make sure that such applicants are psychologically prepared for the testing and interviewing procedure.

10

Interviewing
Management Manpower

AT ONE TIME or another, every organization needs to recruit high-potential managerial manpower. Terminations, retirements, promotions, demotions, transfers, long-term disability, deaths, operational changes, and the expansion of some part of the business enterprise all create vacancies or new positions. For some organizations, the recruiting is continuous; for others, it is an infrequent, concentrated effort. The stakes are high not only for the applicant but also for the organization.

Few would argue with the assertion that the stability, viability, and overall well-being of an organization are very largely dependent on the quality of its managerial manpower. The people who make up the management team help determine management development needs, the complexity of career path projections, the style and implementation of executive authority, the adequacy of the compensation program, the formal and informal training methods, and the policy and precedent framework that best complement the dynamics of executive interaction. Therefore every change that occurs in the management team affects in some way its capability. And, because it takes many years to groom, train, and develop a manager with high potential, the need for identification of quality manpower at the time of employment interviewing is highly critical.

The nature of the management function makes selection difficult. There is no single formula that is guaranteed to identify potential and predict effectiveness in all cases. An interview approach that proved successful for a given individual applying for a specific position may be totally ineffective for another candidate applying for a different job. Moreover, the variety of management positions is vast. Not all organizations define hierarchical levels in quite the same way. Therefore, when job descriptions exist, they are all too often vague and highly abstract. Standards of performance, in a practical sense, do not lend themselves to specific measurement and, often, defy precise explanation. Because of this, the use of nonprofessional interviewers, a common practice with candidates for middle or upper management positions (sometimes a committee or a round-robin approach is used), is extremely ill advised. The nonprofessionals tend to be unduly influenced by the functional and operational responsibilities of their own jobs.

The Problem of Interviewer Perspective

The interviewer is armed with three basic criteria of desirability. He knows his organization wants intelligent men. He wants applicable experience, and he wants maturity. The problem, of course, is in fulfilling these apple-pie standards. It is relatively simple to equate intelligence with IQ and experience with age. But intelligence has many aspects, and no test is valid for all of them. Also there is the problem of how an interviewer perceives intelligence. As for experience, age is certainly a less-than-perfect criterion. Today, rising qualitative levels of education and the rapid pace of technological change all threaten to make the experience of the over-40 manager obsolete. Of the three criteria maturity emerges as the most difficult to measure and perhaps the least valid. Many contend that the mature person is more likely to fall into dissonance with organizational structure than one who is not mature.

Some interviewers, executives themselves, subscribe to the myth that competence is the infallible judge of competence. The executive who has confidence in his own abilities, who has achieved what he considers to be success, and who evaluates his experiences as being highly applicable measures the managerial candidate against himself, his background, his intelligence, and his life style. He is easily influenced by physical appearance, graduation from the "right" school, and membership in the "right" fraternity. Such interviewers find that selection is less than a complex exercise, and they are as ready with rationalizations when one of their handpicked candidates fails as the alcoholic is who wants just one more drink.

Another misconception is that the recruitment source bespeaks the quality of the candidate. Some executives, categorically, do not expect to find the right caliber of top executive talent in their own organizations; others conduct interviews intended (sometimes subconsciously) to prove that the better candidates are those referred by executive search firms that the interviewer considers the best in the field. Many executive interviewers engage in a monolog, expounding on a wide variety of subjects, rarely giving the candidate the opportunity of responding, but at the same time watching his facial expressions closely. If his expression is sufficiently animated, they conclude with a satisfied, "It's been a real pleasure speaking with you."

People-oriented Qualities

The imperfections of the commonly accepted criteria of desirability only underscore the need for meaningful, all-purpose, specific criteria. These cannot be wholly *management-oriented*, in other words confined exclusively to the theory and practice of management, because of the variability of management attitudes and the almost unlimited range of techniques. Criteria must also be *people-oriented*— that is, associated with the human factor. What matters is awareness of, not any specific response to, the feelings and behavior of others. To what extent will the candidate be concerned with the career goals of subordinates, the effects of motivation on production, the role of the work itself in affecting attitudes and behavior, and the effects on quality of work that frustration, stress, and anxiety can produce?

Will he be able to step outside of his role as manager and view the conditions and circumstances of the work milieu in a cause-and-effect relationship? Can he differentiate between the effects on workers of a leader who conducts his job on the basis of his personal goals and needs and those of one who pursues his functional objectives by mediating or integrating the needs of his people with the needs of the organization? Will he be sensitive to the effects of his actions on others, especially on less well-informed employees, who because of his rank may attribute a crushing significance to his slightest gesture of displeasure? Does the applicant expect loyalty and high morale as his due? Does he understand the need to earn these attitudes by dealing fairly with people, communicating with persons on all organizational levels, and recognizing absolutely the human dignity of all workers?

And what are his attitudes toward change? Fear of change is a sign of insecurity. The manager who boasts that he staunchly upheld the old virtues and the well-established ways through thick and thin is advertising a weakness. On the other hand, an irrational fondness for change can be destructive. The best attitude is open-mindedness, an awareness that good can result from a number of approaches, that there is usually more than one right way to do something. The manager must be prepared to analyze the need for change objectively and must be well enough adjusted not to resist change. At the same time he must never lose sight of the effects of change on people.

None of these qualities is easy to determine. For example, to ask the candidate, "Can you step outside yourself or your role of manager and view the work environment objectively?" is to telegraph the answer or at least to confuse an applicant not attuned to behavioral jargon. Open-end questions, hypothetical problem solving, and an interpretative recital by the applicant of some of his most difficult problems and how he solved them are more helpful expedients.

What has been described thus far constitutes a broad area of investigation that should help the interviewer focus more purposefully on the ability of the applicant for a management position to fulfill corporate expectations. Obviously, a prediction of any kind involves risk and the less accurate the prediction, the more risk involved. In the staffing of management positions, high-risk situations must be avoided. As mentioned earlier, the most critical steps are to determine the objectives of the job (and of the organization prior to that), why the organization feels the need for management potential (and whether the need is realistic in terms of corporate growth and promotional and job enrichment policies and practices), and for what the potential will be used. Every time an addition is made to management, there is the expectation that the addition will somehow improve the effectiveness of the management team. While it is true there is less standardization in management than in nonmanagement jobs and that valid criteria for judging management potential are seriously lacking, management cannot escape the obligation of continuous self-evaluation in an effort to perfect such criteria. If management fails to do this, the risk factor reaches the point where selection becomes a wild gamble and the interview deteriorates into a meaningless preemployment rite.

Success and Failure:
A Matter of Organization Milieu

The reliability of performance predictions depends on the relationship between a predictor and the aspect of performance it is supposed to predict. Yet there may be no way to indicate statistically or verbally the perimeters of either predictor or performance. It is possible, however, to search out subtle, sometimes hidden cause-and-effect relationships and build toward conclusions using pursuit paths to piece together smaller, highly relevant behavioral configurations drawn from the applicant's record and interview responses. The resulting pattern is then projected into the prospective employment situation in a given organization.

The significance of the phrase "in a given organization" lies in the fact that there is a lack of agreement in management circles about what constitutes a predictor of management success or failure. A group of executives polled on this point found that they could not agree on even one. The only course open to interviewers, therefore, is to analyze deductively the characteristics, educational and personal, of managers in an organization and relate those characteristics to the organization's evaluation of those executives. As uncertain as this method appears to be on the surface, it is the only approach that poses such fundamental questions as how successful, why successful, and by what criteria.

In our search for meaningful criteria we are inexorably drawn to the problem of evaluating personal traits and characteristics. Obviously there are pitfalls, the most significant of which are lack of precise measurement, myriad semantics problems, and lack of agreement in management quarters on what personal characteristics or traits are meaningful. Again, the best starting place for the interviewer is the selection of personal characteristics and traits he considers applicable to the organization now and in the foreseeable future.

Physical Characteristics

One of the most popular criteria of judgment for many years was physical characteristics. For the most part, however, its popularity has faded—and deservedly so. If there is any correlation between physical characteristics it is very slight. Theories associating the shape of the head, the size and shape of the nose, chin, and cheeks with leadership characteristics, although persistent, have never found the slightest support in any scientific study. One study undertaken at the close of World War 1 purported to demonstrate that business and government leaders were taller and more portly than those not in executive or leadership work, but subsequent studies failed to bear out those conclusions.

The one characteristic of which the interviewer should be aware is vitality or energy, or any of the several attributes that can be linked to endurance and good health. Certainly, the leader in any field, whether government, business, or education, finds his physical resources constantly taxed. Long hours of work, stress on the job, traveling, and hurried lunches produce emotional strain, frustration, and anxiety. The physical toll includes the well-known executive ulcer, heart disease, high blood pressure, and migraines, to name only a few disabilities. But the interviewer should not equate physical size with endurance and energy. A cheery, robust six-footer may be less than the perfect specimen of health.

Interviewers should be alert to some of the more common symptoms of nervousness or psychosomatic illness: fingernails bitten to the quick, twitching, excessive sweating, tearing of the eyes, scaling skin, flushed cheeks, and others. The condition may be a temporary flare-up due to the pressure of the interview, but it pays to investigate. Such information as number of days missed at last job and type of medication currently taken is useful, but it may also be advisable either to consult with the applicant's doctor or to ask the applicant to submit to a physical examination at the company's expense.

Creativity

High on the list of desirable attributes is creativity. Creativity is a rarity. It does not happen often, nor does it occur with scheduled frequency. An applicant may indicate that he "created" this or that program. What he really means is that he developed it. Even though his work may have been original to some extent, essentially it is a modification of the work of other people in other places, a restructuring and reapplication. There is a fine line of distinction here. Probably the major difference between creativity and originality is the value placed on the product.

The employment interviewer should investigate claims of creativity thoroughly. Often what the applicant is describing is only adaptation, restructuring, and development. On the other hand, a high productivity of ideas, even mediocre ones, should not be scorned. With ideas as with actions, practice makes perfect. A person who proposes original ideas at a high rate of frequency can be expected to improve his output qualitatively with time. Of course, the quantity/quality multiple varies with different people.

In evaluating this output, the interviewer should guard against the tendency to dignify every unusual idea, no matter how wild, with the label "creative." Creativity must be utilitarian. Herein lies the difference between the crackpot and the truly creative mind. Originators of impractical proposals are likely to consider themselves geniuses born out of their time but, even if they are right (a remote possibility), the appreciation of future generations will not affect present operations. Originality for its own sake is not creativity.

Some of the signs of creativity are a good grasp of theoretical concepts, sharp perceptions without undue attachment to object imagery, concern with form in the esthetic sense, and a strong sense of inevitability and self-awareness. Although it is to be expected that most creative people are intelligent, creativity can occur in persons of low intelligence. The characteristic that can balance intelligence is the willingness to risk wrong responses in the effort to solve a problem. The creative person is not deterred by a series of failures. Certainly, he experiences frustration, disillusionment, anger, and even withdrawal, but he does not flinch from creative thinking because he knows he will make mistakes and even suffer a series of failures. He expects understanding and patience, and in return he probes a problem with an infinite variety of solutions while maintaining confidence in an ultimately successful outcome.

Stages in the Creative Process

There are several developmental stages to the creative process. Typically, a period of preparation, training, psychological self-development and self-discipline is followed by periods of extreme concentration, anxiety, frustration, and even fatigue. Often there is a withdrawal reaction and a rejection of the problem. The culmination of the creative experience is the moment of exhilarating insight, the so-called blinding flash. Afterward come the testing and unfolding of the idea. The moment of creative insight can occur spontaneously, but this is the exception.

Creative people are independent in thought and actions. Although obviously highly motivated, they find set performance standards and narrow job descriptions defeating and humiliating. They usually do not work well in highly structured situations requiring group coordination and control. Companies that have tried to foster creativity by holding brainstorming or black-box sessions have discovered that these techniques do not achieve the desired objective. The creative type is characteristically indifferent to hierarchical distinctions and designations.

The organization that is not prepared to accommodate creative people should not attempt to recruit them. They require special management know-how, and only the highest caliber of manager (in terms of human behavior orientation and training) is really equipped to use their talents to the fullest advantage. Too many organizations profess a need for creativity, stressing it in their help wanted advertisements and in their instructions to professional executive recruiters; yet, because of their structure and the limited horizons of their management, they are unable to offer any scope for uncommon imaginativeness.

There comes a point at which the interviewer must analyze his organization and determine if, in fact, the work milieu is such that it will be supportive of creative thinking. In other words, he must force himself to step outside his functional role and assume the role of critic. It is not disloyalty or heresy to do this; in fact, it represents the only approach the interviewer can take if he is to be truly effective.

Success Criteria and Validity

It is, of course, possible to test for creativity, but there is not as yet a completely reliable set of test-factor norms. In the past reliance was placed on tests of personality, temperament, and intelligence because many of the criteria of these qualities (for example, redefinition, elaboration, fluency, and problem solving) are also criteria of creativity. Biographical information (about which more will be said later in this chapter) seems to be emerging as a productive source of clues by which to identify the creative person. However, the necessary tests, test evaluation, and biographical data analysis require training somewhat beyond that typically found in the personnel and employment offices of the average company. Often the most practical alternative is to compare the applicant's achievements, work style, contribution, and verbalized approach with what was considered the norm (for the job held) of the applicant's previous employer and with the norm of the prospective employer.

Intelligence

Intelligence is usually high on any list of qualities desired in managers. Certainly above-average intelligence is an asset. However, there is reservation about the connection between intelligence and effectiveness. Specifically it is no longer taken for granted that high intelligence entails high managerial efficiency. On the other hand, a leader should not be less intelligent than his subordinates.

The interviewer dealing with management applicants must not be too easily impressed by a display of facts. It is to be expected that the average executive has been exposed to insights and information; it would be astonishing if it were otherwise. But the matter of intelligence goes far beyond the accumulation of facts and the ability to recall them on cue. An applicant may be a walking almanac capable of expounding on any subject, in absolute detail and accuracy (and incidently, score quite high on general intelligence tests) and be the worst possible choice for a manager.

Intelligence is many-faceted, and it is a mistake to assume that it can be measured in a single simple test designed for IQ alone. For example, one aspect of intelligence is the ability to reason abstractly, to derive a theory from empirical data, or (conversely) to apply a theory to a new problem. When a problem is solved by using a simulated situation or when an employee program is developed in accordance with an untested theory of motivation, the faculty for abstract reasoning comes into play. Another aspect of intelligence is the ability to assimilate and integrate diversified information in a minimum of time. This is a faculty that is constantly becoming more important. Today with reports generated at high speeds in torrential quantities and available anywhere on the globe in a matter of seconds, the executive must produce decisions on complex problems within highly abbreviated time frames.

Adaptiveness

Adaptiveness is yet another aspect of intelligence. Change is the constant of business. The manager comes into an organizational structure with the memory of experiences and with attitudes and insights. The reapplication of this total configuration of experience to a new work milieu requires that he accept new ideas and concepts, new methods and procedures. He must, in effect, modify what he has learned, reapply his experience, and fit this new knowledge into his existing body of knowledge. Finally, there is the elusive quality of judgment, the aptitude for selecting to best effect from alternatives.

Essentially, intelligence is the capacity for schematic thinking. Patterns of thought or schema become a relevant framework into which experiences, perspectives, and cognition are integrated. An interviewer must recognize that the measure of intelligence is in reality a measure of individual differences, with the largest proportion of any population falling into the middle distribution range. Some years ago, what were called general and special factors of intelligence were isolated. While the relevance of group factors was not considered, the importance of the "g" (general) factor was emphasized. This factor was seen as those abilities by which a person can differentiate between different parts of a problem, recognize its objective totality, and deal with abstract unknowns.

Grades earned in school and college are not necessarily indicative of managerial effectiveness. Certainly, the applicant who has received a series of above-average or exceptional marks in school shows signs of commitment. But commitment shown in an academic environment may not be transferable to a nonacademic environment, especially one in which the feedback of achievement is uncertain and irregular, as is often the case in performance appraisal systems in business. Of course, grades earned in a curriculum that can be directly applied to a job situation may be more significant than grades earned in a course of study for which there will not be direct application on the job.

Maturity

Another important factor in overall managerial effectiveness is maturity. Maturity refers to emotional development. A mature person has control of faculties, is able to handle people, and is capable of playing a dynamic role. Maturity is not the same as intelligence. This is not to suggest that brilliant people lack emotional development or aptitude for social situations. The very bright can be quite well adjusted emotionally and socially. But the fact that such people (as determined by their general intelligence test scores) *can* be well adjusted does not mean that they *must* be.

Interviewers are aware of the significance of maturity, but they are often uncertain about how to define it, and they may tend to confuse it with intelligence. Young, unseasoned interviewers, awed by impressive résumés, may equate graying at the temples with maturity. Admittedly there is no formulary of questions and responses by which maturity can be determined in the same way that routine questions on change of address and length of residence can serve to establish stability. But certain indications will emerge in the course of an interview. All that matters is that the interviewer be able to recognize them.

One of the evidences of maturity is the ability to acknowledge one's own strengths and weaknesses, to accept oneself for what one is, without bitterness or resignation, without hopelessness, and with a rational optimism about the future. In other words, a mature person feels comfortable playing the role of himself. This is a form of self-acceptance.

Likewise, the mature person is able to accept others for what they are. He may not surrender to them, but he can handle their weaknesses. In a supervisory role he can criticize subordinates with a minimum of traumatic reaction. He is usually not a one-man team, but he recognizes the need for the support of others, rarely if ever regarding them as a threat on that account. At the same time he exercises selectivity in the acceptance of dependence on and responsibility toward others.

The mature person neither lives in the past, continually reminiscing about youthful achievements, nor dreads the future. It has also been observed that the mature person is a patient problem solver without being a procrastinator. He has no need for procrastination because he has no reluctance toward work. In fact, he very obviously derives satisfaction from his work.

Of course the interviewer should not expect to find the epitome of the completely matured individual. Maturation is a continuing process that is never fully completed.

Maturity, intelligence, aptitudes, skills, and attitudes determine what the management applicant is capable of doing. Measures of these factors obtained through testing and through systematic evaluation of previous employment records, past educational and occupationa' achievements, job titles, job descriptions, references, and the like become what is sometimes called the "can-do index."

Will-Do Factors

Equally significant from the standpoint of performance, but not so easy to isolate, are the will-do factors: values, interests, motivations, and ambitions. When will-do factors harmonize with job objectives, it is to be expected that motivation will be positive. Moreover, strength in the will-do sector can compensate for deficiency in the can-do. For example, an applicant with moderate-to-average skills may excel because his motivation and interest are high. Therefore, the interviewer will get more useful results by exploring the applicant's general interests, his total managerial outlook, and his career strivings rather than by concentrating on narrow can-do factors in relation to an isolated job responsibility.

Personality Traits

The interviewer can expect a high incidence of certain personality traits in executive applicants. Successful businessmen seek to avoid anxiety, want to get ahead, feel comfortable in the presence of authority, accept dependence on company policy, are willing to abide by organizational chains of command, and are marked by a well-developed sense of identity, and to a good degree by objectivity in their thinking.

But the interviewer should not attempt to construct a personality profile of the ideal executive. Personality is not a well-defined entity, but a conglomerate of values, attitudes, and traits that help determine behavior. Instead, the interviewer should focus on those personality characteristics that are most essential from the point of view of managerial effectiveness, with special reference to his own organization. And in so doing, he must look to such broad concepts as energy, drive, motivation, values, need to achieve, self-identity, social confidence, maturity, and intelligence.

Status and Prestige

One of the most interesting traits in today's executive is the need for status or prestige. This trait is of course inherent in mankind, but nowhere is it more effectively and subtly sharpened than in the executive suite. Many companies go to great lengths, even to modifying organizational structure, in order to create titles and establish rewards and recognitions—including such cherished artifacts of daily corporate existence as privileged access to certain facilities or favorable location of office. Naturally these organizations want executives with a goodly share of prestige need in their makeup.

The interviewer must evaluate the applicant's prestige need in relation both to the requirements of the company and to its ability to accommodate that need. If the applicant is prestige-oriented, his occupational history will show that he is a true competitor who is unlikely to rest on his laurels. He will take few if any risks where his status is concerned. Such applicants usually reveal that despite promotions, they have never really achieved a sense of having "made it." Their only real security is in continued striving. The prestige-oriented applicant is likely to have a record of jobs offering either high income potential or large bonuses or commissions, frequently with impressive, even flamboyant, titles. It is not unusual for such applicants to favor glamour industries or companies in which the organizational structure is flexible enough to allow for fairly rapid advancement. Another indication of prestige orientation is a preference for communicating with equals or superiors (lateral or upward communication) rather than with subordinates.

Some interviewers assume that the prestige seeker is necessarily a disruptive element in an organization. Although he requires deference and the trappings of achievement and status, the prestige seeker is too concerned with establishing his own worth to downgrade others —particularly if his origins were humble. However, the interviewer should look into the relations between the managerial applicant and his peers in former jobs for any indications of conflict.

Security

In the evaluation of management applicants, the factor of emotional security cannot be overlooked. The anxious executive can and does affect the anxiety levels and consequently the performance of his subordinates. In an earlier discussion (Chapter 5) a distinction was made between high achievers and failure avoiders. The high achievers have the necessary security to assume a degree of risk in order to demonstrate their abilities and advance their careers. The failure avoiders live in a state of perpetual anxiety that makes risk avoidance paramount to them. Consequently, they willingly sacrifice advancement to security. Typically the failure avoider will do better than the high achiever in the type of job where there is no special pressure. The high achiever, on the other hand, reacts favorably to high pressure: Competition, crash programs, and challenging deadlines have an incentive effect on him.

It has been shown that, while both high- and low-anxiety persons began a task at about the same performance levels, the first failure produces inferior performance by the high-anxiety people, whereas the low-anxiety people (high achievers, risk seekers) actually respond with increased performance. Experimental evidence indicates that, if the high-anxiety group is oriented to failure in a manner that is absolutely free of implied threat to status or an approach that clearly eliminates the personal stake in the outcome, their performance might well dip less dramatically if at all, and the low curve of their performance line probably would be shorter in terms of time before recovery. When an organization does not provide the means of ventilation or resolution of anxiety, withdrawal is likely as personnel seek to avoid anxiety-ridden situations. Some organizational patterns characterized as pathological—that is, in which there is a general avoidance of personal contacts (even direct communication) and responsibility (upward buck-passing)—may reflect this kind of defensiveness.

Failure Avoiders

Failure avoiders often manage to work themselves into surprisingly high-level positions, choosing those that are essential, but where steady, reliable performance rather than creative initiative will suffice to insure tenure. In many cases their security is reinforced by the fact that they are overqualified for their jobs. Inevitably some of these people are able to hide behind the facade of the successful executive. Actually all they have done is ride out the waves of corporate expansion, performing a primary duty or set of functions, the challenge of which is unvarying.

High-anxiety executives are to be found in almost every organization. Yet the long-range effectiveness of their leadership is very much in doubt. That very special quality of executive stretch must, in the long run, evade them. This is not to suggest that such persons are unemployable. It is essential, however, that they not be placed in positions for which they are unfit.

The employment interviewer will be disappointed if he thinks that the failure avoider is easily identifiable as observably tense and over-wrought. Quite the reverse; such persons often appear easygoing. With pleasant dispositions, uncomplaining, and never becoming involved even in heated issues, they rarely present a threat to their fellow employees or their superiors. Thus their own security is not jeopardized.

However, under careful questioning the failure avoider often reveals a startling lack of faith in his abilities, attributing his success to circumstances beyond his control, such as luck or the influence of a dominant person. In addition, the interviewer should analyze biographical data and references. One clue is a history of employment with paternalistic organizations.

Anxiety

In judging the anxiety level of an applicant, the interviewer must not let himself be overly influenced by a few isolated instances of brilliant success or crushing failure, nor should he lose interest in the applicant because his application reveals a history of moderate accomplishment—what is sometimes referred to as a long slate of gray. The interviewer's responsibility, particularly where management applicants are concerned, is to identify patterns of behavior considered to be predictive of effectiveness.

Income and Ego Needs

An applicant may indicate that his salary requirements are open. The implication is that he does not want to close the door too early on a job possibility, preferring instead to demonstrate confidence in his ability and qualifications and in the ability of the prospective employer to recognize them and arrive at an equitable salary arrangement without the necessity of quibbling. This attitude may be little more than a pose. The extent of the applicant's real interest in income can be inferred from how often he has changed jobs for salary reasons and especially from the increases gained—the smaller the increases the more indicative they are of preoccupation with salary. The interviewer should determine what part the applicant played in gaining increases and promotions on previous jobs. Did he ask for such or did he patiently wait? Did his work taper off until he was rewarded or did he accelerate his efforts?

Standard of living is also a good clue. The size and location of the applicant's dwelling; the number, make, and model of his car; his vacation history, and his future plans are all pertinent. Note that such factors are also indications of his status needs. Before condemning an applicant who seems to want too much money for a job, the interviewer should compare the applicant's standards with those of others in the organization currently working in similar jobs or jobs of comparable level.

The applicant's attitude about his family can also be significant. If he is not strongly family-oriented and has no special ambitions for his children, his need for income may be less than that of the applicant who feels full responsibility for the fate and comfort of his family. Some applicants attempt to convey the impression that they are concerned with standard of living and life styles; yet in their off-the-cuff or unguarded comments reveal that they are in fact apathetic to these values.

The drive for status and prestige has already been discussed. An understanding of this drive supplies a certain insight into need for power. One sign of this need may be an affinity for jobs that offer the chance to dominate, manipulate, or control others or in which there is a very high degree of autonomy or contact with well-known or influential persons. (Many power-motivated applicants give themselves away by their weakness for name dropping.) Also symptomatic is the desire to be assigned jobs that affect a large number of people even if the impact on them is moderate.

Power and status needs may be an expression of future-oriented strivings; for example, to attain one day the rank of regional manager or president of the company; or they may reflect a desire to triumph over a past felt to be shameful or degraded. Sometimes the latter motive is at the root of the former; in other words, ambition is a consequence of early deprivation. If he can determine the primary motivating source of the prestige-status-power need, the interviewer will gain an insight that could be relevant in placing the applicant.

Management involves a lifelong process of change, development, obsolescence, revitalization, and practical experience. For the employment interviewer to bring into focus the critical essence of a managerial applicant's qualifications would be an almost impossible task if it were not possible to fragment the analysis of the candidate into workable parts as this discussion has done. It would be impractical, even foolish, to attempt to devise a single analytical method that could take in such factors as intelligence, ability to communicate, desire to manage, integrity, appearance, and imagination. The interviewer should lay down his own criteria on the basis of the needs of the job and the organization (as determined by careful analysis). For each criterion a specific analytical procedure can be formulated. This does not mean that a standard formula for the interviewing of managerial candidates is desirable. Each applicant is different; each manager brings to the organization his own special skills, approaches, and personality, and there is yet to be devised a perfect judgment scale for the measurement of total effectiveness.

Biographical Information

Perhaps one of the most significant analytical methods available to the interviewer of management applicants is the critical study of biographical data. This method is complex, and it requires considerable experience, practice, and knowledge of human behavior if it is to be something more than a witch hunt. But it is well worth the time and effort of study and preparation.

The theory behind biographical studies rests on certain basic assumptions. Every adult who can be considered "normal" experiences certain motivational drives, which may be deeply rooted in childhood experiences. Each person has his own distinctive pattern as unique to him as his fingerprints. Motivational drives do not simply go away. When a need is satisfied, the underlying drive may appear to recede, but it inevitably recurs in the form of a new need, which is an outgrowth of the previously satisfied one. Thus in one form or another motivational drives are active for life, although a drive may be more intense at one period than at another. Such valid constructs have given impetus to studies aimed at finding clues to strengths, weaknesses, and needs in the childhood and adolescent years.

It must be admitted that the use of biographical data to help explain behavior and to predict managerial effectiveness has suffered to some extent from the disrepute into which new methods in science sometimes fall. Fortunately, despite the rebuffs, experimenters have gradually evolved a more sophisticated way of handling biographical information and, although perfection is not within the grasp of the interviewer, it is within sight.

The technique of biographical data analysis had its birth in the widespread feeling of frustration that attended efforts to predict managerial effectiveness on the basis of personality characteristics. Personality assessments were not viewed with enough skepticism, and there was altogether too little effort at validation in terms of the specific employment situation. Personality characteristics could not be defined in precise enough terms to be widely applicable. The pressure for predictive methods did not subside, however, and so the problem was attacked two ways: continued experimentation in an effort to measure personality characteristics more precisely so that they could be described and applied predictively, and a combination of biographical data and specific job analysis to obtain a panoramic view embracing the candidates' interests, personality characteristics, motivations, and abilities and the requirements of the job.

Problems of Predictability

Even though there is relatively high validity to the use of biographical information, the predictability of managerial effectiveness can vary from situation to situation. Some biographical items are more predictive than others, and there is the matter of the intensity of the experience in the history of the person, or, put another way, how much relevant experience is required to constitute predictive data. It is possible to develop a practical system of weights or a value scale by which items in biographical information can be classified according to relevance and, therefore, predictiveness. Thus it is possible to develop general criteria of managerial effectiveness for a specific job responsibility or even for employment within a given company. It must be kept in mind, however, that motivation per se does not reveal itself on an application form or a résumé. Attitudes are not to be isolated like bacteria on a laboratory slide. Biographical data analysis serves to detect different personal characteristics and psychological forces and to measure them indirectly. Such indirect methods are proving to be more reliable than direct measurement.

In the process of exploring the applicant's family relations, his socioeconomic background and how he interprets it, and his life goals and self-concept and how they were influenced by that background and developed through the years of school and employment, a network of interrelated and mutually supportive correlates of behavior is brought to light. This network lends itself to effective interpretation.

But the use of such a system demands preparation. It requires research to develop valid biographical criteria applicable to a given employment situation. The starting point for such research is often a series of simple questions as: What common characteristics are shared by the successful managers in the organization? What are the statistical correlation and validity of such criteria? What gross patterns of life experiences seem to be shared? What personal qualities, job skills, or experiences seem most valued in the organization? What attributes, life styles, patterns of behavior, and expectations did top management most frequently designate as important to the management team —and to what extent did such indicators reflect the self-concept of these top managers? Note that in these preliminary and fundamental questions a relative-value scale (validated and statistically controlled by frequency of response, if by no other way) begins to emerge. As validation criteria are improved by performance appraisal methods, testing, interviewing, or analysis by professional psychologists, the biographical data begin to yield greater insight, and intricate patterns of behavior that very likely have remained with the individual emerge.

Although the approach suggested here as a beginning yields excellent results, it has its pitfalls. It is purely empirical and relies on statistical correlations between life experiences and job relevance.

A search of hundreds of bits of input might yield only a few correlates related to specific job requirements. The interviewer should also be aware of another approach in which theoretical constructs and logical deductions determine the relevant criteria. Assume, for example, that earnings over a given period is among the best criteria for productivity in a salesman, particularly if significant circumstances surrounding the work have changed relatively little, as, for example, product market, general economic conditions, and geographical differences. Similarly, for management personnel, the best criterion might be job titles in relation to the size of the company as measured by profits, number of employees, or physical plant. It might even be the number of persons directly supervised or the number of employees affected by the service performance. In production work, the criterion could be quality control standards in relation to production quotas.

These criteria are subjected to a theoretical or logical test, which must be statistically validated but which involves investigation and analysis of the job and the organization in relation to expectations. An invaluable correlate is the relationship between what was sought and what was actually accomplished in the person's history. Was an important educational and occupational experience a second or a third choice? Did the person really want to enter XYZ College, or had he first attempted to gain entrance into ABC University? Had he really wanted to be a physician but, failing in that effort, decided on accounting instead? Did he really want a promotion and transfer, or was he given no choice? Are his occupational experiences reflections of achievement or of default?

The Use of Known Criteria

The interviewer will probably select a combination of what he considers relevant methods of analyzing an applicant against known criteria. Such methods may well include, in addition to interviewing, results of tests (subjective and objective, job skills, general ability, and others); the comparative analysis of the applicant and others in the organization in similar positions in the hierarchy who are considered high achievers. When patterns of achievement seeking are compared and analyzed, the achievement need may be better understood. Obviously, managers who are quite proud of their backgrounds are high-achievement seekers, too. Their success needs, however, may require a higher level of accomplishment. A person who is interested in buffering himself from the past or, to put it another way, in covering his tracks typically may require very little in the way of significant power, status, recognition, and other tangible evidence of social worth to ease the hurt of his early years.

Managerial Effectiveness and Work Style

Managerial effectiveness is linked closely to work style. Obviously, different management functions require different work styles; for example, one job may call for close attention to detail; another for broad concepts. The interviewer therefore should not assume that because an applicant has a preference for the broad approach that his work can be expected to be sloppy or incomplete. He may be a master at delegation and organization. Similarly, the applicant who strongly resents carelessness, who insists on perfection in himself and others, and who is methodical and meticulous in attention to detail may be excellent at record keeping, report work, meeting deadlines, and maintaining documentation. It is up to the interviewer to decide whether the applicant's particular style is best suited to the requirements of the vacant position. Probably a well-balanced combination of these two extremes is the ideal, but the realities of recruitment and selection are such that this ideal rarely occurs. However, it is not essential, since it is almost always possible to find an applicant with the work style needed for a particular job.

Many organizations prefer managers who have narrowness of purpose, who cannot be easily swayed from a set course of action, and who, rejecting the frills and fancies, roll up their sleeves and tackle the job. Other organizations prefer the socially sensitive, service-oriented type. Obviously, the choice between such extremes cannot be capricious and if such a choice is necessary the requirements of the job will usually dictate.

The service-oriented person is basically altruistic. He has demonstrated community- or civic-mindedness. Probably he has participated in social service activities either in connection with his employment or voluntarily on his own time. He seems to champion and to understand the underdog. To the service-oriented applicant the impact of the company's products or services on society is as important as output and profit, and quality of services is sometimes emphasized to an extreme degree. This type of manager may be expected to act in accordance with his principles rather than his economic or career interest in any disputes between the employees and the company.

In contrast to the service-oriented type is the nonaltruistic person. He may show no record of social service or of activity in church, charitable, or civic affairs. He is primarily interested in his job, in doing it well, and in getting the recognition he deserves. He is little concerned with hardship, hard luck, or near misses. Yet he can be just as high-principled as his service-oriented counterpart. His refusal to participate in social service may reflect his sincere skepticism as to its social value. In his dealings with others he is willing to take it on the chin and dish it out in the same way.

These two types are well known throughout the business world, and both have their well-deserved place in the organization. It is incorrect to label one good and the other bad. Each can be a success if placed on a job that best suits his style and outlook on life in an organization that values the orientation each will give to his work. Both can fail, too, if misplaced. Every organizational structure imposes its own very special tyrannies on the people who labor in it. Only within the context and framework of a given structure can any management applicant be judged.

The interviewer who has practiced his art for any length of time knows that every applicant carries with him the remembrance of those responses he found successful on a previous job. In other words, every organization leaves its mark on an individual. For example, self-descriptions can be quite enlightening in explaining the relationship of roles and attitudes. When a group of managers and laborers were asked to describe themselves, managers usually used words and phrases that were consistent with their image of management, leadership, control, and organization. Workers used expressions typical of those who take orders but who rarely give them. The interviewer may find that, in addition to biographical data analysis and other analytical and interview techniques, the free-flow conversational approach under the direction of the interviewer can produce valuable insights when dealing with self-description.

One of the most difficult problems in the interviewing of management applicants is the matter of the reliability and validity of the interview. Certainly the problem exists with all interviews regardless of whether conducted with clerical, laboring, or managerial employees. However, with the management applicant the problems are compounded because, as pointed out earlier, the standards of performance are ill defined. This is probably due to unclear management functions, grossly insufficient knowledge about causal effects related to work needs and attitudes, and the effects of various management techniques on human beings. When reliability is mentioned in connection with interviewing, it means the degree of trust that can be placed in the interview for purposes of decision making. A kind of reliability can be achieved simply by asking two or more persons to interview a number of applicants and record their responses by ranking the applicants in order of their suitability to fill a specific vacancy. After each interviewer has ranked the applicants, a coefficient of correlation between the ranked lists is performed.

Validation imposes greater demands on the interviewer. Validity is the ability of the interview to generate data predictive of the applicant's performance. The standard method of validation is to maintain continuous comparison between predictions and subsequent performances.

Many studies have been performed in an effort to increase reliability and validity in interviewing. In one of particular importance a pair of interviewers were directed to determine the cause of poverty among a group of welfare seekers. The first interviewer, who was socially oriented, found that the most common causes for destitution were the effects of industrial blight and, to a lesser degree, drinking. The other interviewer, a temperance advocate, found that industrial blight was only a very small factor and attributed the overwhelming cause to alcoholism and moral breakdown. These results point of course to the conclusion that interviewer attitudes can affect reliability and validity.

It is quite possible, particularly in management interviewing, to overload the interviewer or subsequent decision maker with too much information. Too much testing and interviewing and overlong periods of analysis and problem-solving exercises are largely to blame. Excessive input of personality data increases the likelihood of underrating highly relevant and significant clues.

Applicant Bias

The problems that arise in the interviewing of minority applicants have already been discussed. But a special problem arises when the minority applicant is also a managerial applicant. This reaction may be termed "applicant bias." Applicant bias is a defense mechanism by which the applicant shields himself from the uncertainties and ambiguities inherent in the interview situation, which he perceives as threats to his self-concept. The object of the bias is the interviewer, who is seen as either less qualified than the applicant to make valid judgments about the applicant's abilities and potential or else as lacking the proper sensitivity or life experiences to understand the applicant's needs, motives, and behavior. Often such applicants see themselves as special cases whose backgrounds contain enough of the atypical to entitle them to be dealt with in a nonroutine manner.

Black applicants are particularly likely to suffer from applicant bias. Their qualifications, however excellent, are usually of a fairly recent order, consisting of concentrated educational experiences on the adult level—special training courses, business schools, and so forth. Their backgrounds are probably lacking in the life experiences hitherto usually associated with executive life styles and work habits. Consequently, it takes a skilled, unbiased interviewer to judge objectively the black applicant's qualifications. Naturally, these applicants have every right to be skeptical about whether the interviewer fits that exceptional description.

Although applicant bias manifests itself most clearly with blacks, it is not confined to this group. It is common among managerial applicants of all descriptions who have attained admirable records in executive management, together with substantial salaries, only to find themselves deprived of a job through merger, corporate politics, or their superiors' need to find a sacrificial lamb when a new product failed or when profits dipped and markets softened. Accordingly applicant bias is usually less prevalent among lower-level managers, laborers, and clerical workers because they are less likely to encounter ambiguity in regard to expectations, job responsibility, and standards of performance and of required educational and occupational experience.

Sometimes an applicant with strong managerial experience and a sense of having been successful experiences role conflict during the interview because he must relinquish any semblance of a leadership role and defer to the leadership of the interview. Similarly, applicant bias goes hand in hand with a sense of role-playing limitations. The applicant has placed himself in the role of seeker; he feels he must negotiate with the giver on the latter's terms. Typically, applicants tend to exaggerate and overemphasize the role they think they should play, becoming submissive or passive. At the same time they may see themselves as the victims of the "system," which they interpret as being, at best, a vague, uncertain, ill-defined guessing game. If, however, the interviewer hands down a favorable decision, the applicant's distrust and resentment tend to fade, and he may even become an avid supporter and defender of the system.

Applicants experiencing the syndrome of applicant bias can become highly agitated by questions whose answers they feel are obvious. To such an applicant, routine questions miss the bigger issues at stake, tend to belittle him, waste time, and snare him. The black applicant may suspect that such questions reflect a subtle form of discrimination. When it comes to job-skills, aptitude, and intelligence tests, the agitation is, if anything, more severe.

Applicant bias may be reflected in efforts to appeal to the interviewer's ego. Still lacking confidence in the interviewer's ability to understand him and judge him fairly, the applicant may attempt to appeal to the interviewer personally. Expressions like "As you probably know" or "I'm sure you understand" reveal the underlying anxiety. Responses to interview questions are not simply answers. They also take the form of explanations intended to educate and enlighten the interviewer. The interviewer who is not prepared for this kind of response reacts unfavorably and may regard the lengthy explanations as rationalizations or efforts to fill credibility gaps.

The interviewer cannot treat these problems lightly. His only chance of reducing applicant bias (he cannot eliminate it) is through the use of relevant, well-thought-through interview pursuit paths that demonstrate his ability to deal with the situation at hand. His questioning cannot follow formularized patterns. He will not accomplish anything by using first names. To the executive manager who has ranked far above the interviewer it is demeaning. To the black, it is another, less blatant form of "boy." To withdraw from the challenge and to give the applicant only superficial, patronizing attention is equally ineffective.

The interviewer need not be an expert on race relations, behavioral science, or executive management to handle these situations. He must, however, be a well-rounded, generally knowledgeable person with a good understanding of relevant areas of human interaction with which he must deal. He must be flexible in attitude and approach and, above all, in dealing with management applicants he must not be so presumptuous as to assume that he can comfortably ply his art, secure in the thought that in time he can amass a catalog of applicable postulates such as "if A, then B."

An objective, well-planned interview supported by (a) knowledge about the job to be filled and the organization in which the job must function; (b) testing procedures controlled for relevance, standardization, and validity; and (c) a professionally skilled interviewer conversant with the fundamentals of human behavior as a means of understanding (but not psychoanalyzing) the applicant is far more reliable than any single method that attempts to probe beneath the surface, as it were, seeking minute projective particles of information of questionable correlation.

Selected Readings

Allen, L. A., *The Management Profession.* New York: McGraw-Hill, 1964.

Anastasi, T. W., Jr., *Face to Face Communication.* Cambridge, Mass.: Management Center of Cambridge, 1967.

Argyris, C., "Understanding Human Behavior in Organizations: One View Point," in Haire, M. (ed.), *Modern Organization Theory.* New York: Wiley, 1959.

Black, J. M., *Developing Competent Subordinates.* New York: AMA, 1961.

Blake, R. R., and Mouton, J. S., "The Experimental Investigation of Inter-Personal Influence," in Bidderman, A. D., and Zimmer, E. (eds.), *The Manipulation of Human Behavior.* New York: Wiley, 1961.

Blauner, R., "Work Satisfaction and Industrial Trends in Modern Society," in Galenson, W., and Lipset, S. M. (eds.), *Labor and Trade Unions.* New York: Wiley, 1960.

Blough, R. M., "Business Can Satisfy the Young Intellectual," *Harvard Business Review,* January–February 1966.

Cambern, J. R., and Newton, D. A., "Skills Transfers: Can Defense Workers Adapt to Civilian Occupations?" Washington, D.C., vs. Department of Labor, *Monthly Labor Review,* June 1969.

Costello, T. W., and Zalkind, S. S., *Psychology in Administration.* Englewood Cliffs, N.J.: Prentice-Hall, Inc., 1963.

Drucker, P. F., *Concept of the Corporation.* New York: The John Day Company, Inc., 1964.

Emory, C. W., and Liand, P., *Making Management Decisions.* Boston: Houghton-Mifflin, 1968.

Gross, M. L., *The Brain Watchers.* New York: Random House, 1962.

Hackman, R. C., *The Motivated Working Adult.* New York: AMA, 1969.

Haire, M., *Psychology in Management* (2d edition). New York: Mc-Graw-Hill, 1964.

Herzberg, F., "One More Time: How Do You Motivate Employees?" *Harvard Business Review,* January–February 1968.

Herzberg, F., Mauser, B., and Snyderman, B., *The Motivation to Work* (2d edition). New York: Wiley, 1959.

Korzybski, A., "The Role of Language in the Perceptual Process," in Blake, R. T., and Ramsey, C. V. (eds.), *Perception: An Approach to Personality.* New York: The Ronald Press, 1951.

Leavitt, J. J., "Unhuman Organizations," *Harvard Business Review,* July–August 1962.

MacKinnon, D. W., "The Identification and Development of Creative Personnel," *Personnel Administration,* January–February 1968.

Mahoney, T. A., Jerdee, T. H., and Nash, A. H., "Predicting Managerial Effectiveness," *Personnel Psychology,* Summer 1960.

Mandell, M. M., "The Selection of Executives," in Dooher, M. J., and Marting, E. (eds.), *Selection of Management Personnel.* New York: AMA, 1957.

Maslow, A. H., *Motivation and Personality.* New York: Harper and Brothers, 1954.

McClelland, D. C., *The Achieving Society.* Princeton, N.J.: D. Van Nostrand Company, Inc., 1961.

McGregor, D., "The Staff Function in Human Relations," *The Journal of Social Issues,* Summer 1948.

Paul, W. J., Jr., Robertson, K. B., and Herzberg, F., "Job Enrichment Pays Off," *Harvard Business Review,* March–April 1969.

Peskin, D. B., *The Art of Job Hunting.* New York: World Publishing Company, 1967.

Porter, L. W., "Job Attitudes in Management: I. Perceived Deficiencies in Need Fulfillment as a Function of Job Level," *Journal of Applied Psychology,* 1962, 46.

Porter, L. W., and Lawler, E. E., *Managerial Attitudes and Performance.* Homewood, Ill.: Richard D. Irwin Inc., 1968.

Rao, K. V., and Russell, R. W., "Effects of Stress in Goal-Setting Behavior," *Journal of Abnormal and Social Psychology,* 1961.

Rice, A. K., *Productivity and Social Organization,* in Kelly, J., *Organizational Behavior.* Homewood, Ill.: Richard D. Irwin Inc., and The Dorsey Press, 1969.

Sayles, L. R., and Strauss, E., *Human Behavior in Organizations.* Englewood Cliffs, N.J.: Prentice-Hall, Inc., 1966.

Schien, E. H., "Management Development as a Process of Influence," *Industrial Management Review*, School of Industrial Management, Massachusetts Institute of Technology, May 1961.

Simon, H. A., *The New Science of Management Decision*. New York: Harper and Row Publishers, 1960.

Stagner, R., "Dual Allegiance as a Problem in Modern Society," *Personnel Psychology*, 1954.

U.S. Commission on Civil Rights, "Employment Testing: Guide Signs, Not Stop Signs," U.S. Government Printing Office, Washington, D.C.

Van Buskirk, C., "Performance on Complex Reasoning Tasks as a Function of Anxiety," *Journal of Abnormal and Social Psychology*, 1961–62.

Van Zelst, R. J., "Sociometrically Selected Work Productivity," *Personnel Psychology*, 1953, v, 3.

Vernon, P. E., *Intelligence and Attainment Tests*. London: University of London Press, 1960.

Vidulich, R. N., and Kaiman, I. P., "The Effects of Information Source Status and Dogmatism Upon Conformity Behavior," *Journal of Abnormal and Social Psychology*, 1961.

Warner, W. L., and Havighurst, F. J., and Laeb, M. B., *Who Shall Be Educated?* New York: Harper and Brothers, 1944.

Weitz, J., "Job Expectancy and Survival," *Journal of Applied Psychology*, 1956.

Welch, J., Stone, C. H., and Patterson, D. G., "How to Develop a Weighted Application Blank" (*Research Technical Report II*), Industrial Relations Center, University of Minnesota. Dubuque, Iowa: William C. Brown Company, 1952.

Wells, F. L., and Ruesch, J., *Mental Examiners Handbook* (Revised edition). New York: New York Psychological Corporation, 1946.

Wertheimer, M., *Productive Thinking*. New York: Hartford, 1945.

Whyte, W. F., "The Import of Money," in Gellerman, S. W., *Motivation and Productivity*. New York: AMA, 1963.

Wickert, F. R., "Turnover and Employees' Feelings of Ego Involvement in the Day-to-Day Operation of a Company," *Personnel Psychology*, 1951.

Wilson, J. W., "Toward Better Use of Psychological Testing," *Personnel*, May–June 1962.

Woodworth, R. S., and Schlosberg, H., *Experimental Psychology* (Revised edition). New York: Holt, Rinehart and Winston, Inc., 1954.

Zaleznik, S., "The MBA: The Man, the Myth and the Method," *Fortune*, May 1968.

Index

ability tests, 213–214; *see also* testing; tests

abstraction: communication process and, 106–107; extensional orientation and, 109–110; functions of, 105–111; levels of, 104–105; nonidentity and, 108–109

achievement: motivation and, 156–157; need for, 122; -oriented people, 159; potential and self-concept, 122; risk taking and, 156; social mobility and, 159

action-oriented behavior, 48

adaptiveness, intelligence and, 225–226

adaptive tests, 200–201

address changes, 4

adjustive reactions, in college students, 189

aggression, anxiety and, 134

alienation, in college students, 188

Allen, L. L., 197 n.

anger, 132–133

Anshen, M., 71 n.

anxiety: defined, 125; job performance and, 130–131; in management applicant, 231; mechanisms, 133–136; motivation and, 124–129; performance and, 124–129; "rapport" game and, 170; retaliation in, 135; sublimation of, 135–136; success or failure and, 127, 133–136

apathy, in college student, 189

applicant: anxiety in, 126–136; aspirations and expectations of, 124; assumptions about, 42; attitude reinforcement in, 52–53; as "bad apple," 133; "bad habits" of, 54; bias, 238–240; biographical data on, 21–22,

157–162, 233–236; career selection by, 33–34; -centered interview, 171–172; "chewed out for making error" complaint, 132; communication with, 14–15; "cool" type, 27–28; current and future capabilities of, 9; desirable qualities in, 222–225; discriminating, 33; feeling and response under pressure, 11; first impressions of, 36–37; games played with, 168–171; generalizations about, 37–38; goal of, 131; "halo effect" and, 38–40; "ideal" impression sought by, 48; impressions vs. actualities in, 27; income and ego needs of, 231–232; incongruities in, 42; individual differences in, 26; interview granted to, 9–10; as job hopper, 119; job needs and, 117; job vacancy and, 28; as "loser," 18; maturity in, 226–227; minority-group, 176–180; misleading attitudes in, 55–56; "money game" and, 27; motivations of, 21, 27, 28–29, 121–124, 140–163; new role of, 52–53; parent-child relations and, 29–30; perception of, 35–47; personality traits in, 228–232; placement of, 2; "potential" of, 18; previous "failures" of, 17; prime and nonprime answers by, 84, 89–91; prior disciplining of, 131–133; problem-solving situations with, 77–79; "rapport" with, 170–171; reaction formation in, 29–30, 128; "right person for right job" criterion for, 9; "sales type," 129; self-esteem or ego in, 32, 48, 144, 154–155; self-evaluation by, 113–116; self-image of, 33–34; shrewd, 49; social background of,

44; success or failure predictions for, 26; testing of, 9–10, 31, 201–202, 198–216; as test taker, 207–208; as threat to interviewer, 44–45; "total impression" of, 58; as troublemaker, 129; wants and need fulfillment in, 32–33, 143; will-do factors and, 227–228; work history of, 58; *see also* black applicants; management applicant

application forms, uses of, 91

aptitudes, job needs and, 117

aptitude tests, 199

Argyris, C., 28 n.

attitude: action-oriented, 48; changing, 55–56; defined, 47; divergent, 53; environment and, 51–52; "internalizing" of, 54; interpretation and, 50–53; life role and, 51; manpower scarcity and, 57; "official" management, 26; perception and, 49; reinforcement, 52–53, 60; self-image and, 56–57; undesirable, 56–57; utilitarian function of, 49; value-expressed, 50–51

attitude change, 53–58

attitude formation: vs. attitude change, 59; cognitive dissonance and, 59–61; group effects in, 54; perception and, 47–49; perceptual process and, 35–61

awareness, understanding and, 103

Bayesian approach, in probability theory, 74

behavioral analysis, importance of, 26–32

behavioral concepts, job placement and, 30–32

behavioral science, principles of, 6

Bendix, R., 159 n.

biographical information: on management applicant, 233–236; motivation and, 21–22, 157–162

black applicants: applicant bias in, 238–240; communication with, 178–179; cultural and social backgrounds of, 215–216; testing of, 212–216; *see also* minority applicants; minority groups

black students: conflict in, 194–195; credibility and, 196–197; recruitment of, 193–197

branching, in interview programming, 84–85

Brown, J. K., 183 n.

Bruner, J. S., 22 n.

Bureau of Labor Statistics, U.S., 8

campus recruitment, 181–197; behavioral approach to, 185–192; of black students, 193–197; boycotts, 184; changing trends in, 181–182; credibility gap and, 196–197; objectives in, 183–184; "security" as goal in, 191; selection criteria in, 190–192; student unrest and, 184–185; worker role in, 192–193

Cantril, H., 45

career choice, self-image and, 33–34

Civil Rights Act of 1964, 212, 214

closed-mind syndrome, 110–111

cognitive dissonance, 59–61

cognitive processes, 63

college students: alienated, 187–189; black, 193–197; career orientation and expectations of, 186–187; commitment vs. adjustment in, 193; identity needs of, 185–186; loyalty in, 189–190; recruiting of, 181–197; role as worker, 192–193; self-concept of, 193

communication: abstractions and, 106–107; with black applicants, 178–179; closed mind in, 110–111; gap, 15; interviewing as, 14–16; language and, 15, 100–103; need for, 99–100

computer programs, decision making and, 70–71

conflict: conformity of attitudes, 53; job performance and, 130–131; origins of, 129–133

contravaluant hypothesis, 41

conversational approach, in employment interview, 174–175

corporation: growing complexity of, 8–9; insulation of life in, 117–118

counseling, 24–25; vs. interviewing, 23; as problem solving, 24

creative thought, in problem solving, 75–76

creative process, stages in, 223–224

creativity, desirability of, 222–223

Dailey, C. A., 36

Dearborn, D. C., 46

decision making, 62–74; alternatives in, 65–66; computer and, 70–71; consequences of, 73; data needed in, 70–71; vs. decision theory, 68–69; defined, 63, 68; fallacies in, 66–67; false analogies in, 67–68; general theory of, 64–72; goal orientation and, 71–72; inertia in, 65; levels of, 68; motivation and, 69; prediction and, 73–74; solution finding and, 72

decision theory, 64–72
disciplinary action, effects of, 131–133
drugs, reaction formation and, 30
Duncker, K., 20

Edwards, W., 69 n.
effect, law of, 16
ego: defense and attitude, 50; fulfillment, 136, 143; involvement and
turnover, 142; needs, 143–144; needs
of management applicant, 231–232
employment, decline in, 8
employment interview, see interview
employment interviewer: alternatives
of, 16–17; applicant bias in, 238–240;
attitude change in, 55–56; attitude
of, 17–19; cognitive style in, 22; company pressures on, 45–47; contravaluant hypothesis and, 41; creativity
and, 222–223; decision making by,
64–72; ego-involved attitude of, 55;
evaluation by, 16–25; facial expressions and, 36, 178; "first impressions"
of, 36–37; gaming by, 165–167;
"good–bad" attitudes of, 17–18; inept,
81–82; information needed by, 25;
language of, 100–101; management-
oriented, 219–220; manpower planning approach of, 25; motivation of,
45; nervousness and, 222; as norm,
42–43; occupational background of,
1; people-oriented qualities in, 219–
220; perception of, 40–41; perceptual
selectivity of, 41–47; personal beliefs
vs. management attitude in, 26; personality traits of, 228–232; perspective of, 218–220; previous "failures"
of, 16; probability approach in, 74;
programming by, 83–89; responsibility of, 15, 46; selection of, 41; as student of human behavior, 40–41; techniques of, 164–180; testing and, 199–
205; test results analysis by, 210–212;
"title" given to, 23; value expression
by, 105
employment pattern, 4
environment: attitude and, 51–52; motivation and, 162–163; reality and,
59–61; stimuli from, 97
equal employment opportunity (EEO),
5, 11
Equal Employment Opportunity Commission, 212, 214
executive talent, shortage of, 8; see also
management applicant; manager
experience: problem-solving behavior
and, 19–20; success and, 120–121

extensional orientation, abstraction and,
109–110

facial expressions, perception and, 36,
178
facts, understanding and, 103
failure: anxiety and, 127, 133–136;
avoidance of, 18, 230; evaluation of,
113–139; interviewer's attitude on,
17–18; on job, 3; job hopping and,
118–120; organization milieu and,
221–224; penalty for, 16; satisfaction
and, 136–139; understanding and,
116–121
false analogies, 67–68
false cause, fallacy of, 66–67
family: interactions and personality, 29;
of management applicant, 234–235;
as primary social unit, 157
father, reaction formation and, 29
Federal Bureau of Narcotics, 30
Festinger, L., 59, 130
Finlator, J., 30
first impressions, 36–37
fixity, in college student, 189
forced choice, as interview technique,
175
Freud, S., 29, 128
frustration, anxiety and, 127, 134
functional approach, vs. utilitarian, 3–4
functional fixedness, 19–21

game theory, 165–166; goals and, 167–
168; identity in, 168
gaming: with black students, 194–195;
in interview, 165–167; give-and-take
in, 168–171; role playing in, 167–171
generalization: dangers of, 37; in test
results, 210–212
generation gap, drugs and, 30
Gestalt theory, perception and, 40–41
give-and-take game, 168–171
goal orientation, decision making and,
71–72
go–no-go game, 169
good–bad attitudes, 17–18
Griggs v. Duke Power Co., 213
Grove, B. A., 38–39
group interviewing, 175–176
growth cycle, motivation and, 150
Guilford, J. P., 68

Habbe, S., 183 n.
habit formation, problem solving and,
79–80
Haire, M., 28 n., 98 n.

halo effect: perception and, 38–40; self-evaluation and, 115
Hartley, E., 22 n.
Harvard Business Review, 71
hatred, 132–133
Henry, W. E., 125 n.
Herzberg, F., 144
hostility, 132–133
"how-we-do-it" game, 170

immaturity, signs of, 128–129
income: levels and attitudes, 37–38; needs of management applicant, 231–232
information: biographical, 21–22, 157–162, 233–236; prime vs. nonprime, 62–63; selective control over, 62–63
insulation, anxiety and, 126
intellectual abilities, testing and, 203
intelligence: adaptiveness and, 225–226; defined, 226; desirability of, 225; judgment and, 203–204; tests and testing, 31, 201–202
interviewing: applicant-centered, 171–172; applicant motivation in, 21–22; attitudes, 47–49; as communication process, 14–16, 99; conjunctive, 1, 198–216; constants and variables for, 24; counseling vs., 23; decisions made in, 13; defined, 11–14; forced choice in, 175; "gaming" in, 13, 165–171, 194–195; inept or misdirected, 11; interviewer-oriented, 173; interviewer's motivation in, 45–46; job vacancy and, 24; listening in, 15; of management applicants, 217–240; matter "at stake" in, 12–13; methodology, 210–212; minorities and, 11, 176–180; misconceptions, 23; nature of, 22–24; objective, 13, 24; participants in, 12; penetration, 9; perception of applicant in, 4; physical posture in, 2; placement of applicant in, 2; prime and nonprime answers in, 84, 89–91; "prize" in, 12–13; programming of, 83–98; vs. psychological test, 10; purpose of, 13; question response variations, 5; "red flag" zones in, 26; reference points in, 42; responsibility in, 15, 46; "right person for right job" criterion in, 9; rigidity of standards in, 66; as structured social situation, 2; structuring of, 41; superior–inferior relationship in, 172; survey of, 7–34; utilitarian vs. functional approach to, 3; see also interviewing; interview programming

interviewer, see employment interviewer
interviewer-oriented interview, 173
interviewing techniques, 1–2, 164–180; conversational approach, 174–175; group, 175–176
interview programming, 83–98; branching in, 84–85; definitions and methodology in, 53, 83–84; goals and unproductive paths in, 96–98; for interviewing managers and technicians, 92; prime and nonprime responses in, 84, 89–91; pursuit path in, 86; value scale in, 94–96; written or unwritten program in, 91
IQ, 201–202; intelligence and, 218
isolation, as job satisfaction, 146

job, anxiety over, 124–125
job challenge, vs. success or failure, 137–138
job constraints, work rules and, 152
job description, employee counseling and, 24
job dissatisfaction: isolation as, 146; motivation and, 141;
job enlargement, 24–25
job enrichment: vs. job enlargement, 145–146; motivation and, 150
job evaluation, 25
job experience, success and, 120–121
job hopping, 118–119
job interest levels, testing and, 205–209
job objectives, of college student, 186–187
job performance: anxiety and, 130–131; evaluation of, 115–116; self-evaluation in, 113
job placement, behavioral concepts in, 30–32
job satisfaction: measurement of, 141–142; motivation and, 144, 161–162; self-esteem and, 154; vs. success or failure, 136–139; turnover and, 141–142
job satisfiers, 137
job skills, see skills
job vacancy: candidates for, 10; interview as result of, 24; motivation and, 28–29; promotees and, 10
judgment: perception and, 47; testing for, 203–204

Katona, G., 20–21
Kelly, J., 184 n.
Kerr, W. A., 38–39
knowledge, attitudes and, 53–54

"knowledge of people," 3, 37
Korzybski, A., 15

language: awareness and, 103; communication and, 100–101; reality and, 15; semantics and, 102–103
Lawler, E. E., 163 n.
learning: kinds of, 21–22; problem solving and, 20–21
Lindzey, G., 130 n.
Lipset, S. M., 159 n.
listening, by interviewer, 15, 16
love, giving and receiving of, 143
lower class, motivation of, 158–160
loyalty: of college students, 190; job hopping and, 119

Maccoby, E., 22 n.
Maier, N. R. F., 19 n.
management applicant: bias in, 238–240; biographical data on, 233–236; as failure avoider, 230; family life of, 234; income and ego needs of, 231–232; known criteria on, 235–236; self-description by, 237; validation in, 238
management: -oriented tests, 204–205; power, interviewing and, 217–240; style and motivation, 152–153; see also management applicant
managers: community-minded, 236–237; effectiveness of, 31, 233–235; high-potential, 9; job experience of, 120–121; maturity in, 226–227; performance evaluation, 114–116; personality traits of, 228–232; potential measurement, 206–207; "professional," 7–8; security needs of, 229–230; self-description by, 237; service-oriented, 236; shortage of, 8–9; types of, 152–153; work style and effectiveness, 236–238
manpower: attracting and identifying, 7; business community need for, 7; development program, 8; planning approach, 25; resources squandered, 12; shortage and attitudes, 57; shortage implications, 8–9
Margetts, S., 30 n.
maturity, 226–227
McClelland, D. C., 122 n.
McGregor, D., 27 n.
meaning, words and, 15
Michigan Bell Telephone Company, 142
middle class, motivation of, 158–160
minority applicants: interviewing, 176–180; sensitivity of, 179–180; testing, 212–216; see also black applicants; minority groups
minority groups: employment of, 177–178; as factor in labor market, 11; see also minority applicants
mirror effect, 39
Morgenstern, O., 165–166
motivation: anxiety and, 124–129; applicant, 21; decision making and, 69–70; job experience and, 121; job skills and, 161–162; management style and, 152–153; screening or placement in relation to, 140–163; self-image and, 154; social class and, 158–160; social interaction and, 147–149; success or failure as, 121–122; supervisory style and, 152–153; technological processes and, 153; turnover and, 141–143; work environment and, 162–163; work as, 149–157
motivators vs. satisfiers, 151–152

n achievement, 122
National Industrial Conference Board, 183 n.
national origins, stereotypes of, 39; see also minority groups
need fulfillment, 33
needs vs. wants, 143
nervousness, 4, 222
Neumann, J. von, 165–166
neurotic behavior, discipline and, 132–133
Newcomb, T., 22 n.
nonachiever, motivation of, 123
nonidentity, abstraction and, 108–109
non-zero-sum game, 195

offensive listening, 16
organizational structure, problems of, 5
organization milieu, success/failure chances and, 221–224

parent-child relations, of job applicant, 29–30
Patten, T. H., Jr., 183 n.
Patton, A., 8 n.
Pearson, A. E., 183 n.
peer attitudes, roles and, 147–149
penetration interviewing, 9
perception: attitude formation and, 46–49; behavior and, 47; distortion of, 35–41; emotional stress and, 45; environment, 40; judgment and, 47; learned responses and, 46 n.; pitfalls in, 43–45; problem of, 35; reality and,

57–58; self-adjustment and, 43; self-identity in, 43

perceptual process: attitude formation in, 35–61; cognitive dissonance and, 59–61

perceptual selectivity, 41–47

performance: anxiety and, 124–129; failures and, 17; ill-defined standards in, 114; managerial, evaluation of, 114–116

personality: family interactions and, 29; tests, 199 (see also testing); traits, in interview, 228–232

"persuasion" game, 169–170

physical characteristics, 36, 221–222

placement, motivation and, 140–163

planning, decision making and, 63

Porter, L. W., 163 n.

posture, in interview, 2

potential, in applicant, 18; managerial, measurement of, 206–207

"pregnant pause" effect, 125

prestige/status needs of management applicants, 228–229

prime response, in interview programming, 89–91

private life, job satisfaction and, 138

probability theory, 74

problem solving, 75–83; categories of facts in, 80–81; creative thought and, 75–76; defined, 63; genuine, 78–79; goal of, 75; habit formation and, 79–80; habitual behavior and, 78; interviewer ineptitude and, 81–82; kinds of, 20–21; past experience and, 19; possible solutions in, 76–78; risk in, 80–81

productive thinking, 19

productivity, risk taking and, 155–157

programming, see interview programming

projection, mirror effect in, 39–40

promotion: disinterest in, 150–151; frustration over, 134; interviewing and, 11

psychological testing, 1, 9–10; see also testing

psychosomatic illness, 222

punishment, fear of, 132

pursuit path, in interview programming, 86

rapport game, 170

reaction formation, 29–30; anxiety and, 128; in college students, 189

reality: language and, 15; perception and, 57–58

real-life situation, attitude formation and, 59

references, reliability and, 10–11

regression, 132–133

reliability factor, 103

reproductive thinking, 19

resignations, motivation for, 141–145

risk: in problem solving, 80–81; productivity and, 155–157; taking and achievement, 156

role playing, 148, 167–171

Ross, I., 143 n.

"sales type" applicant, 129

satisfiers vs. motivators, 151

Schein, E. E., 183 n.

Schelling, T. C., 195 n.

screening, motivation and, 140–163

security needs: emotional, 144–145; in management applicant, 229–230

selection techniques, limitations of, 9–11

selection tests, 199–205; see also testing

self-adjustment, perception and, 43

self-analysis, failure and, 164

self-concept: of college students, 193; environment and, 157; motivation and, 122–123, 154

self-definition, of college student, 186

self-description, by management applicant, 237

self-development, action-oriented, 48

self-esteem: job satisfaction and, 154–155; motivation and, 144; value system and, 48

self-evaluation: job performance and, 113; morale and, 113–114; peers and supervisors in, 114–115; performance standards and, 114

self-image: of applicant, 33–34; attitude and, 51–52; of college students, 186; motivation and, 154–155

semantics barrier, 99–111; abstraction levels and, 104–105; minimizing of, 110

Simon, H. A., 46

skills: deficiency and conflict, 129; demand for, 161; inventory, 1, 4; job openings and, 33; in problem-solving situation, 20; transient, 161–162

social certitudes, theory of, 147

social class, 157; differences in, 158–160

social interaction, motivation and, 147–149

social mobility, 159

social stratification, 157

socioeconomic group, motivation and, 158–160

solution finding, task delineation and, 72

Standards for Educational and Psychological Tests and Manual, 213

status: as ego need, 144; and prestige needs, in management applicant, 228–229

stereotypes, perception and, 37

student(s), *see* campus recruitment; college student

subjectively expected utility (SEU), 69

sublimation, anxiety and, 135–136

success: anxiety and, 127, 133–136; aptitudes vs. job needs in, 117; aspiration level and, 126–127; criteria and validity in, 224–228; evaluation of, 112–139; "excess" of, 116–117; job experience and, 120–121; need for, 121; organization milieu and, 221–224; private life and, 138; satisfaction and, 136–139; understanding and, 116–121

success–failure: conditions, 17; predictability, 26

superior–inferior relationship, in interview, 172

supervisors, types of, 152

task delineation, solution finding and, 72–73

technology: environment and, 6; motivation and, 153

testing, 198–216; generalizations from, 210–212; vs. interview, 10; job-interest levels and, 205–209; management-oriented, 204–205; for managerial potential, 206–207; methodology in, 211–212; of minority-group applicants, 212–216; programs in, 31; results of, 209–212; "see-through" effect in, 207–208; validity in, 213–214; *see also* tests

tests: astuteness in taking, 207–208; cultural and social impact in, 215–216; intelligence, 201–202; limitations of, 10; psychological, 9; selection, 199–205; standard methods and uses of, 202–203; value of, 208–209; *see also* testing

thinking, productive and reproductive, 19–20

Thorndike, E. L., 16

training: failure and, 118; problem-solving behavior and, 19–20

transient skill, motivation and, 161

troublemaker, applicant as, 129

turnover: ego involvement in, 142; motivation in, 141–143

upper middle class, motivation of, 159–160

utilitarian approach vs. functional, 3–4

utilitarian value, in decision making, 69

value-expressive functions and attitudes, 50–51; *see also* attitude

values: abstraction and, 105; attitudes and, 50–51

verbal ability, 205

voice quality, 4

wants vs. needs, 143

Wickert, F. R., 142 n.

"will-do" factors, job objectives and, 227–228

withdrawal, in college student, 189

words: connotative and denotative, 100–101; dynamics of, 101–102; emotions triggered by, 108; facts and, 101–102; meaning and, 15; physical response to, 108; responses to, 100–101, 108

work: environment and motivation, 162–163; group influence, 133; as motivator, 149–157; rules and job constraints, 153–155; style and managerial effectiveness, 236–238

"you-the-jury" game, 169

Zandor, A., 143 n.

zero-sum games, 166–169, 195